The Islamic Impact

Frontispiece. Page of broken *shikasteh* script. From an album of calligraphy. Iran, 18th century, by Muhammad Reza. Springfield, Massachusetts, *Museum of Fine Arts,* No. 59 Ms 70.

The Islamic
IMPACT

Edited by Yvonne Yazbeck Haddad
Byron Haines
Ellison Findly

SYRACUSE UNIVERSITY PRESS · 1984

Library of Congress Cataloging in Publication Data
Main entry under title:

The Islamic impact.

  Includes bibliographical references and index.
  1. Islam—Addresses, essays, lectures. I. Haddad,
Yvonne Yazbeck, 1935–   . II. Haines, Byron.
III. Findly, Ellison Banks.
BP20.I752   1984   297'.197   83-18274
ISBN 0-8156-2304-6
ISBN 0-8156-2299-6 (pbk.)

Contents

~~~~~~

Contributors

Eqbal Ahmad is a Fellow at the Institute of Policy Studies, New York, New York.

Willem A. Bijlefeld is Professor of Islamic Studies and Director of the Duncan Black Macdonald Center for the Study of Islam and Christian-Muslim Relations, Hartford Seminary, Hartford, Connecticut.

Walter Denny is Professor of Art History, University of Massachusetts, Amherst, Massachusetts.

John L. Esposito is Professor of Islam and Chairman of the Department of Religious Studies, College of the Holy Cross, Worcester, Massachusetts.

Lois Ibsen al Faruqi is at Temple University, Philadelphia, Pennsylvania.

Yvonne Yazbeck Haddad is Associate Professor of Islamic Studies, Hartford Seminary, Hartford, Connecticut.

Charles Issawi is Professor of Economics, Near Eastern Studies Department, Princeton University, Princeton, New Jersey.

Akbar Muhammad is Associate Professor of African and Islamic History, State University of New York, Binghamton, New York.

Seyyed Hossein Nasr is Professor of Islamic Studies, Department of Religion, Temple University, Philadelphia, Pennsylvania.

Annemarie Schimmel is Professor of Indo-Muslim Culture, Harvard University, Cambridge, Massachusetts.

Jane I. Smith is Associate Dean for Academic Affairs, Lecturer in Islamic Studies, Harvard Divinity School, Cambridge, Massachusetts.

Acknowledgments

T HIS BOOK brings together several studies by scholars in the field
   of Islamic Studies. Seven of them were delivered as lectures in
the series "The World of Islam" sponsored by the Task Force on
Christian-Muslim Relations of the National Council of the Churches of
Christ in the U.S.A., the National Conference of Christians and Jews,
Trinity College, The Duncan Black Macdonald Center for the Study of
Islam and Christian-Muslim Relations of Hartford Seminary, and Mas-
jid Muhammad No. 14 of Hartford. Three chapters (on law, music and
art) were solicited for this book. The project was supported by a grant
from the Connecticut Humanities Council, the state committee of the
National Endowment for the Humanities. Other financial support was
received from the Islamic Science Foundation, United Technologies
Corporation, Exxon Corporation, the Intercultural Studies Program of
Trinity College, and the World Affairs Center, Inc. The viewpoints and
recommendations expressed are those of the authors and do not necessarily reflect those of the Connecticut Humanities Council, the National Endowment for the Humanities, or other sponsoring
organizations.

   The organizing committee wishes to thank the Wadsworth
Atheneum, the Greater Hartford Consortium for Higher Education,
the University of Hartford, and the Hartford Graduate Center for co-
sponsoring the event; Ms. Marjorie Anderson of the World Affairs
Center and Ms. Ruth Billyou of the Greater Hartford Consortium for
Higher Education for their assistance in the publicity efforts associated
with the project; Dr. James F. English, President of Trinity College,
Dr. Stephen Trachtenberg, President of the University of Hartford,
Dr. John Dillenberger, President of Hartford Seminary, Mr. Charles

Tracy Atkinson, Director of the Wadsworth Atheneum, Mr. Oliver F. Johnson, President of the World Affairs Center, Inc., Dr. Edythe J. Gaines, Commissioner of the Public Utilities Control Authority, State of Connecticut, Mr. Henry Parker, Treasurer for the State of Connecticut, and Dr. Peter K. Breit, Professor of Politics and Government, University of Hartford, for chairing the sessions, and Dr. Leslie Desmangles of the Intercultural Studies Program of Trinity College for his special endorsement.

The publication of this book is the result of the efforts of a number of people and agencies. In addition to the particular support given to the project, United Technologies Corporation has made a special contribution toward the publication of this book. The editorial assistance, especially of Ms. Barbara Haines, has been invaluable. Ms. Roseann Lezak has shouldered major burdens not only with respect to the lecture series itself, but also in the typing of the many drafts of the manuscripts. Assistance in typing from Ms. Mary Bragg, Ms. Elizabeth D'Amico, Ms. Gay Weidlich, Ms. Patricia Jacques, and Ms. Velga Adamson is also noted. Ms. Cecelia Larson prepared the line drawings. Mr. Charles Sardeson, of the Hartford Office of the National Conference of Christians and Jews, was not only the instigator of the whole project, including the book, but an indispensable ally in its implementation. For all these contributions, the editors and the authors, express their acknowledgment and thanks. Without this multifaceted help, neither the project nor the book would have been possible.

Hartford, Ct.   YYH
Fall 1983   BH
                                                                        EF

The Islamic Impact

Introduction

Yvonne Yazbeck Haddad

$\mathcal{T}$HE AUTHORS who have contributed chapters to this volume focus on the impact of aspects of Islamic culture within their own areas of expertise in order to provide a comprehensive statement on the subject. They analyze the manner in which Muslims in the past have attempted to nurture, synthesize, and implement the prescriptions of the faith in fashioning their world. They report on current efforts to recapture the impetus and dynamism of that faith to create a new Islamic civilization, one that is grounded in the teachings of the Quran, attempting to imbue all human institutions and cultural expressions with an Islamic character.

The essential belief of Muslims is grounded in the revelation of the Quran which affirms that Islam is the religion of God which He ordained for the welfare of humanity, "Religion with God is Islam" (S. 3:19). To be a Muslim is to live a life of submission and surrender to the will of God.

Islam is a religion of the Book. The Quran, Muslims believe, was revealed to the Prophet Muhammad by God for the guidance of humanity. Its divine origin has endowed it with ultimate authority. It is considered to be the final arbiter of all truth governing the various aspects of life. Throughout the centuries, the Quran has been at the center of all Islamic intellectual activity, having an impact on philosophy, lexicography, jurisprudence, law, theology, art, and calligraphy, among others. Committed to memory by many Muslims in childhood, it forms the collective conscience of the community, a constant reminder to the believers of the divine will.

1

The revelation in the Quran is believed to be the last and most complete in a series that God made available to the world through His messengers. In fact, the Quran teaches that God has never left humanity to fend for itself. His guidance was given to Adam when he descended from the Garden. When Adam's progeny veered from the path of truth, God sent other messengers to call people to return to Islam, the worship of the One God. "He has prescribed for you that religion He commended to Noah and that which We revealed to you and commended unto Abraham, Moses, and Jesus" (S. 42:13). The history of revelation ends with the message given to Muhammad which has been preserved in perfect form, thus rendering further messengers unnecessary: "Today I have perfected for you your religion and completed my grace unto you and have accepted for you Islam as a religion" (S. 5:3).

In a certain sense, then, Islam is the religion of the Prophet Muhammad. He is considered the seal of the prophets, the bearer of the final message from God. God and His messenger are linked together in forty specific references in the Quran, urging the believers to have faith in both. Obedience to the messenger is itself obedience to God. Furthermore, the primary act of worship incumbent on every Muslim, the confession of faith, witnesses to God's uniqueness and Muhammad's primary role as His messenger. The Quran enjoins the believers to take the prophet as a "good example" (S. 33:21). This has led Muslim scholars to carefully and faithfully collect anecdotes about Muhammad's life and teachings which form the corpus of the Hadith, a vital source of authoritative precedent of what constitutes true Islam. The Prophetic example, throughout the centuries has served Muslim communities as a guide for daily life and a restraint against assimilation into surrounding cultures.

The prescriptions and proscriptions of the Quran, supplemented by the traditions of the Prophet, form the essential core of Islamic law which was developed to legislate proper behavior with attention given to the minutest detail of human activity. Where there was no clear commandment or precedent, the consensus of the scholars and analogical reasoning were utilized to develop Islamic standards of response to meet various situations that confront the believer.

Islamic law became the norm by which Muslims sought to administer and supervise a righteous order. The law dealt with all aspects of life, including the proper relationship of man to God, the prescribed acts of worship incumbent on all adherents to the faith, which were known as the pillars of Islam. From this vantage point, Islam is the praxis of the believers. A Muslim is one who bears witness to the unity of God and the apostleship of Muhammad. He is expected to perform the prescribed prayer five times a day, tithe 2.5 percent of his assets, fast daily from pre-dawn to dusk during the whole month of Ramadan, and go to Mecca on pilgrimage at least once in his lifetime, if he can afford it.

Islamic law is also concerned with the regulation of proper human relations: of husband to wife, of child to parent, of believer to non-believer, and so on. It provides guidance on economic, cultural, social, and political behavior. In time it became the custodian of the ethical foundation of the totality of Islamic society, acquiring an infallible status, commanding corporate obedience because of its divine origin.

Even in its formative period, however, there were those who felt that the mere fulfillment of religious obligations was insufficient since strict adherence to the prescriptions of the law would lead to formalism—a sterile existence with no spiritual content. Rather than marking the perimeters of life, Islamic law was perceived as a mere stepping stone into the spiritual dimension of existence whose ultimate goal is union with God, a union which the righteous will achieve in the hereafter, a union which the Sufis, the mystics of Islam, felt was within the reach of mortals while in this world. Seen from the perspective of the Sufis, Islam is the experience of God.

To realize this experience, they emphasized the necessity of the constant awareness of God which can be achieved by various means including prayer, meditation, and the remembrance of His name. In this they followed the example of the Prophet Muhammad who spent days meditating prior to his reception of the revelation. They were also heeding the injunctions of the Quran to recall, remember, and recite the name of God. The spiritual life they sought was initiated by asceticism—the renunciation of the world, its cares, and its allurements, by assuming a life of poverty and abstinence, placing full trust in God's sustenance, and by focusing one's consciousness on Him.

Over the years, new means of attaining the experience of God were explored and developed by various Sufis—among them chanting, whirling, and other physical and spiritual disciplines. Their effort at communicating their joy and fulfillment led to their becoming the chief vehicle for the propagation of the faith. They wrote volumes of poetry and prose that ranged in topics from warnings to the believers about the pitfalls of being "world-centered," with graphic descriptions of the fate awaiting them in hell, to rapturous descriptions of their "God-oriented" experience. This was defined by some as love, by others as knowledge, and still others as union. Most of them manifested a negative attitude toward the material world, for in their striving to discipline the self to be a worthy receptacle of divine grace, they were anxious to eliminate the world from their consciousness, seeking the experience of God in their lives.

This attitude led some Sufis at times to ignore the law, which earned them the wrath of the legal establishment anxious to maintain uniformity in public morality. But over the years, the influence of Sufism became quite pervasive; it was able to count legists and jurists among its practitioners, insuring thereby a spiritual dimension to the juridical expositions of the pillars of the faith.

The relation between law and mysticism fluctuated between being one of conflict and compatibility throughout Islamic history, with reformers tending to advocate a return to a strict adherence to the law when there is an apparent setback in the fortunes of the Muslim community. This does not mean that Sufism advocated anarchy; rather, Sufi orders in various Muslim countries have at times been the vanguard of reform. In all cases, these orders called for a disciplined life as well as adherence to the law.

This has not saved the Sufis from severe criticism and condemnation by both the modernists at the turn of this century and the revivalists today. Mysticism is perceived by both as a menace to communal revitalization. To the former, its threat was seen in the Sufi's quest for personal communion with God at the expense of other considerations. The focus on personal salvation led to the renunciation of the material world, calling it transitory since the seeker sought reward in the hereafter. To reformers anxious to industrialize and westernize their countries, Sufism was an obstacle, at best a palliative, distracting the believers from the serious business of modernizing educational, legal, political, cultural, and economic institutions and proceeding to build a new society.

Advocates of the politics of Islamic revival agree that Sufism is a distortion of Islam; with its undue emphasis on the spiritual dimension of life, they see its deviation more clearly in its antinomian attitude. For them, the revival of Islamic potency is contingent on corporate commitment to the religion and a faithful obedience to its law.

The importance of Islamic law in defining what can be considered properly Muslim and thus in the maintenance of an Islamic ethos in culture and society can be grasped when one realizes that after the death of the Prophet, in the world view of Islam, it was the community of believers that was entrusted with the preservation of God's guidance. Other groups, including Jews and Christians, were perceived to have previously veered from the truth by falsifying the revelations their messengers preached. Through obedience to the law of God Muslims are a constant living witness to His will.

This awareness has recently given impetus to efforts throughout the Muslim world to return to what is considered to be the essential core of Islam, shedding the accretions of centuries of redefinitions as well as the westernizing efforts that were championed in the early part of the twentieth century under the tutelage of European colonial powers. From this consciousness has grown a new urgency to rummage and sift through the heritage, the repository of Islamic knowledge, to rediscover the authentic Islamic statement on trade, business practices, economic and political theories, art, music, family and penal law—in fact every aspect of life.

The quest for authenticity is increasingly becoming the primary concern of a growing number of Muslims throughout the world. This is due in part to the spectacular events that led to the downfall of the Shah of Iran and the assumption of political power by those advocating the fusion of politics and religion in the administration of society. Their harnessing popular support through religion serves as a proven method for those anxious to bring about change in other countries. These include among others, members of the liberalizing and westernizing elites of the 40s and 50s who are dissappointed by the repeated failure of their governments to bring about the reforms they sought.

The search for the Islamic position has also captured the imagination of the growing number of educated young people, especially those majoring in science and technology, who appear to be impatient with the slow pace of development of their political, social, cultural, and economic resources aimed at gaining parity with western nations. It appears to have gained the allegiance of those disappointed with the apparent inability of current governments in nation states to operate independently in the interest of their own people without succumbing to outside pressures that make them veritable instruments of "big-power" politics.

In the Arab context, the search for an Islamic solution seems to have touched a sensitive chord in a large sector of the population who have wearied of proposed solutions to the problem of Israel. They reflect a growing perception that nationalism and socialism, in vogue for a while, have failed to liberate Palestine or provide justice for its displaced people. They see Islamic revival as the only alternative, not only for the recovery of dignity and assertion of identity, but also as a potent force capable of mobilizing the masses in a united effort to affirm the collective will. In some cases this perception is not new; it takes into account the fact that the majority of Muslims live in rural areas and are governed by religious traditions, their lives rotating around seasonal festivals. The new politics of Islamic revival is expected to wean the populace from inertia and the feeling of despair and to act as an incentive to further technological development of society, while preserving inherited values.

The politics of Islamic revival has been championed as a response that seeks the welfare of the Muslim people rather than serving the interests of the ruling elites. While affirming that Islam insures the right to private property, its advocates generally call for an equitable redistribution of wealth to meet the needs of the believers rather than the pleasures of the wealthy. They insist that the various constitutions and laws adopted by national governments throughout the Muslim world need to be replaced by Islamic law as the primary guide to all aspects of life. They advocate the restoration of Islamic education as a cure for the anomie that permeates Muslim society, severed from its roots by the adoption of Western education and the abandonment of the heritage which had produced the glorious past.

The scramble for the recovery and restoration of the idealized authoritative past has centered on the importance of community solidarity and the necessity of placing the welfare of the group above that of the individual. While adherents insist that each person is accountable for his commitment in word and deed to the obedience of God's will on earth, the believers are reminded that the Quran says, "You are the best community brought forth to humanity commanding what is good and forbidding what is evil and believing in God" (S. 3:110). This is not an affirmation of election by God granting the Muslims license to legislate morality; rather, it is God's selection of a community willing to function as an instrument of His will on earth.

1

Islam and Politics

Eqbal Ahmad

$\mathscr{I}$ N WRITING about Islam and politics, one faces special difficulties. The field of Islamic studies, strewn with ancient potholes and modern mines, is dominated by apparently different but complementary adversaries—the "traditionalist" Ulema and the "modern" Orientalists. Their methods are different; so are their intentions. Yet, with few exceptions, both tend to view Islam's relationship to politics in fundamentalist and textual terms. Both emphasize the absence of separation between religion and politics in Islam. Both hold an essentially static view of Islam and interpret change and innovations produced by social and economic forces as impingements on established, therefore ordained, religious standards. Both treat Muslim history, especially its most creative periods—that is, the Umayyads in Spain, the Moghuls in India, the Safavids in Persia—as deviations from the norm. The interplay of the Westerners' academic orthodoxy and the Ulemas' theological orthodoxy has set the terms of prevalent discourse on Islam.

A second problem concerning perceptions and prejudices should be put forth. The Islamic civilization is the only one with which the territorial, religious, and cultural boundaries of the West have fluctuated for fourteen centuries. Islam's relationship with the West has been continuous, frequently intimate, marked by protracted and violent confrontations and fruitful, though often forgotten, collaboration. During the century that followed the prophethood of Mohammad, the dramatic expansion of Islamic dominance occurred largely at the expense of Christendom. Subsequently, the West and Islam remained locked in a relationship of antagonistic collaboration that included

7

seven centuries of Muslim rule in Spain, unsuccessful invasion of France, and an inconclusive occupation of Sicily. The long and bitter confrontation during the Crusades, and later the Ottoman domination of the Balkans further solidified in the West the adversarial perceptions and menacing images of Islam and Muslims. Even the prophet Mohammad and the Quran were not spared several centuries of vilification and abusive misrepresentation. In turn, medieval Muslim writers misrepresented and misjudged Judaism and Christianity. However, because Islam venerates Biblical prophets as predecessors of Muhammad, their polemics fortunately stopped short of vilifications *in extremis*. To the Western world's credit, the "medieval canon" of Christian discourse on Islam (up to the eighteenth century) has been admirably documented.[1]

This unique history of the West's encounter with a non-Western civilization undoubtedly left on both sides a heritage of prejudice and resentment. Yet, in this pattern of hostility, there were periods of accommodation. While our cultures were traditional, agrarian, and medieval, there existed a structural symmetry between them which accounted for a degree of equality in the exchange of ideas as well as products. Winners and losers manufactured and used the same weapons, traded in comparable goods, debated on familiar intellectual premises. There was a certain congruence of class interests and shared attitudes among the aristocrats, craftsmen, traders, and scholars. The commonality of outlook between Saladin the Great and Richard the Lionhearted is known to almost every Muslim and Christian child even today. Students of European and Muslim history can recall numerous such examples. But the symmetry which had constituted the basis of an intimacy and antagonistic collaboration between Islam and the West disappeared in modern times. Nothing in the past was as damaging to Muslim-Western understanding as has been the structurally unequal encounter of traditional, agrarian/pastoral Muslim societies with the industrial and capitalist West. Its many ramifications include, as we shall presently see, modern Islam's peculiar, disjointed relationship to politics.

A dramatic reversal in the relationship between the Muslim world and the West began with Napoleon Bonaparte's invasion of Egypt in 1798 and the establishment of British dominion over Moghul India during the eighteenth and nineteenth centuries. It ended with the break-up of the Ottoman empire, which was the last of the Muslim empires, and the colonization by European countries of virtually all of the Muslim world from East Asia to West Africa. It was a traumatizing development for the Muslims. This was not merely due to the fact that for the first time in the confrontation between Islam and the West they were the colonized, not the colonizers; rather, this latest encounter of Islam with the West was felt as a deeply dehumanizing and alienating experience. Modern imperialism was unique in history in that it was a complex and highly integrated system in which pre-industrial and pastoral civilizations were either destroyed (as was the case with the great civilizations of the Western hemisphere) or subjugated (as were the countries of Asia and Africa) to serve the needs of the mercantilist and industrializing Western metropoles. The legitimizing principles of this system (that is, the White Man's burden, the *Mission Civilisatrice* or the Manifest Destiny) were based on the assumption of the inferiority of "native" peoples, their lesser existence, and diminished humanity. Devaluation of the colonized civilization, debasement of its cultural heritage, and distortion of native realities have been part of the moral epistemology of modern imperialism. These were important elements of the "corporate institution" which Edward Said and others have recently analyzed as "Orientalism."[2]

As the process of decolonization began, the Western need to justify domination over the "natives" was lessened. A certain détente in the organized libel against Islam and Muslims was expected. The expectation was credible, given the growth of ecumenical sentiments in the United States and Europe and the ease in communications provided by technological development and international exchange. After centuries of interruption, the possibility had reappeared that Western scholars and their Muslim counterparts would begin to recognize and reassess the limitations and biases of their intellectual work and also begin to examine critically but positively the meaning of the Islamic experience in history and society. The trend that emerged between the world wars, first in France, then in Britain and the United States, suggested that a change in this direction had started. In France, the works of Louis Massignon encouraged the rise of a "revisionist" school which included scholars of Islam such as Jacques Berque, Maxime Rodinson, Yves Lacoste, and Roger Arnaldez. In Britain and the United States, their counterparts were to be found in H. A. R. Gibb, Wilfred Cantwell Smith, and Norman Daniel. Unfortunately, this welcome trend was overwhelmed by those with vested ideological interests.[3]

Far from producing a detente in the post-colonial era, the Cold War and the Arab-Israeli conflict added to the Western discourse on Islam an element of manipulation and malevolence. Cold War academic functionaries and pro-Israeli Middle East "experts" have rendered difficult an appreciation of contemporary Muslim problems. These include distortions, misrepresentations and libels, not mere criticism. Critical writing needs to be distinguished from racial and ideological hostility. There is a desperate need for critical analyses of the Muslim world's contemporary predicament. From Morocco through Syria, and Iraq to Pakistan and Indonesia, Muslims are ruled by armed minorities. Some describe themselves as socialist and democratic, others as Islamic; yet others as Islamic, socialist, and democratic. Nearly all Muslim governments are composed of corrupt and callous elites more adept at repressing the populace than protecting natural resources or national sovereignty. They are more closely linked to foreign patrons than to the domestic polity. The recent rise of fundamentalist, neo-totalitarian Muslim movements is an aberration, not a norm in Muslim history. However, it is predicated upon the failure of the current regimes and the absence of visible, viable alternatives. These are hardly the times for expert praise and paeans. But a critical scholarship is the opposite of heartless and opportunistic employment of expertise.

It is a nemesis of biased scholarship that the societies and systems they serve ultimately suffer from their distortions. An understanding of Muslim politics and the anguish and aspirations of Islamic, especially Middle Eastern, peoples has slipped beyond the grasp of most "experts." Hence, historic trends toward major developments—that is, the outbreak of an epoch-making revolution in Algeria, an Arab military rebound in October, 1973, or Anwar Sadat's dramatic and disastrous *demarche* for peace—went unnoticed by them until events hit the headlines. In 1978, big men in the United States, from Jimmy Carter to Walter Cronkite, were surprised by the failure of the experts to perceive the revolutionary process in Iran, which had been long in the making. The failure, nevertheless, was as predictable as the Iranian revolution. The Shah was deemed a friend of the United States as well as of Israel; he was "modern," anti-Islam, and generous to the experts. Foremost Iranian experts explained the Shah by distorting Iran and its history. Thus Professor Leonard Binder, a distinguished professor at the University of Chicago wrote, "Here is a nation, Iran, that has not ruled itself in historical times, that has had an alien religion (Islam) imposed upon it, that has twisted that religion (Shi'ism) to cheat its Arab tormentors, that can boast of no military hero . . . that has been deprived by its poets and mystics, of all will to change its fate.[4]

Professor Marvin Zonis, another well-known expert on Iran,

found the "kingly grace" of the "Shahanshah" (King of Kings) toward "foreign scholars . . . both courageous and laudable . . . the monarch's control over the internal situation is at its zenith. It is undoubtedly true that no Iranian ruler however exercised as much power or commanded as responsive a political system as does Mohammed Reza Pahlavi in 1974, 'urban guerrillas' and censorious foreign critics notwithstanding."[5] Examples are nearly as numerous as experts. Superficially trained, attached to disciplines and methods in flux, governed by the preferences of governments and foundations, and lacking empathy with the *objects* of their study, the area experts of the post-colonial era have all the limitations of conventional Orientalists but few of their strengths.

   A historically rigged intellectual tradition, then, continues to dominate Western perspectives on Islam. Its impact on Muslims too has been considerable. It has made the traditionalist Ulema more obdurate and closed to new methods of critical inquiry. It has led educated Muslims to neglect substantive contributions of Western scholarship to theological ideas and historical interpretation. Above all, it has stunted the creative and critical impulses of modernist Muslims by activating their defensive instincts.

In writing about Islam for a largely Western audience, a Muslim faces hard choices between explanation and exploration. One's instinct is to explain the errors, deny the allegations, and challenge the overwhelmingly malevolent representations of Muslim history, ideals, and aspirations. For a century, since Syed Ameer Ali wrote *Life and Teachings of Mohammed,* most modernist Muslim writers have, to varying degrees, surrendered to this instinct.[6] There is a certain poignancy to their effort, for these colonized, Western-educated Muslims were desperate to communicate to the West, in Western terms, pride in their devalued culture, distorted history, and maligned religion. For their labors they have been dubbed modern Islam's "Apologist" school. Thus, another vast body of contemporary literature on Islam merely symbolizes the futility of corrective and defensive responses to the Orientalists' representation of Islam. This is reason enough to resist giving in to this urge.

It is commonly asserted that in Islam, unlike in Christianity and other religions, there is no separation of religion and politics. In strict textual and formal legal terms, this may be true. But this standard generalization is not helpful in comprehending Muslim political praxis either historically or contemporaneously. In its most fundamental sense, politics involves a set of active links, both positive and negative, between civil society and institutions of power. In this sense, there has been little separation, certainly none in our time, between religion and politics anywhere. For example, Hinduism played an important role in the ideological and organizational development of the Indian national movement. Mahatma Gandhi's humanitarian and idealistic principles of passive resistance and non-violence drew on Hindu precepts like Ahimsa. The Mahatma was challenged by fundamentalist religious parties like the Arya Samaj and the Hindu Mahasabha, and died at the hands of a Hindu fundamentalist political assassin. In Southeast Asia, including Vietnam, Buddhism and Buddhist institutions have been a potent force on both sides of the political divide.

In the United States, where the two major political parties have become increasingly indistinguishable on the basic issues of war and peace, the Christian churches have emerged as the primary platforms of political discourse, disputations, and even militancy. The political activism of Christians in the United States ranges widely from the right-wing Reverend Jerry Falwell's Moral Majority through the centrist liberalism of the National Council of Churches, to Dorothy Day's populist humanism and Father Daniel Berrigan's militant pacifism. In Latin American countries—including Argentina, Chile, El Salvador, and Brazil—government-sponsored assassination squads have been carrying out their murderous missions in the name of preserving Christian values and virtues. On the opposite side, bishops are killed and nuns are raped for their advocacy of justice and democracy.

As for Judaism, we have witnessed its full-fledged politicization with a fundamentalist ideology successfully staking out its claims over Palestine on the Bible's authority. The Bible is still being invoked to justify the expansion of Israel into "Judea and Samaria" (that is, the West Bank and Gaza) and further dispossession of Christian and Muslim Palestinians from their ancient homeland. Since the outcome of the struggle for power in revolutionary Iran remains uncertain and since in Pakistan a self-proclaimed "Islamic" dictator rules in isolation, Israel and Saudi Arabia must be counted as the two truly theocratic states in the Middle East. Both have a contradictory existence: one as an "Islamic" monarchy; the other as a sectarian "democracy" whose Christian and Muslim subjects are treated, under law, as second-class citizens. Given these facts, it is obviously tendentious to ascribe to Muslims, as media commentators and academic experts so often do, a special proclivity to engage in religiously motivated politics.

In a narrower perspective, the relationship of politics and religion may be discussed in terms of the links between religion and state power. In this sense, separation between state and religion has existed in the Muslim world for at least eleven of Islam's fourteen centuries. The organic links between religion and state power ended in A.D. 945 when a Buwayhid Prince, Muiz al-Dawla Ahmad, marched into the capital city of Baghdad and terminated the Abbasid Caliph's dual role as the temporal and spiritual leader of the Islamic nation. For a time, the Caliph served in various parts of the Muslim world as a legitimizing symbol through the investiture of temporal rulers—Sultans, Amirs, and Khans—among them, successful rebels and usurpers. The Buwayhids, who ruled over Iraq and Fars as Amirs, kept the Caliphate in subjection for 110 years until they were displaced in A.D. 1055 by Tughril, the Seljuk Warrior. In 1258, the Mongols sacked Baghdad, killed the Caliph and his kin, and terminated the Abbasid Caliphate, which had been for two centuries a Merovingian cipher. Although the Caliphate was revived and claimed—at different times in various places, by a variety of rulers—it never quite mustered the allegiance of a majority of Muslims. Power, in effect, remained secularized in Muslim practice.[7]

One is generous in dating the effective separation of religion and state power from the Buwayhid intervention of A.D. 945. The fundamentalist Ulema take a somewhat more conservative view. They believe that no Muslim state has been Islamic since the accession to power of the Umayyad dynasty in A.D. 650; to them, the Islamic state effectively ended with the first four Caliphs who had been companions of the Prophet Muhammad. However, the minority Shiite Ulema, who believe that legitimate succession belonged only to the blood relatives and descendants of the Prophet, definitely do not regard two of the four Caliphs (Umar and Uthman) as legitimate rulers. The orthodox Ulema's rejection of the Islamic character of Muslim states after 650 is based primarily on three factors. The first concerns the presumed impiety of all but a few exceptional rulers (that is, Umar Ibn Abd Al-Aziz, 717–720). The second relates to the historic prevalence of secular laws and practices in Muslim statecraft. The third involves the actual fragmentation of the Islamic world into multiple political entities—historically, Sultanates, emirates, Khanates, Sheikdoms, empires, and now, republics. All theologians agree on the principles of a single Umma (Muslim nation) and a single Caliph (or Imam) as essential to a truly Islamic polity governed according to divine laws and the example of the Prophet.

Lacking all three conditions of the ideal Islamic polity, Muslim peoples have for more than a millennium accepted as legitimate the exercize of state power by temporal governments, as long as they observe the basic norms of justice and fair play, and rule with some degree of consent from the governed. This generalization applies also to the overwhelming majority of Ulema and local religious leaders. In fact, the most renowned theologians of Islam—that is, al-Mawardi (974–1058), al-Baghdadi (d. 1037), al-Ghazzali (1058–1111), and Ibn Jamaa (1241–1333)—have developed a large body of exegeses to justify, explain, and elaborate on this historic compromise between the Islamic ideal and Muslim political realities. Thus, in all religious communities, there is a repository of millennial traditions in Islam that tend to surface most forcefully in times of crisis, collective stress, and anomie.[8] Times have rarely been as bad, as stressful, or as disorienting for the Muslim peoples as they are now. Hence, all the contrasting symptoms associated with deep crises of politics and society—rise of religious fundamentalism, radical and revolutionary mobilization, spontaneous uprisings and disoriented quietism—characterize Muslim politics today.

A fusion of religion and political power was and remains an ideal in the Muslim tradition. But the absence of such a fusion is a historically experienced and recognized reality. The tradition of statecraft and the history of Muslim peoples have been shaped by this fact. The many manifestations of this reality are important in comprehending the Muslim polity. A few of these need to be mentioned here. As a religious and proseletyzing medieval civilization, the Islamic Umma evinced a spirit of tolerance towards other faiths and cultures that has been rare in history. It is important for us to acknowledge—for the sake of historical veracity as well as for a desperately needed reinforcement of non-sectarian and universalist values in Muslim civilization— that non-Muslims, especially Christians, Jews, and Hindus, have been an integral part of the Islamic enterprise. In the pre-colonial period, Muslim law and practice reflected a certain separation and autonomy of religious and social life along confessional lines. Admittedly, there were also instances of excesses against and oppression of the non-Muslim population under Muslim rule. Yet, the greatest achievements of Islamic civilization in science, philosophy, literature, music, art, and architecture, as well as statecraft, have been the collective achievements of Christians, Jews, Hindus, and others participating in the cultural and economic life of the "Islamicate." In fact, the most creative periods of Muslim history have been those that witnessed a flowering in the collaborative half of our ecumenical relationships. This secular

fact of Muslim political praxis, from Indonesia and India through th
Fertile Crescent and Egypt to Spain, is generally neglected in the writings both of the Ulema and the Orientalists. Yet, it is more relevant to
understanding Islam's relationship to politics than the antics of any
current "Islamic" political leader.

Throughout history, Muslims, like other people who live in complex civilizations, have evinced paradoxical tendencies in relation to
politics. In dissident movements, Islam has sometimes played a crucial
role by galvanizing group support for opposition leaders around a reformist, often puritanical creed, attacking the corruption and profligacy
of a ruling class. The latest case in point is Ayatullah Khomeini's
Islamic Movement in Iran. An early example is the austere movement
of Ibn Tumart, which in the twelfth century gathered enough support in
North Africa to displace the Almoravid dynasty in Morocco and Spain.
A later example is the puritanical Wahhabi movement of the eighteenth
century, which gained tribal support in the Najd, especially of the tribe
of Saud, and thence spread to the Arabian peninsula. In power, such
reformist movements have betrayed a proclivity to softening and secularization. The Almohad, for example, patronized the rather secular
and speculative Philosophical School including Ibn Rushd, known in
the West as Averroes (1126–1198).

On the other hand, the Muslim community has resisted state
sponsorship of a creed or even a school of religious thought. Thus, two
of the greatest Muslim rulers encountered popular resistance when
they unsuccessfully attempted to sponsor an official creed. The Abbasid Caliph, al-Mamun (786–833), son of Harun al-Rashid (of the *Arabian Nights!*) and founder of the House of Wisdom in Baghdad (where
many of the translations and commentaries on Greek works were completed and later contributed to the European Renaissance) adopted the
Mutazilite doctrines as official creed. This rationalist school of religious thought in Islam was beginning to flourish when it received the
sponsorship of the state. At the time, the Caliphate was in its prime.
Resistance to it mounted rapidly in the Islamic community. It was thus
that the Mutazilites acquired the dubious distinction in Muslim history
of engaging in the first significant practice of repression on theological
grounds. Similarly, Akbar the Great (1542–1605), the most illustrious
of the Moghul Emperors in India met with widespread resistance from
his Muslim subjects when he promulgated his own eclectic creed *Dine
Ilahi* (1582). Fortunately, Akbar was skeptical and open-minded
enough to refrain from forcing his eccentric, ecumenical creed on the
populace.

  Historically, the Ulema as a class prospered and played a conservative role as mediators between political power and civil society,
much like the clergy in Christendom. During the first two centuries of
Islam, a significant number of theological scholars abjured any
identification with power, declining to serve even as judges. Thus,
Imam Abu Hanifa (d. 767), founder of one of the four schools of Sunni
Islamic law was flogged for refusing the judgeship of Baghdad. In later
years many served as legal advisers to governments and as judges. The
institution of Waqf (private and public endowment of property to
mosques and schools) which were invariably administered by the
Ulema, and their role as educators and as interpreters of religious law,
insured for them a lucrative and prominent place in society next to the
military and bureaucracy. As a class, therefore, they betrayed a certain
bias in favor of stability and obedience to temporal authority. Thus, al-
Mawardi, al-Baghdadi, and al-Baqillani—great theological authorities
to this day—held that an unjust and unrighteous ruler should not claim
obedience, and that the community would be justified in transferring its
allegiance to a contender. However, they opposed rebellion and civil
war. The great philosopher-theologian, al-Ghazzali—the equivalent in
Islam of Thomas Aquinas—and his successor Ibn Jamaa, invoked the
Doctrine of Necessity to counsel that public tolerance of even a bad
ruler was preferable to anarchy and civil strife. Professor Anwar Syed
has rightly concluded that the theologians "endorsed the secularization
of politics in return for a pact of mutual assistance between the government and the Ulema."[9]
  Recognizing their historical role as well as their present discontent, most contemporary Muslim governments have tried various
schemes that offer a modicum of security and status to the Ulema; in
almost all instances they have been successful in coopting the clerical
class. It is noteworthy that the most iconoclastic of contemporary
Muslim rulers—Habib Bouguiba (1903–   ) of Tunisia—has encountered the least resistance from the Ulema. This is so not only because
he has enjoyed considerable popularity among the masses as the
liberator of Tunisia, but also because, unlike Kemal Ataturk (founding
father of modern Turkey) or Mohammed Reza Khan (1877–1944, founder of the Pahlevi dynasty in Iran), Bourguiba did not attempt to
suppress forcibly religion and traditional Muslim institutions. Rather,
while instituting modernist reforms, he allowed the Ulema a certain
visibility and status as religious leaders.
  The political quietism of the Ulema has not been shared by all
sections of the Muslim intelligentsia, and by no means by the majority

of the Islamic community. There has, in fact, been a perennial tension between the moral imperatives of Muslim culture and the holders of power. It is difficult to recall a widely-known Muslim saint who did not collide with state power. Popular belief may have exaggerated the actual confrontations with contemporary rulers of men like the Persian saint, Mevlana Jalaluddin Rumi (1207–1273)—best known to the West as the founder of the mystic order of "whirling dervishes"—the Indian Khwaja Muinuddin Chishti (1142–1236), and the Moroccan saint, Sidi Lahsen Lyusi (1631–1691). But in this case, popular belief is the more significant indicator of political culture. It is equally important to emphasize that in each instance the collision was not incidental, a mere adding of lustre to the growth of a legend. Rather, it was a principal landmark in the making of a saint, in distinguishing the exceptional Muslim from the ordinary. In this conception of sainthood there is an admission, on the one hand, of the difficulty of achieving an alignment of piety to power and an affirmation, on the other hand, of a Muslim's obligation to confront the excesses of political authority.

The political culture of Islam is, by and large, activist and insurrectionary. Scholars have described the Muslim heartland from Pakistan to Mauritania as lands of insolence. Historically, rebellions have been as endemic here as were wars in Western Europe, and the target of insurrection has often been the state's authority. Until recently, all but a few Muslim polities were typically divided between what the Maghrebins ("Western" Arabs of North Africa) aptly named *Bilad al-Siba* (the Country in Rebellion) and *Bilad al-Makhzan* (the Country of the Treasury). There are exceptions to the rule, but normally, both popular rebellions and dynastic movements of opposition have been led by temporal figures. When involved in dissident politics, religious figures and groups were generally associated with the mystical schools, that is, with the pietist and populist, rather than the orthodox, theological tradition in Islam. However, as with state power, Islam has played a certain role in the legitimization of revolt. If the state-oriented Ulema cited religious injunctions against disobedience and contumacy, rebels too invoked the Quran and the Prophet's traditions, calling upon Muslims to struggle (Jihad) against tyranny and oppression.

An explanation for the perenniality of the insurrectionary strain in Muslim societies lies, at least partly, in the fact that wherever Islam took hold, it had its origins in a counter-tradition, a dissident point of view. In many regions such as North Africa and Central Asia, the spread of Islam was dialectically linked with social revolt. In other places, such as the Indian subcontinent, Islam's egalitarian precepts

and emphasis on social justice (both widely violated in practice) offered an escape to the disinherited from the harsh realities of oppression. In its exemplary form, Islam is a religion of the oppressed.
Hence, to this day it retains a powerful appeal among the poor and
oppressed throughout the world. It is currently the most rapidly growing faith in Africa and the East Indies. In the black communities and
prisons of the United States, too, Islam has a significant presence.
Even in independent India it is still finding new converts among the
Harijans (literally, Children of God, Gandhi's preferred name for the
Untouchables). The religious and cultural force of Islam continues to
outpace its political capabilities.[10]

Historically, then, the Islamic community has lived in separate
polities ruled by a wide variety of temporal authorities ranging from
tribal chieftains to modern republics. These secular political entities
have been ethnically, linguistically, and often religiously diverse. They
have been subject to constant change brought about by dynastic chal-
lengers and popular insurrections and, occasionally, by somewhat religiously motivated reformist movements. Given its heterogeneity,
observers of the Muslim world are impressed by the evidence of unity
in Islamic peoples' cultural, social, and political life. There is evidence
also of a strong Islamic affinity across territorial and linguistic divides.
This sense of solidarity has been based not merely on religious beliefs
and practices but on a shared consciousness of history, and a commonality of values. In this respect, the Islamic civilization was, and to a
lesser extent, remains inherently political. The values and linkages that
defined the unity of the historically diverse Muslim community have
been political in the deepest sense of the word. It should suffice here to
mention only a few factors that produced, over the centuries, the patterns of unity-in-diversity—what scholars have called the "mosaic" of
Muslim cultures.

For centuries a complementary tension, creative in its impact on
society and individuals, had existed between particularist and universalist loyalties and *loci* of Muslim political life. Typically, a Muslim
held two sets of identity: one—immediate, social, and spatially particular; the other—historical, ideological, cultural, and global. Almost all
Muslims lived in intensely community-oriented societies which, paradoxically, eschewed isolation. The paradox had a political dimension.
The interests and demands of local authority—that is, the extended
family, tribe, city, guild, and ethnic or linguistic group—in principle
competed with the universal expectations of the Umma, the vast Islamicate, that is, the worldwide community of people who embrace the

teachings of the Quran and practice Islam. The stability and quality of Muslim life had depended on the extent to which these two identities were reconciled. The achievement of such a reconciliation had been a preoccupation of politics in the Islamic civilization. Its attainment was by far the greatest accomplishment of civil society in the Muslim world. The processes by which this was achieved included a certain decentralization of power, a toleration of differences, and pluralism in religious and cultural life. Thus, while the Umma was one, and ideally united, its diversity was presumed. Rather, it was honored and extolled, for indeed it was the sign of God's mastery and creativity (S. 30:22). Also, the Prophets had declared "differences within the Umma to be a blessing."

A complex web of laws, activities, and institutions had contributed to the development of a common identity and culture in the Muslim world. A shared system of law, education, aesthetics, and religious organizations (especially religious fraternities or mystical orders) had assured the growth and continuity of a unifying ethos that cut across the political, ethnic, and linguistic boundaries of the Islamicate. For example, the divided and diverse Umma was assured a certain structural unity by a common adherence to laws (Sharia) which were based on the Quran, the Sunna (Traditions of the Prophet), and Ijma (Consensus of the Community). Typically, the Sharia served less as a guide to governmental conduct than as a regulator of societal relationships—of property, business transactions, marriages, and public morals.

For centuries, Muslims from the Pacific to the Atlantic Oceans were not merely born and buried according to similar rituals; more importantly, they were likely to be punished for crimes or failure to honor a contract, to have a grievance redressed, or a property dispute settled, get married or divorced, and make business transactions in accordance with similar, though not always identical, laws and codes of conduct. Similarly, the educational system of the Muslim world was based on a shared tradition of jurisprudence, philosophy, mathematics, ethics, and aesthetics. Hence, it was not uncommon for jurists and scholars to serve in more than one country in a life-time, for artists and architects to have lived and worked in various kingdoms, for elites to intermarry across political boundaries, for nomadic tribes to move from one ruler's domain to another. The passport was inimical to the spirit of the Islamicate. The phenomenon provided the framework for a sharing of values, the growth of an extra-territorial ethos, a source of collective identity.

This state of affairs lasted until the eighteenth century when

Western imperialism started to "territorialize" the Muslim world. Thereupon began its parcelling out into colonies and spheres of British, French, and Dutch influence. The differences and hostilities of European nation states came to be mirrored in Muslim lands. For the first time in its long and eventful history, Islamic civilization began to be defined by reference to another. Neither its wars nor peace, neither prosperity nor sufferings were of its own making. A people habituated to a history of success were reduced to serving another's history. The myriad links which had assured the Islamic culture its unity-in-diversity were severed. Its fragmentation, institutionalized in multiple ways, was completed by the creation of highly centralized, "independent" nation states governed by the post-colonial military-bureaucratic elites, each a disfigured copy of its colonial predecessors. The "mosaic" of Muslim culture was destroyed. The remarkable continuity which, over centuries of growth and expansion, tragedies and disasters, had distinguished Islamic civilization was interrupted. This change, labeled modernization by social scientists, has been experienced by contemporary Muslims as a disjointed, disorienting, unwilled reality. The history of Muslim peoples in the last one hundred years has been largely a history of groping—between betrayals and losses—toward ways to break this impasse, to somehow gain control over their collective lives, and link their past to the future.

In discussing the role of religion in contemporary Muslim politics, four points should be emphasized. First, the contemporary crisis of Muslim societies is without a parallel in Islamic history. Second, throughout the nineteenth and twentieth centuries the role of Islam in politics has varied in time and place. Third, the evidence of continuity with the patterns of the past has been striking. Fourth, in the 1980s, the trend is toward the growth of fundamentalist, neo-totalitarian Muslim movements. The phenomenon is contrary to the political culture and historical traditions of the Muslim majority. The still limited but growing appeal of the fundamentalist parties is associated with the traumas of Muslim political life, and the absence of viable alternatives to the existing state of affairs. A brief discussion of these points follows.

When a civilization reaches a point of fundamental crisis and perceptible decline, we see three responses. One may identify these as: (a) restorationist, (b) reconstructionist, and (c) pragmatist.

The restorationist is one that seeks the restoration of the past in

its idealized form. This is the thrust of fundamentalism, of such movements as the Muslim Brotherhood in the Arab world, the Jamaat-i-
Islami in Pakistan, the Sharekat Islam in Indonesia, and the Islamic
government of post-revolution Iran. So far, these have been minority
movements in the Muslim world. Without an exception, they have
failed to attract the large majority of workers, peasants, and the intelligentsia. This was true even in Iran where the shift toward the current
fundamentalist ideology began *after* the seizure of power.

The reconstructionist is one that seeks to blend tradition with
modernity in an effort to reform society. This is the thrust of the
modernist schools which have, intellectually and ideologically, dominated the Muslim world since the middle of the nineteenth century.
The most influential writers and thinkers of modern Islam—Jamaluddin
Afghani, Shibli Nomani, Syed Ameer Ali, Muhammad Abduh,
Muhammad Iqbal, Tahir Haddad, among others— have belonged to
this school of thought; in political life their influence had been considerable until the rise of military regimes in many Muslim countries.
This was true also in Iran where until after the Shah's fall no significant
group of Ulema had openly challenged the eminent Ayatullah Naini's
formulation in support of the democratic and constitutionalist movement (1904–1905), a position that was endorsed by the leading theologians of the Shia sect of Islam. For five decades, successive
generations of Iranian religious leaders had reaffirmed this position.
During the 1977–78 uprising against the Shah, all the politically prominent clerics of Iran, including Ayatullah Khomeini, had claimed to
favor a pluralistic polity and parliamentary government. The first ap-
pointment by Khomeini of a social democratic government with Dr.
Mehdi Bazargan as Prime Minister had seemed to confirm this claim.
Above all, it should be noted that the mobilization of the Iranian revolution toward Islam had been the work of such lay Muslim intellectuals
as Dr. Mehdi Bazargan, Jalal Alé Ahmad and Abul Hasan Bani Sadr.
The most important populizers of Islamic idealism were Ali Shariati, a
progressive layman, and the Ayatullah Mahmud Taleghani, a radical
religious leader. Although the Ayatullah Khomeini had been an important opposition figure since 1963, he was far from being the central
figure he became in 1978. In January 1978, as the revolution began to
gather momentum, the Shah's regime did Khomeini the honor of singl-
ing him out for its most publicized and personal attack. From this point
on, he became the counterpoint to the hated but central figure of the
Shah. An explanation of his meteoric rise to charismatic power lies in
the complex character of Iran's disorganic development, which lent

one of the objectively most advanced revolutions of history a millenarian dimension.

The pragmatist denotes an attitude of viewing religious requirements as being largely unrelated to the direct concerns of states and governments and of dealing with the affairs of the state in terms of the political and economic imperatives of contemporary life. The regulation of religious life is left to the civil society and to private initiatives. This approach has not been opposed by the reconstructionist school of intellectuals. As discussed earlier, it parallels the historical Muslim experience; as such, it is accepted both by the masses and the majority of the Ulema. Thus, wherever popular attitudes have been tested in open and free elections, pragmatist political parties and secular programs have gained overwhelming victories over their fundamentalist adversaries. In this realm of real politics one finds the resonances of the historical patterns discussed earlier. A few examples follow.

The paradoxical historical pattern involving on the one hand a preference for the temporal exercize of power and for a this-wordly political exchange, and on the other hand, popular vulnerability to religious symbols and slogans in times of social stress and collective anxiety, is replicated in modern times. Thus, throughout the twentieth century, the political heroes of the Muslim world, the liberators and founding fathers of contemporary Muslim nations, have been secular, generally Westernized individuals. To name only a few and the familiar, Kemal Ataturk (1881–1938), the founder of modern Turkey, Muhammad Ali Jinnah (1876–1948), the founding father of Pakistan, Ahmad Sukarno (1901–70), first president of Indonesia, Gamal Abdul Nasser (1918–70), first president of the republic of Egypt, Habib Bourguiba (1903–   ), of Tunisia, and the Seven Historic Chiefs of the Algerian Revolution, are regarded as the most popular and decidedly historic Muslim leaders of this century. The movements and political organizations they led were secular and heavily influenced by modern, largely Western, ideas. Today, the most popular movement in the Arab world, the Palestine Liberation Organization, claims a "secular and democratic" polity as the basis of its program; two of its three most prominent leaders are Christians.

By contrast, religious sectarianism is being most aggressively displayed in the Near East by two exclusionary ideologies and movements, the Phalangists and Zionists—one Maronite Christian, the other Jewish. Their shared antipathy to the secular, democratic, and universalist ideal underlay the ironic alliance between Israel and the Phalange, that is, between the Jewish state and the first fascist movement to make a successful bid for power in the post-World War II period. This same phenomenon also explains, perhaps, the fact that in the Occupied Territories Israeli authorities have been particularly harsh on the Christian population, and in an effort to destroy the unity of Christian and Muslim Palestinians, the government of Israel has been encouraging the growth of fundamentalist Muslim groups in the Occupied Areas, allowing them considerable freedom to organize. This freedom is denied the ecumenical and secular Palestinian nationalist movement.[11]

Another historical pattern repeating itself in our time is the resistance to state-decreed religion in the two countries where an official version of Islam is being imposed on citizens by the state. In Iran, thousands of people have been executed and jailed for their opposition to Ayatullah Khomeini's Islamic regime. Significantly, the Iranian resistance today is made up primarily of former activists and supporters of the opposition to the Shah. It includes the youthful Mujahideen movement, influenced by Islamic radicals Ayatullah Mahmud Taleghani and Dr. Ali Shariati, the followers of Abdul Hasan Bani Sadr (first president of Iran after the revolution), the nationalists who had previously supported the Constitutional regime of Prime Minister Mohammed Mossadegh, and many disillusioned former supporters of Ayatullah Khomeini. Were they to be given the freedom of choice, a majority of Iranian people would probably rid themselves of the fundamentalist tyranny in favor of a pluralistic and democratic regime of the sort the Iranian revolution, including the leaders of its Islamic wing, had promised them. In Pakistan, there is a certainty that if General Muhammad Zia ul-Haq were to fulfill his promise of a free election, the secular political parties would win it by an overwhelming majority—a certainty which has led General Zia to violate for more than six years the solemn promises he made to hold free elections within ninety days of his *coup d'etat*.

The centrality of Muslim peoples' predicament lies in the nature of their latest encounter with the West. The colonial encounter was unique in history in that it entailed the transformation of land and labor into commodities, in the literal, capitalist meaning of the word. Inevitably, it caused the erosion of economic, social, and political relationships which had contributed the bases of traditional Muslim order for more than a thousand years.

Unlike capitalist development in the West, in the Muslim world it occurred under foreign auspices for the benefit largely of the metropolitan power. Hence, it involved uneven and disorganic change. Consequently, the vast majority of Muslim people still live in structurally archaic, increasingly impoverished societies, but they are organically linked with the modern, industrial, metropolian world. They are the men and women—the Mustazafeen, the weakened ones—among whom the Algerian and Iranian revolutions had the strongest appeal. Germaine Tillion, a French anthropologist, who worked among the Algerians, has described them as "living on the frontiers of two worlds—in the middle of the ford—haunted by the past, fevered with the dreams of the future. But it is with their hands empty and their bellies hollow that they are waiting between their phantoms and their fevers."[12]

The trauma of Muslim life today is augmented by the fact that the resource-rich, strategically important heartlands of Islam are still subject to conquest and colonization. For the Palestinians, the era of decolonization opened in 1948 with the loss of the greater part of their ancient homeland. Now, they are being systematically dispossessed from its remnant, the West Bank and Gaza. In Lebanon, the refugees who fled in 1948, mostly from the Galilee, are being terrorized in Israel's pursuit of its policy of "dispersion." Jerusalem, a holy city and touchstone of Arab cultural achievements, has been unilaterally annexed, as has been the Golan Heights. Since the creation of the United Nations, only three of its members lost territories without being able to regain them. All three were Arab states. Only at the cost of betraying others and of isolating itself from its Arab/Islamic milieu did Egypt reclaim in 1982 the territories lost in 1967. Now Lebanon has joined the list of occupied countries; its ancient cities—Tyre, Sidon, Nabatiyyeh—are ruins. Beirut, the cultural capital of the Arab world, became the first capital city in the world whose televised destruction was watched by the world week after week. No Arab, no Muslim government budged except to suppress popular support at home. Their lucrative business with the United States—the sole sustainer of Israel—continued as usual. Never before had been so tragic the links between wealth and weakness, material resources and moral bankruptcy. Never before in the history of Islamic peoples had there been so total a separation of political power and civil society.

In the breach there is a time bomb. When the moral explosion of the masses occurs, it will undoubtedly have a reference to the past. But its objective shall be the future. The past is very present in the post-colonial Muslim societies. That it is a fractured past invaded by a new world of free markets, shorn of its substance and strength, incapable of assuring the continuity of communal life does not make it less forceful. Its power derives from the tyranny of contemporary realities, and the seeming absence of viable alternatives. For the majority of Muslim peoples, the experienced alternative to the past is a limbo—of foreign occupation and dispossession, of alienation from the land, of life in shanty-towns and refugee camps, of migration into foreign lands, and, at best, of permanent expectancy. Leaning on and yearning for the restoration of an emasculated, often idealized past is one escape from the limbo; striking out, in protest and anger, for a new revolutionary order is another. Occasionally, as in Iran, the two responses are merged. More frequently, they are separated in time but historically, organically, linked. Hence, in our time, religiously-oriented millenarian movements have tended to be harbingers of revolution.

The "hopes" that underlie popular support of religious movements in our time, Islamic or otherwise, are not really of the "past." The slogans and images of religio-political movements are invariably those of the past, but the hopes that are stimulated by them are intrinsically existential hopes, induced and augmented by the contemporary crisis, in this case, of the Muslim world. The often publicized ideological resurgence of Islam (social scientists and the American media spoke as much of "resurgent" Buddhism in the 1960s) is a product of excessive, uneven modernization and the failure of governments to safeguard national sovereignty or to satisfy basic needs. In the "transitional" Third World societies, one judges the present *morally,* with reference to the past, to inherited values, but materially in relation to the future. Therein lies a new dualism in our social and political life; the inability or unwillingness to deal with it entails disillusionment, terrible costs, and possible tragedy. One mourns Iran, laments Pakistan, fears for Egypt.

NOTES

1. See Norman Daniel, *Islam and the West: The Making of an Image* (Edinburgh: The University Press, 1958).
2. Edward Said, *Orientalism* (New York: Pantheon Books, 1978).
3. For a discussion on this question, see Stuart Schaar, "Orientalists in the Service of Imperialism," *Race and Class* 11 (Summer 1979).

4. Leonard Binder, *Iran: Political Development in a Changing Society* (Berkeley: University of California Press, 1962), pp. 61–62.

5. Marvin Zonis, "The Political Elite of Iran: A Second Stratum?" in *Political Elites and Political Development in the Middle East*, ed. Frank Tachau (New York: Halsted Press, 1975), pp. 212–13.

6. Syed Ameer Ali, *Life and Teachings of Mohammed or the Spirit of Islam*, 3rd ed. (London: W. H. Allen, 1899).

7. I owe this and the following point to Anwar H. Syed, *Islam and the Dialectic of National Solidarity in Pakistan* (New York: Praeger, 1983), chapter 2.

8. The literature on millenarian movements is quite extensive. A few basic works are: Vittorio Lanternari, *The Religions of the Oppressed* (New York: Knopf, 1963); N. Cohn, *The Pursuit of the Millennium* (London: Secker and Warburg, 1957); S. L. Thurpp, ed., *Millennial Dreams in Action: Comparative Studies in Society and History*, Supplement II (The Hague: Mouton, 1962).

9. Anwar H. Syed, *Islam and the Dialectic of National Solidarity in Pakistan*, Chapter 2.

10. See James Kritzeck and William H. Lewis, eds., *Islam in Africa* (New York: Van Nostrand-Reinhold, 1969). On the appeal of Islam among poor blacks in the United States, see the very powerful *Autobiography of Malcolm X* (New York: Grove Press, 1965); Archie Epps, ed., *Speeches of Malcolm X at Harvard* (New York: Morrow, 1968); Essien-Udom, E. U., *Black Nationalism: A Search for Identity* (Chicago: University of Chicago Press, 1962). Relatively little is known about the continuing conversion of Untouchables to Islam. For a brief description and refernences, see *World View: 1983* (New York: Pantheon, 1983), pp. 113–14.

11. For example, due to property expropriations and repression, in Jerusalem alone the Christian population had been reduced from 25,000 in 1967, to 7,000 in 1980. Similarly, Palestinian Christians constitute a disproportionate number of political prisoners in Israel.

12. Germaine Tillion, *Algeria: The Realities* (New York, Knopf, 1958).

2

~~~~~~

The Adaptation of Islam to Contemporary Economic Realities

Charles Issawi

*T*HIS CHAPTER will address four broad questions. First, what are the causes of the present discontent, or why were the Middle Easterners and North Africans dissatisfied with the economic evolution which their countries experienced in the course of the nineteenth and early twentieth centuries under Western rule? What were the factors that enabled them to do something about their discontents in the 1960s and 1970s? What was the stock of Muslim economic and social ideas, ideals, and practices on which they could draw when reshaping their societies? And finally, what institutional changes have they actually carried out?

DISCONTENTS

To a detached outsider who compares the present state of the Middle East and North Africa with what it was in 1800, or even 1914, the progress achieved is overwhelming. Where camel caravans moved at under three miles an hour, trains, cars, and planes now speed passengers and goods to their destinations. Great harbors and airports have been built. An impressive and ever widening array of factories has been established. And the region has become the center of the world's

27

oil industry and the largest depository of liquid funds in the international money market.

Nor is the progress purely economic. In 1914 only Turkey enjoyed independence; today all the countries of the region do. In 1914 about five to ten percent of children of primary school age attended school; today the figure is more than 70 percent; similarly, literacy has risen from 5 percent to nearly 50. Life expectancy has risen from under thirty years to fifty-five or sixty. Levels of living have distinctly improved. For the first time in several centuries, Middle Easterners are making a significant contribution to world science, literature, and art.

Middle Easterners, however, dwell much more on their misfortunes than on their blessings. Two features of the process of development that took place in the last 150 to 200 years have caused it to appear flawed in their eyes. First, a disproportionate share of the fruits of progress have accrued to foreigners and members of minority groups. Secondly, the social bonds that held the Middle Eastern society together were loosened or snapped. This chapter touches lightly on both, having been discussed at length elsewhere.[1] Regarding the fruits, Europeans (French, British, Belgians, Italians and others) and members of minority groups (Armenians, Greeks, Jews and Arab Christians) controlled practically all the urban activities: banking, insurance, foreign trade, industry, transport, etc. In North Africa and Palestine they also owned a large amount of land. Until the 1920s in Turkey, Iran, and Egypt and until the 1950s in North Africa, Muslims felt excluded from modern economic activities and could not but regard capitalism as an alien and exploitive process. By the time a small Muslim bourgeoisie had come into being it was too late; shortly after its foreign or minority counterparts, it was swept away by radical upheavals.

Regarding social bonds, traditional Muslim society, with all its shortcomings, was a tightly knit fabric. Tribal and communal ties of kinship and ownership held together the rural and nomadic populations, who made up more than 80 percent of the total. Guilds and religious fraternities performed the same function for urban craftsmen and merchants, and kinship and neighborhood ties were also strong in the towns. Finally, traditional Muslim ideology, expounded by the Ulema, the learned, religious leaders, was accepted by all and cemented the whole society.

The absorption of the region in the world capitalist market broke or loosened all these bonds. Private property in land soon resulted in social differentiation in the villages and, conjoined with the rapid population growth due to better hygiene, resulted in a large and increasing landless proletariat. The crafts were gradually eliminated by the competition of foreign goods but until very recently little modern industry rose to replace them; this too meant a growing urban proletariat. As already mentioned, the bourgeoisie was overwhelmingly of foreign origin or from minority groups. With the increasing secularization of society the Ulema were replaced by a new, Western-trained intelligentsia of lawyers, journalists, and teachers who, like their Western counterparts, were critical of traditional society and sought radical solutions. The outcome has been the revolutions of the 1950s to 1970s, most of which were led by the army.

FACTORS THAT MADE CHANGE POSSIBLE

Decolonization

European (mainly British and French) imperialism in the Middle East and North Africa reached its apogee just before the First World War with the occupation of Morocco by France and Spain and Libya by Italy, and the partition of Iran between Britain and Russia.

In the previous hundred years, the French had occupied the rest of North Africa, the British had established their role over Egypt, the Sudan, and large parts of the Arabian Peninsula, and the Russians had conquered Central Asia and Transcaucasia.

Following the First World War, there was a further extension of foreign rule: Britain received League of Nations mandates over Iraq and Palestine and France over Syria and Lebanon. Other potential rivals—notably Russia and Germany—had been eliminated, while British hegemony in the Middle East, and French in North Africa, seemed assured; in fact their position had weakened. Turkey, Iran, Saudi Arabia, and Yemen had become fully independent, and in the interwar period large concessions had to be made to rising nationalism in Egypt and Iraq.

The Second World War completely undermined the Western position in the Middle East and North Africa; by the 1960s all the countries of the region had achieved independence. This process was greatly helped by the United States and Soviet Union, both of whom were anxious, but for different reasons, to eliminate British and French political and economic hegemony in the region. Concurrently, or a little later, the peoples of the region were able to take advantage of the Cold War to eliminate the United States position of strength in, for instance, Iraq, Syria, and Libya and Soviet positions in Egypt. This freedom of movement enabled them to effect sweeping changes in their economy; in particular, they were able to take over practically all foreign investments and businesses in the region.

Accompanying these political changes was an important socio-economic shift: an exodus of some 2,000,000 European settlers from Algeria, Tunisia, Morocco, Libya, and Egypt. A similar exodus took place among the minority groups in these and other countries such as Iraq, Yemen, and Syria.

Oil

Exportation of oil started just before the First World War, but the industry began to yield large revenues to the governments of the region only in the late 1950s. By 1960, the Middle East and North Africa were receiving some $1.5 billion a year in oil revenues and by 1970 $5.5 billion. The oil price revolution of 1973, and the subsequent sharp rises in price, multiplied the revenues many times over. In 1979 the region received the unbelievable sum of $163 billion, and in 1980 the figure was more than $220 billion.

But it was not only a question of revenues. In the course of the 1970s, the governments of the oil-producing countries took over control of the industry. Now, it is they who determine how much shall be produced, not the companies. It is they, at OPEC meetings, who set the price. And, when the occasion arises, it is the governments who specify the countries to which oil will be sold and which will be denied, e.g., in 1973 the United States and the Netherlands.

And the oil revenues have, in turn, created another form of power. OPEC, and in particular its Arab component, is now almost the only segment in the world economy that enjoys a large surplus in its foreign trade and balance of payments. The funds that have thus accrued to the Middle Eastern countries have been invested in various international money markets—New York, London, Frankfurt, Zurich, and Paris—and the wishes of their owners have to be taken into account. The foreign exchange reserves of the Saudi Arabian government are now greater than those of any government in the world, and some of the other Middle Eastern governments also have huge reserves. In 1980, Saudi Arabia's foreign exchange holdings were officially, and probably conservatively, put at $110 billion. Recently, its financial quota in the International Monetary Fund has been greatly increased and with it its voting rights. All of this naturally generates power, which can be used for purposes deemed desirable by the society.

TRADITIONAL IDEALS, IDEAS, AND PRACTICES

Islam, like Christianity or any other great religion, is a vast and complex entity containing many divergent, and sometimes even incompatible, elements.

Dominant themes which have formed the minds and policies of the Muslim Middle East are (1) property; (2) community and state; (3) equality; and (4) the charging of interest, which takes us to the center of economic theory and ideology.[2]

Property

Here we encounter a strange paradox. On the one hand, Islam lays great stress on the right to property. Indeed the notion of the property contract is so central to Islamic law that many other social relations are assimilated to it. Thus in Islam marriage is a civil contract, an essential part of which is the payment by the bridegroom of a stipulated sum of money to the bride's family. Again, much of the medieval Islamic discussion of birth control centers on the notion of property rights; some schools of jurisprudence insisted that if a man wanted to practice certain forms of birth control he had to pay his wife a monetary compensation.

Yet at the same time there is no doubt that, in the Islamic Middle East, ownership of property was a far more precarious matter than in Christian Europe. From the early caliphate on, the history of the Middle East is replete with accounts of the confiscation of the property of merchants, officials, and others. The property basis of Middle Eastern "feudalism" was also much weaker than that of European: landed estates (or more strictly rents or taxes levied on them) were usually grants made by the monarch in return for military or other services and, in principle, lapsed at the death of the grantee. In practice some were inherited, but estates seldom remained in the same family for many generations. And Middle Eastern "feudalists" usually lived in cities, not on their estates, further weakening the tie between them and their property.

It is not too far-fetched to say that the property basis of the Middle Eastern family structure was weaker than that of the European. This is not to ignore the fact that family feeling and solidarity is very strong indeed in the Middle East. But, with few exceptions, Muslim families do not show the durability and continuity of European families. We do not see the phenomenon described by Schumpeter: "The bourgeoisie worked primarily to invest and it was not so much a standard of consumption as a standard of accumulation that the bourgeoisie struggled for and tried to defend against governments that took the short run view."[3]

Many reasons may be suggested for this difference in family structure. One is the general fluidity of society and the less marked lines of social stratification to be discussed later. Another is polygamy, accompanied by the absence of discrimination between children of wives and those of slaves. Another may be the retention of property rights by Muslim women after marriage, in contrast to European women until quite recently. Still another is inheritance laws; unlike Europe, Islam did not practice primogeniture; all children inherit, females receiving half the share of males, though in practice women were sometimes excluded; moreover, parents could not disinherit their children and could will only a small part of their estate.

The Middle East thus does not have the equivalent of a strong bourgeoisie, secure in its property rights, which could generate the equivalent of European capitalism. Perhaps the most striking example is the different history of the Hansa merchants in northern Europe and the Karimi merchants in the Indian Ocean area. The commerce of the Karimis extended from China to North Africa and, considering the high price of the spices and other articles in which they traded, their turnover may have been equal to or greater than that of the Hansa. Yet whereas the Hansa dominated the politics of northern Europe for several centuries, the Karimis seem to have had very little power against the Muslim states and the fact that they vanished, leaving no records and only scattered references in contemporary histories, perhaps best illustrates their weaknesses.[4]

Muslims have, then, in principle a deep respect for property but in practice a strong tradition of insecurity and expropriation. This tradition surfaced again in the 1950s.

Community and State

From the very beginning Islam has had a very strong sense of community. It has sought to provide for the needs of its poorer members through the *zakat,* or charity tax, imposed on all forms of wealth. This principle remains very strong and the duty of the community to provide for the needy is taken for granted. It is used to justify some of the nationalizations and sequestrations carried out in various Arab countries and Iran.

Another important aspect is the relation between wealth and power. At the risk of oversimplification, one can say that in the West, during the modern capitalist period, wealth generated power. But in the Middle East the opposite has been true. The great fourteenth century Arab historian and social scientist, Ibn Khaldun, pointed out that rank and prestige made it possible to accumulate wealth.[5] A contemporary Turkish sociologist, Serif Mardin, develops the idea as follows:

Imagine a society where the central value, the most effective—and more avidly sought after—social lever, is political power—a system where political power affects economics not only directly through the government's control of the market mechanism but where a very large proportion of the arable land is controlled by the state. Imagine a society where status is the primary determinant of income rather than the reverse, as has been the case in Western "capitalistic" society; where "prebendal" rewards are one of the main sources of wealth, but every type of wealth is legitimate only if the state recognizes it to be so. This is a society where the social mechanisms for the perpetuation of private property, such as corporate personality, are extremely limited, where law is not an adjunct of market transactions but has grown primarily from criminal law, where officials receive extraordinarily generous salaries although their life earnings are confiscated at their death.[6]

The social structure of the Middle East state, from the late Middle Ages on—that is, in the Mamluk and Ottoman periods—had some important economic consequences. Until about the twelfth century, the Middle Eastern governments were predominantly civilian and did not seek to interfere in the economy but let traders and craftsmen pursue their occupations. As a result, the economy flourished. But after that, to the accompaniment of numerous disasters, such as the Crusader and Mongol invasions and the Black Death, power passed on to the military who relied on the bureaucracy. The result was an economic policy that ignored the interests of the producers—craftsmen, farmers, traders—and concentrated on raising taxes and seeing to it that cities were supplied with food and other provisions (since the urban mob would otherwise be troublesome) even if the long-term interests of the producers suffered. This meant heavy taxation, confiscation, forced deliveries, and the overregulation of producers.

Thus, once more, we do not have in the Middle East the counterpart of the European bourgeoisie, which, by the late Middle Ages, was in a position to make its voice heard and its interests safeguarded not only in the city-states of Italy and the Netherlands but also in the national monarchies of England and France.[7] In the Middle East the functions of a middle class were for long performed by foreigners and members of minorities; the bourgeoisie was therefore regarded as alien and exploitative, and was easily crushed—together with its Muslim elements—by the military regimes in the 1950s and 60s.

Equality

This subject can be dealt with very briefly. Ideologically, Islam is a highly egalitarian religion. It does, of course, contain some basic discriminations and inequalities between Muslims and unbelievers, between freemen and slaves, between men and women. Within the community of free Muslim males, distinctions were light and blurred. There were no castes as in India, no social estates as in Europe, no consecrated priesthood as in Christianity, no hereditary nobility as in most parts of the world. At most, one can say that the Ashraf (descendants of the prophet Mohammad) enjoyed a certain dignity and prestige.

Moreover, Muslim society was very fluid. As anyone reading the *Arabian Nights* soon finds out, a porter or fisherman can, by a stroke of fortune or through the whim of the ruler, be elevated to the highest degree of honor and wealth. By the same token yesterday's all-powerful vizier or opulent merchant can equally rapidly be stripped of his position and cast in jail. And history records, down to the nineteenth century, many examples of social mobility which are at least as fantastic as those of the *Arabian Nights*. For example, the Persian reforming prime minister Mirza Taqi Khan, 1848–51, known as Amir-i Kabir, was the son of a cook; his downfall and murder were even swifter than his rise.[8]

The egalitarian ideal was not translated into social practice. Little was done to help the poor, and the contrasts in wealth and power remained very large. Moreover, many jurists justified inequality as socially beneficial. Of course in this respect Middle Eastern society was no worse than others. But the yearning for equality remained strong and was to find expression in the 1950s.

The Charging of Interest

The Islamic attitude toward the charging of interest sprang from the same roots as, and was almost identical with, the early Christian scholastic attitude.

Like the Scholastics, Muslim theologians and jurists started from the Judeo-Christian and Aristotelian idea that usury was wicked. Unlike sheep or trees, money does not breed, and, therefore the charging of interest for a loan is wrong. There has been much discussion as to whether the Arabic word *riba* designated every kind of interest or only usurious interest, but the evidence points to the former, broader, interpretation.

However, interest has been a fact of life for thousands of years, and every society has had to accommodate itself to it. For example, Hammurabi's code (paragraph 88) sets a rate of 20 percent for loans of grain or silver money.[9] In Europe, a partial and temporary way out was to leave moneylending to the Jews. But Christians also wanted to participate and did engage in moneylending, which was highly profitable, and the growing volume of commercial and financial transactions necessitated the development of some form of banking and money market.

Hence, by the fifteenth and sixteenth centuries, we find an important distinction being made between money and money capital. Coins may be sterile, but money capital can be used to expand production and earn profits. Therefore, it was only fair that the lender should be compensated for the profit he could have made on the capital: what a modern economist would call the opportunity cost of the capital.[10]

Something very similar happened in Islam. In principle, money-lending was left to Christians and Jews, but the historical evidence is clear that at all times many Muslims also engaged in it.[11] Moreover, by the early Middle Ages Islamic trade had reached very large proportions, stretching from China to West Africa and covering a great variety of objects.

All this necessitated the development of credit: to finance the circulation of goods, to provide means of payment across vast areas by means of bills, letters of credit, and cheques, and to supply capital for setting up or expanding business firms. As Avram Udovitch has shown, this was accomplished by various forms of partnership. If A sells B goods on credit, A is entitled to charge a higher price, that is, to make a profit. Or if A invests money in a partnership with B under which B carries out various transactions, A is entitled to part of the profit.[12]

These examples bring out one very important point. A is entitled to a profit—or what we would in some cases prefer to call interest—because he is sharing in the risk incurred by B. Risk-taking is entitled to a reward. We shall now see the use to which this concept is being utilized in modern times.

PRESENT-DAY INSTITUTIONAL CHANGES

Two main types of change may be distinguished: what we may call the statist and the private property approach.

Statist

Over the greater part of the Middle East and North Africa the state has, since around 1960, taken over the bulk of economic activity: banking, insurance, land and sea transport, communications, and large scale manufacturing and mining. Banking and insurance—the greater part of which had been in foreign hands—have been nationalized and are now run by the state. Most railways had either been built by the state (as in Egypt, the Sudan, Iraq, Iran, and Saudi Arabia) or had been taken over in the interwar period; the remaining ones were nationalized after the Second World War. So was maritime navigation and river shipping. Telephones, telegraphs, and radio and television broadcasting have always been government activities.

In the Middle East and North Africa manufacturing and mining were usually started by foreigners, with some help from minority groups. In Turkey and Iran a substantial public sector was developed in the 1930s accounting for nearly half of total output and employment. But in the 1950s and '60s practically all large scale factories and mines were nationalized in Egypt, Iraq, Syria, Algeria, South Yemen, Libya and, very recently, also in Iran.

The government also exercises control over foreign trade and has many instruments with which to direct agriculture, e.g. price setting, compulsory deliveries, credit allocation, sale of fertilizers and machinery, etc. Internal trade is also closely regulated by the government.

One can, therefore, say that by now only Israel, Lebanon, Turkey, Kuwait, Tunisia, Saudi Arabia, and Jordan have a large private sector. And even in them, particularly in oil countries where the state has huge revenues, the public sector is growing rapidly.

The roots of this shift are three-fold: socialism, nationalism, and the Islamic or Middle Eastern tradition.

Socialism

In the Middle East and North Africa, as almost everywhere in the world, socialism has had a great appeal to large sections of the population, for reasons good and bad. It is enough to say that while *"socialism"* continues to be a term of praise, *"capitalism"* has become a dirty word over most of the region and that "Arab socialism," whatever that may mean, is in vogue. Of course, most Marxists deny that Algeria or Egypt or Iraq are socialist at all and call them "state capitalist" countries, whatever *that* may mean, as it appears to be a contradiction in terms.

Nationalism

Nationalism is even more powerful and elemental. In the course of the nineteenth and early twentieth centuries, the greater part of the "modern" sector—foreign trade, finance, mechanical transport, industry, etc.—belonged to foreigners or members of minority groups. Resentment against such people built up and when the opportunity came, their property was nationalized or sequestrated. The impetus thus generated continued, and the property of the fledgling Muslim bourgeoisie was soon taken over.

Islamic or Middle Eastern Tradition

The claims of the Muslim community on the individual are very great indeed, and the Middle East has no equivalent of the Western tradition of individual rights, protected by an array of legal and political institutions against the encroachment of the state.

Similarly, there is the old Islamic notion of equity and egalitarianism, which stresses the claim of the poor on society, and condemns the ostentation of the rich. But in the Middle East and North Africa in the last hundred years or so there has been a great amount of conspicuous consumption by the rich, and since, to make matters worse, ostentation took a Western form, including alcohol and the mixing of the sexes, the wrath of devout Muslims against the rich has been very great indeed. Recent events in Iran provide a striking example, but similar attitudes prevail among the Muslim Brotherhood in Syria, Egypt, and elsewhere, and new, even more fundamentalist, groups are springing up in Egypt, the Sudan, and other countries, for example, the Mujahidin in Iran and the Takfir wa Hijra group in Egypt. But even among more moderate Muslims "there is a desire for reversion to a simpler morality and to what is conceived to be traditional Islamic conduct."[13] The economic views of all these groups are usually very radical.

The old tradition of the Middle Eastern military and bureaucracy has also helped. As in the past, soldiers and bureaucrats run the state, and pay little attention to the needs of producers. The result has been a cumbrous and over-regulated economy. Middle Easterners are fully aware of the arbitrariness, inefficiency and corruption of their bureaucracy. But, as in Western Europe and the United States, nothing seems able to stop its inexorable growth. "In the Shah's Iran, merchants saw in Islam protection for traditional business and the rights of private property against a predatory government and the modern industrial sector," which they opposed with the more zest because it was secular and Western oriented.[14] But, as usual, revolution proved no remedy in this respect. However, even the most inefficient engine will sputter along, if injected with a sufficient amount of fuel. Thanks to massive infusions of oil money and foreign aid, the economy has kept going and has even succeeded in ameliorating the condition of at least the urban masses. This kind of socialism is probably there to stay for quite a long time.

The Private Property Approach

Opposition to Arab socialism—which has a secular as well as a Muslim face—has sprung from two main sources: the governments of the oil rich Arabian countries, notably Saudi Arabia; and the Muslim Brotherhood and such similar groups as a formulation of their ideals was provided in 1977 by a professor at Kuwait University:

1. Complete respect for private ownership.
2. Elimination of wealth centralization and accumulation and emphasis on medium-sized economic units in order to avoid painful roles of capital.
3. Islamic legislations to protect capital of individuals and wealth of nations.
4. Special care for poor and needy social classes.
5. Complete harmony between labor and capital to provide optimal solutions leading to peace on earth for all mankind.
6. An economic policy based on Islamic devices.[15]

Putting the matter in more general terms, Islamic economics has the following characteristics:

First, there is an urge to redistribute wealth. Quite a bit has been accomplished in this direction since the early 1950s: the expropriation of foreign wealth in Egypt, Algeria, and elsewhere, including oil; land reform in Egypt, Syria, Iraq, Iran, and Algeria; the sequestration and confiscation of large firms and of shares and bonds in almost every branch of business; and in some countries, notably Iran and Libya, the handing over of private dwellings to homeless people. But, as reformers since the time of Solon and the Gracchi have found out, inequality is a very stubborn animal to deal with. Somehow or other, a new class always seems to emerge; some people somehow manage to live well. And, if nothing else, population growth on the order of 3 percent a year is enough to ensure that a large number of young, restless, and destitute people are thrown on the market each year. Hence, the call for equality is bound to become increasingly strident.

Second, there is the call for industrialization. In this there is nothing peculiarly Muslim. All over the developing world, industrialization is seen as the panacea that will cure all of society's economic, social, and political ills. Indeed, in the long-run, industry offers the best hope for these countries. But two remarks are in order. First, in their zeal for industry, Middle Easterners—again in large if not good company—have overlooked the equally urgent need for agricultural development. As a result, agriculture has in many countries failed even to help keep pace with population growth, much less with the rapidly rising demand for food caused by growing incomes. Hence, the Middle East and North Africa—which until the Second World War and even after was a net exporter of cereals—has become the largest importer, per capita, in the world. In 1978 imports of grain amounted to nearly 23 million tons, costing over $4.2 billion; by now only Turkey is a significant exporter.

The second remark is a repetition of the good Arabic saying: "Praise be to God who changes [things] but who [himself] does not change." Until very recently, anyone who hinted that the industrialization policies were ill considered and were being carried out at the expense of agriculture and the food supply was classified as a reactionary and arch-imperialist, in the tradition of Lords Cromer and Curzon. But now it is the radicals who continue with increasing virulence, bringing these accusations against westernized rulers as they did against the Shah and Sadat.

The third characteristic of Islamic economics is a certain wariness of and hostility to private consumption and individualism. It is not that Islam is inherently averse to consumption and enjoyment. The Quran (Rodwell's translation) says: "O children of Adam! wear your goodly apparel when ye repair to any mosque and eat ye and drink; but exceed not, for He loveth not those who exceed. Say: who hath prohibited God's goodly raiment, and the healthful viands which He hath provided for his servants?" (S. 7:29) and again, in verse 160 of the same Surah, "Eat of the good things with which we have supplied you."

Indeed Muslims have often criticized Christianity as an otherworldly, ascetic religion, "too heavenly minded to be any earthly good," and contrasted it unfavorably with their own. But a zealous Muslim today would argue that, given all the unfulfilled needs in the world in general and in the Muslim community in particular, and given the scarcity of resources, luxury consumption should be strictly limited. Similarly there is a wariness of men's greed and acquisitiveness and the feeling that individualism should be kept on a tight rein, if necessary, by curtailing what are regarded in the West as essential liberties. It is in these respects that contemporary Islam is most critical of the West in general, and the United States in particular, regarding them as indulging and pampering individual desires well beyond the permissible limits, and at the same time stimulating desires with an endless barrage of advertising.

But hostility to the West does not necessarily mean receptivity to the East though Marxism does exert a certain appeal because of its emphasis on equality and community. For if the basic Islamic category is not the individual, neither is it the class but, to repeat, the community. The whole concept of class struggle is regarded as a mischievous misdirection of attention and energy. Equality and justice must be sought and achieved by, for, and within the Islamic community, whether defined as roughly corresponding with some of the present states or including the whole Muslim world.

After all these generalities, it may be desirable to give a few concrete examples of how Islamic principles are being applied in some countries, notably the oil-rich states of Arabia. Two fields may be singled out—fiscal policy and banking.

In fiscal matters, vast state revenues have been channelled to the private sector in the form of subsidies of foodstuffs and essential goods, a large array of social services, generous advances for building houses and setting up businesses, and in Kuwait the purchase by the government of real estate from individuals at very high prices and its resale or leasing to them together with funds to erect a house or other building.

Thus we have a unique phenomenon in history. In the past, all over the world, the chief concern of the state was to transfer resources from the private sector to the public. Here we have the public sector transferring resources to the private.

Another form of transfer may be briefly noted: from the oil-rich countries to poorer areas. Here the record is quite impressive. In 1980 net Arab OPEC aid totalled $6.8 billion, or 2 percent of the combined GNP of the Arab oil states. The main disbursing agencies are the Islamic Development Bank, with headquarters in Saudi Arabia, which finances trade; the OPEC fund, which lends for balance of payments purposes; and the various national funds (Kuwait Fund, Saudi Arabian Fund, Abu Dhabi Fund) which lend for infrastructure development.[16]

The aid has been disbursed in concentric circles. Proportionally, by far the greater part has been given to the poorer Arab countries, Syria, Jordan, Sudan, Egypt, Tunisia, Morocco, Somalia, Yemen, etc.

The next circle consists of non-Arab Muslim countries, notably Pakistan, Turkey and some African states. Finally, a small amount has been extended outside the Muslim community, for example to India. Large amounts have also been given, or loaned, to various international organizations, such as the World Bank, International Monetary Fund, and United Nations agencies.

As regards banking, one should distinguish sharply between the rapid growth of what one might call "ordinary," or Western-type banks belonging to Muslim states and strictly Islamic banks. Until the First World War, all the banks operating in the Middle East and North Africa were either branches of foreign banks—like Barclay's and Crédit Lyonnais—or foreign owned and managed, like the Ottoman Bank and the National Bank of Egypt. In the 1920s and '30s a few banks, owned and staffed by nationals and using the national language, were established, like Bank Misr in Egypt, Ish Bank in Turkey, Bank Melli in Iran, and the Arab Bank in Palestine. In the 1960s, with the sharp increase in oil money, there was a large expansion of banking, especially in the Gulf. New banks were founded, such as the National Bank of Kuwait, the National Commercial Bank of Libya, the Qatar National Bank, the Bank of Oman, and the National Bank of Dubai. Many of these and other banks began to participate actively in world finance, and Beirut and Kuwait emerged as major financial centers.

The explosion of oil revenues in 1973, and again in 1980, greatly accelerated the development of banking. International banking markets evolved in Kuwait, Bahrain and the United Arab Emirates. Joint ventures were set up with foreign banks, for example the Union des Banques Arabes et Françaises and the Banque Arabe et Internationale d'Investissements, both based in Paris; the European Arab Bank in Brussels; the Saudi International Bank in London; and the Arab Latin American Bank operating out of Peru. In Paris there are now 35 wholly or partly Arab-owned banks and in London 29, and an entry has been made in other centers such as New York, Singapore, and Tokyo.

Altogether, Arab banks now represent a truly impressive set of institutions. A recent list made by *The Banker* shows that 17 of the 500 largest banks in the world are Arab. The combined assets of the 50 top Arab banks exceed $150 billion; not surprisingly, almost all are domiciled in oil producing countries. Many of them are consortia, in which other Arab, or Western banks participate, and their own governments supply a substantial share of capital.[17] These banks play a very active part in the international money market. They are estimated to have supplied 10 percent of all syndicated international bank credits in 1980 and about 27 percent in 1981.[18] Their customers include a wide variety of countries, from the most advanced to the least developed.

The strictly "Islamic banks" developed in the 1970s; in Egypt, (Nasir Social Bank), Saudi Arabia (Islamic Development Bank), Kuwait (Kuwait Finance House), Sudan (Faisal Islamic Bank), Bahrain, Dubai, Jordan and elsewhere. There is even one in Calvinist Geneva—the Bahrain-registered Dar al-Mal al-Islami. Their combined assets run into the billions of dollars and are growing rapidly.

All of these banks provide, on a fee basis, many of the services available at a Western bank, such as travelers' cheques, foreign exchange transactions, demand deposits, etc. Their peculiarity is that they neither pay nor charge interest. As for payment, neither depositors nor shareholders receive interest; instead they share in the profits made by the bank, receiving a "dividend." As we have seen, this is in line with Muslim medieval theory and practice. It is also quite a profitable business for depositors. For example, in Kuwait in 1980 the dividend paid to depositors was equivalent to an interest rate of 11.25 percent, which compared favorably with current rates on deposits in that capital-soaked country.

Regarding loans and advances, the guiding principle is risk-sharing. For example, both the bank and the borrower may provide capital and share the profits. Or the bank provides all the capital to an agent-manager, who receives a share of profits and may be authorized eventually to buy out the bank. Or the bank finances trade by actually buying the commodity, transporting it to the customer and selling it to him at a mark-up. The profit, not being interest, is legitimate. Or finally, in case of need, consumption loans may be made. For these an administrative fee may be charged, which again is not regarded as interest.

Here is a rather amusing example of the way Islamic injunctions can be turned against Muslim authorities. Starting a long time ago as money changers the Al Rajhi family built up the third largest financial institution in Saudi Arabia. They are very willing to accept interest-free deposits from pious Muslim customers. Not unnaturally, the Saudi Arabian Monetary Agency considers that Al-Rajhi Company for Currency Exchange and Commerce is a bank and, therefore, should be under its jurisdiction and keep reserves with it. "Not so" says Al Rajhi, "we make profits, not interest and therefore cannot be considered as a bank." This is because the company engages in operations that yield a profit, not interest, e.g. buying a tankerload of oil for a customer, holding it for a few days and selling it to the customer with payment delayed until the goods are received.[19]

I may conclude with a somewhat unexpected phenomenon, also in Saudi Arabia: Banks for Women. Under Muslim law women have always had the right to own property and some estimates put women's share of the private wealth of Saudi Arabia as high as 30 to 40 percent. As a result, some thirteen banks catering exclusively to women—and run entirely by women—have sprung up in the last two years and their business is thriving. A somewhat jaundiced male explanation, given by a Saudi Arabian is: "I think the real purpose of the ladies' banks is not to provide any services they did not have before in the existing banks. It is to give all these smart women something to do!" But it is certainly a fact that women feel free to use these banks whereas few if any deal with the ordinary ones, asking their male relatives or servants to do their banking.[20]

In conclusion, there are some very interesting experiments under way in the region. They have been made possible only by the abundance of oil money. But since, barring an earth-shaking cataclysm, oil money will continue to flow into the region for several decades, we can expect to see further attempts to adapt Islam to contemporary economic realities or, as a Muslim might prefer to put it, further attempts to fit contemporary economic institutions into an Islamic mold.

NOTES

1. See Charles Issawi, *The Arab Legacy* (Princeton, N.J.: Darwin Press, 1981) and Charles Issawi, *An Economic History of the Middle East and North Africa* (New York: Columbia University Press, 1982).

2. The most thorough and comprehensive account of both traditional and contemporary Islamic views is Khurshid Ahmad, ed., *Studies in Islamic Economics* (Jeddah: International Centre for Research in Islamic Economics, King Abdul Aziz University, 1976).

3. Joseph Schumpeter, *Capitalism, Socialism and Democracy* (London: Allen and Unwin, 1950), pp. 160–61.

4. See *Encyclopaedia of Islam,* 2nd ed., "Karimi," and references cited.

5. Ibn Khaldun, *al-Muqaddimah,* ed. M. Quatremère (Paris: Benjamin Duprat, 1858), II: 286; translation in Charles Issawi, *An Arab Philosophy of History* (London: John Murray, 1950), p. 86, and Franz Rosenthal, *The Muqaddimah* (New York: Pantheon Books, 1958), II: 326–28.

6. Serif Mardin, "Turkey: The Transformation of an Economic Code," in Ergun Ozbudun and Aydin Ulusan, eds., *The Political Economy of Income Distribution in Turkey* (New York: Holmes and Meier, 1980).

7. This point is developed in "Europe, the Middle East and the Shift in Power," in my *Arab Legacy,* pp. 111–32.

8. See Feridun Adamiyyat, *Amir-i Kabir wa Iran* (Tehran, 1334); Carter Findley, *Bureaucratic Reform in the Ottoman Empire* (Princeton, N.J.: Princeton University Press, 1980), p. 37.

9. James Pritchard, ed., *The Ancient Near East* (Princeton, N.J.: Princeton University Press, 1958), I: 147–48.

10. Joseph Schumpeter, *History of Economic Analysis* (New York: Oxford University Press, 1954), pp. 64–65, 101–107, and references cited. To this day the taking of interest disturbs the conscience of a few Christians—see C. S. Lewis, *Mere Christianity* (New York: Macmillan, 1960), p. 81.

11. For evidence on the activity of Muslims in moneylending in the sixteenth–eighteenth centuries see, for Turkey, Halil Inalcik, "Capital Formation in the Ottoman Empire," *Journal of Economic History* (March 1969), and Ronald Jennings, "Loans and Credit in the Early Seventeenth Century Ottoman Judicial Records," *Journal of the Economic and Social History of the Orient* (April 1973); for Iran, J. Chardin, quoted in Maxime Rodinson, *Islam et Capitalisme* (Paris: Le Seuil, 1966), p. 57; for Egypt, see Stanford Shaw, *The Financial and Administrative Organization and Development of Ottoman Egypt* (Princeton: Princeton University Press, 1962), pp. 56–57; for Syria, A. N. Poliak, *Feudalism in Egypt, Syria, Palestine and Lebanon* (London: Royal Asiatic Society, 1939), pp. 68–69, and Abdul Karim Rafeq, "Economic Relations between Damascus and the Dependent Countryside," in A. L. Udovitch, ed., *The Islamic Middle East* (Princeton: Darwin Press, 1981), pp. 674–75.

12. A. L. Udovitch, *Partnership and Profit in Medieval Islam* (Princeton: Princeton University Press, 1970); Hammurabi's code has a provision (paragraph 98) that investors in trade ventures should share losses and not just receive a fixed profit—see Joan Oakes, *Babylon* (London: Thames and Hudson, 1979), pp. 58–59.

13. Shaul Bakhash, "Reformulating Islam," *New York Times,* October 22, 1981.

14. Shaul Bakhash, "Reformulating Islam," *New York Times,* October 22, 1981.

15. Fareed El Naggar, "The Methodology of Islamic Economics and Systems Theory Model," *Middle East Management Review* (January 1977).

16. *The Economist,* November 21, 1981; supplement on Middle East Banking.

17. *The Banker* (December 1981); International Monetary Fund, *IMF Survey,* February 3, 1982.

18. *IMF Survey,* February 3, 1982, and *Economist,* November 21, 1981.

19. *The Economist,* November 14, 1981, p. 108.

20. "Saudi Banks for Women Thriving," *New York Times,* January 27, 1982.

3

~~~~~~

Islamic Education and Science

A SUMMARY APPRAISAL

Seyyed Hossein Nasr

*B*OTH ISLAMIC EDUCATION and science cover such a vast expanse of intellectual space and historical time that it is hardly
possible to do justice to them in this short appraisal except by pointing
out some of the principles and salient features which have always
characterized them as authentic manifestations of the Islamic spirit and
notable aspects of Islamic civilization. If some of the achievements of
Muslims in these domains are mentioned, it is with the purpose of
providing necessary examples to elucidate those principles and features and not with the aim of enumerating the achievements of Muslims
in these fields in an exhaustive manner. Needless to say, even a catalo-
guing of what Muslims have accomplished in these fields would require
volumes.[1]

Both Islamic education and the science which developed in Islamic civilization over the centuries are Islamic in character whatever
may have been their historical origin. The living organism which was
Islamic civilization digested various types of knowledge from many
different sources ranging from China to Alexandria and Athens, but
whatever survived within this organism and was made to grow as a
living being was transformed thoroughly into the Islamic mold. Whatever may have been the origin of the "material" for education and the
sciences, the form was always Islamic, and both Islamic education and
the Islamic sciences are related in the most intimate manner to the
principles of the Islamic revelation and the spirit of the Quran which is
the central theophany of Islam.

The Quran contains, according to the traditional Islamic perspec-

47

tive, the roots of all knowledge but not, of course, scientific facts. Although it contains the principles of knowledge, it is not a text book of science in the manner that is claimed by certain modern apologists who have tried to find this or that particular scientific fact or theory in the verses of the sacred Book. The Quran is the "recitation." It is also understood by some commentators to mean "the gathering," namely the treasury in which is gathered all the pearls of wisdom. The sacred Book is also called "discernment," for it is the supreme instrument of knowledge whereby truth is distinguished from falsehood. It is "the mother of all books," for all authentic knowledge contained in "all books" is ultimately born from its bosom. It is "the guidance," for in it is contained not only moral guidance but also educational guidance, the guidance which educates the whole being of man in the most profound and also complete sense.[2] No wonder that the Quran, the Word of God, has always been the *alpha* and *omega* of all Islamic education and the sciences, being at once their source and goal, their inspiration and guide.

Enwrapped in the perpetual presence of the Quran, the life of the Muslim was witness to a continuous process of education based on the form and spirit of the Quranic revelation as contained in the sacred Book and reflected in the very substance and being of the Prophet. From the affirmation of faith, "There is no deity save God," uttered into the ear of the newly born child until the moment of death, the words of the Book and the sayings of the Prophet molded the mind and soul of the Muslim, providing for him the primary content as well as ambiance of his education and the principles and goals of the sciences. The quest after knowledge and its veritable celebration[3] were dominated from beginning to end by a conception of knowledge based upon its sacred quality and nature. In Islam knowledge was never divorced from the sacred[4] and the whole educational system, and the sciences whose cultivation it made possible, breathed in a universe of sacred presence. Whatever was known possessed a profoundly religious character not only because the object of every type of knowledge is created by God, but most of all because the intelligence by which man knows is itself a divine gift, a supernaturally natural faculty of the human microcosm, even the categories of logic being the reflections of the Divine Intellect upon the plane of the human mind.[5]

Being related to holiness, hence wholeness, Islamic education had to be concerned with the whole being of the men and women whom it sought to educate. Its goal was not only the training of the mind but also the whole being of the person. That is why it was not called only instruction or transmission of knowledge but also training of the whole being of the student.[6] The teacher was not only the transmitter of knowledge, but also a trainer of souls and personalities. This was true to such an extent that the term teacher itself came to gain the meaning of trainer as well. It came to be imbued with ethical connotations which in the modern world have become almost totally divorced from the question of teaching and the transmission of knowledge, especially at higher levels of education. The Islamic educational system never divorced the training of the mind from that of the soul and the whole being of the person. It never considered the transmission of knowledge or its possession to be legitimate without the possession of appropriate moral and spiritual qualities. In fact the possession of knowledge without these qualities was considered so dangerous that the Persian poet Sanai called a person who possesses knowledge without moral and spiritual virtue a thief and asserted "If a thief comes with a lamp, he will be able to steal more precious goods."[7]

Although Islamic education encompassed the whole life of the traditional Muslim, there are distinct phases and periods to be detected in this organic whole. There was first of all the early family education in which the father and mother both played the role of teacher and educator in religious matters as well as in elements pertaining to language, culture, social customs, etc.[8] This period which was usually longer than the pre-kindergarden period in the West today, was followed by the Quranic schools, corresponding more or less to elementary and early high school, then the Madrasah, which can be said to correspond to secondary and early college education and finally the Jamiah, or highest formal education. In many parts of the Islamic world the Madrasah incorporated the Jamaiah and included at once what would correspond to secondary, as well as college and university education.

The earliest Quranic school not only acquainted the child with the religious foundation of his or her life, society, and civilization but also served as introduction to the mastery of language. Although of course the situation for Arab children differed from non-Arab Muslims, there is no doubt that in both cases literacy was impregnated with religious meaning and the very process of reading and writing was seen as a religious activity. The word *pen* itself, with the help of which the child wrote his or her first words, was also the instrument of revelation by which God has even sworn in the Quran. Likewise, book as such was first of all *the* Book, namely the Quran with all that the term implies in the Islamic context. The habit of illiterate traditional Muslims to respect any piece of printed material when printing first came to the

Islamic world was based on this attitude of identifying the written with the sacred.

Outside the Arab world, children were taught their own language but since both the alphabet[9] and much of the basic vocabulary dealing with both religious and moral ideas were drawn from Quranic Arabic, the two types of training did not oppose but complemented each other. Many children were also taught at home rather than at a school located physically in a mosque. This was particularly true of girls although in many places girls did also attend formal schools outside the home and even Madrasahs.[10] Furthermore, many children received an oral education of a high quality based upon the Quran and traditional literature, so that literacy was not at all synonymous with formal education. The remarkable literary knowledge of certain "illiterate" Muslims even today testifies to the strength of the less formal, oral education which usually starts at an early age.[11]

As far as the Madrasah is concerned, it became a formal educational institution early in Islamic history and developed into a full-fledged college and university system by the fourth/tenth century. The radiance of such institutions and their significance was so great that soon they began to become a noticeable element throughout most of the Islamic world and in fact played a fundamental role in the foundation of the European centers of higher education, a role that is only now becoming fully recognized.[12] The Madrasahs ranged from fairly modest and small schools with one or two hundred students to major universities such as the Qarawiyyin in Fez in Morocco which is over 1100 years old, the al-Azhar,[13] founded over a millennum ago in Cairo and still the greatest seat of Sunni learning, or the Shiite Madrasah of Najaf,[14] established some nine hundred years ago. It even developed into a university system with several campuses as in the case of the Nizamiyyah established in Baghdad as well as in Khurasan by the Seljug minister, Khwajah Nizam al-Mulk. Almost always the Madrasahs, which were endowed and where students received free room and board as well as other expenses, were constructed with great care in a beautiful setting. To this day in most Islamic cities, after the mosques, the madrasahs, which in fact were always related geographically to the centers of worship, are the most notable architectural masterpieces to be found. Some of them like the Qarawiyyin, the Mustansariyyah of Baghdad and the Chahar Bagh of Isfahan are among the greatest achievements of Islamic art. Since in Islam knowledge was never divorced from the sacred and Islam saw in the sacred, especially in its numinous aspect, the aura of Divine Beauty, Islamic education was always imparted in an ambiance of beauty.[15] Great care was taken to create an atmosphere in which the sacred quality of knowledge and the religious nature of all educational pursuit in the traditional context was confirmed rather than denied by the atmosphere in which the act of teaching and learning took place.

The main activity of the Madrasahs concerned the religious sciences, especially the Divine Law, its principles, jurisprudence, etc. The study of the Law was itself based on the careful study of the Quran and its commentaries, of the traditions of the Prophet, and of the sacred history of Islam, which is related to both the Quran and the traditions. These studies in turn required complete mastery of Arabic and all the literary disciplines connected with it. They also led to the study of theology in its manifold schools which developed beginning in the first Islamic century and which reached a period of intense activity in the Baghdad of the third/ninth and fourth/tenth centuries. These disciplines together were called the transmitted sciences and they dominated the educational activity of most Madrasahs.

There were, however, a series of other disciplines including logic, mathematics, the natural sciences, and philosophy which according to Muslim thinkers could be arrived at by human intelligence and were not transmitted as were the religious, linguistic, and historical sciences. Hence they were called the "intellectual sciences," intellectual in contrast to and as complements of the transmitted sciences. This division of the sciences became reflected in the curriculum of the Madrasahs,[16] many of which taught at least some of the intellectual as well as the transmitted sciences at least until a few centuries ago. In certain parts of the Arab world the intellectual sciences ceased to be taught after the eighth/fourteenth century, while in Persia and such Turkish centers as Istanbul as well as in the Indian subcontinent they were taught until much later, philosophy continuing to be taught seriously in Persia until today. But there is no doubt that when the modern Western educational system was brought to the Islamic world in the nineteenth century, there was practically no Madrasah which had preserved its former vitality in different fields of knowledge, especially in mathematics, and the natural and medical sciences.[17]

Moreover, even during the height of activity in the Islamic sciences, there is little doubt that in the domain of the intellectual sciences except for logic and philosophy, the natural and mathematical sciences were taught to a large extent outside of the Madrasahs. This seems at least to be the conclusion when one reflects upon the curricula that have survived from the earlier period. One can, therefore, state with some assurance that as far as the intellectual sciences are concerned, the activity of the Madrasah in traditional Islamic society was complemented and abetted by two other types of activity: one of scientific institutions and the second of private circles. Islam developed such scientific institutions as teaching and research hospitals and observatories, in both of which instruction for a professional cadre was carried out extensively. Already in the third/ninth century hospital of Baghdad where the famous Persian physician Muhammad ibn Zakariyya al-Razi (the Latin Rhazes) taught and treated patients, there are records of how medical students were trained both theoretically and practically, how they had to undergo a stage of internship and finally how they were examined and given the professional status of a physician.[18] Likewise, in the major observatories which were established by Islam for the first time as scientific institutions, instruction in mathematics and astronomy as well as related disciplines including logic and philosophy were carried out as seen in the first of these major observatories under Khwajah Nasir al-Din al-Tusi in Maraghah.[19]

As for private circles which exist to this day in Persia and are referred to as "outside instruction or lesson," they had always been prevalent as a means of teaching the less common disciplines to a group of chosen students both to avoid the anathema of those religious scholars who might object to the subject being taught and to have a more intimate ambiance for the transmission of certain of the intellectual sciences. This type of instruction has been especially important in the teaching of Islamic philosophy and must be considered in any serious study of the traditional Islamic educational system.

Another institution whose impact upon Islamic education has been immense is the Sufi center. In such centers whose function is to provide a place for the transmission of the highest form of knowledge, namely Divine Knowledge or what could be called *scientia sacra*,[20] there has always been an educational activity of a most intense nature. Sufism has always been concerned first and foremost with the training of the human soul so as to enable it to become a worthy receptacle of Divine Presence.[21] It has therefore been concerned with education as training on the highest level. But Sufism is also concerned with a knowledge which is imparted to the disciple by the master, or more exactly is made to be born from within the depth of being of the disciple with the help of the master. This knowledge, although in essence metaphysical, also possesses cosmological and psychological dimensions. Moreover, since Sufism has usually expressed its teachings in the form of literature and music of the highest order, the Sufi centers have been also places for artistic education. Finally, it must be remembered that in certain periods of Islamic history, such as after the Mongol invasion when the formal educational system was destroyed, Sufi centers also took the task of formal education upon themselves, and in some areas of the Islamic world for long periods of time they were the sole educational institutions which were still functioning. Altogether, Sufi centers must be considered as among the most basic institutions of Islamic education in addition to being the place of assembly of the friends of God where the ecstasy of Divine Union is experienced and celebrated.

No discussion of Islamic education would be complete without mention of the practical education connected with the crafts and the arts.[22] Within the guilds as well as through individual instruction in homes or ateliers of master craftsmen, not only were the techniques for the production of objects of art ranging from carpets to tile work transmitted to the student, but a science was also taught which had both a microcosmic and macrocosmic significance. It concerned the soul of the student who, while making an object of traditional art, was also molding his own soul, as well as the objective norms concerning the object at hand along with the symbolism involved in the making of the object in question. Islamic art is a science as Islamic science is an art.[23] Not all those who learned to weave carpets or make tiles were consciously aware of the profound metaphysical and cosmological significance of the symbolism of patterns, forms, and colors with which they were dealing. Nevertheless, something of the science involved was transmitted from the beginning, the knowledge becoming more explicitly elucidated as the student advanced in the mastery of his craft and came to gain a more immediate awareness of the nature of the materials with which he was working and the principles by which his art was ennobling the material he was molding or making.

There is no doubt that a vast oral tradition was transmitted over the centuries which enabled architects to construct domes of incredible beauty and durability or to create gardens with perfect harmonic ratios. A science of a high order was somehow preserved and transmitted as long as the traditional arts survived and in fact to the extent that they survive today. This process could not be called anything else but educational, and this type of teaching which concerned technological and scientific knowledge as well as an artistic one cannot but be considered as a major component of the traditional Islamic educational system.

All of these modes of traditional education are undergoing a major crisis as a result of the introduction of alien systems of education from the West and the partial destruction of many of the traditional channels for oral and more formal education. Although the traditional system in its various facets survives to one degree or another in most of the Islamic world, no satisfactory solution has been found so far to integrate into this system the disciplines which the modern world imposes upon the Islamic world. In fact, the crisis in education in the contemporary Islamic world is at the heart of the malaise which this world displays in these turbulent moments of its history.

As far as the intellectual sciences which the Islamic world produced through this educational system are concerned, their development constitutes both an important chapter in the history of science in general and a dazzling achievement of Islamic civilization itself of which it was an integral part. The rapid geographical expansion of Islam from the vast plains of Western China to the snow-covered mountain peaks of southern France made it heir to most of the sciences of antiquity. Already within the first century of its existence when it was building the very foundations of classical Islamic civilization, Islam was confronted with the learning of the Graeco-Alexandrian world as it had been cultivated not only in the school of Athens but especially in Alexandria and its offshoots in Pergamon, Antioch, Edessa, and other cities of the Near East.[24] Islam became heir to the sciences of the Persians and to a large extent Indians through the university center of Jundishapur where both Indian and Persian sciences including astronomy and medicine had been taught extensively before the rise of Islam. The center in fact continued to flourish until the foundation of Baghdad by the Abbasids when it was finally transferred to the new capital.[25] Islam also inherited some of the Babylonian and the more esoteric elements of the Hellenic and Hellenistic sciences through the Sabeans of Harran.[26] It even had contact with China, and traces of Chinese alchemy began to appear in Islamic sources already by the second/eighth century. As the last religion of mankind, Islam became heir as well to nearly all the sciences of the ancient world upon whose basis it constructed a number of sciences, which while being profoundly Islamic[27] had also integrated in an unprecedented manner the scientific heritage of many different civilizations which had come before it.

The merely physical presences of these centers of learning could not, however, have been sufficient to cause such a major movement within the Islamic world to transmit these sciences to the Muslims and to translate their sources into Arabic. The Muslims had no military, economic, or political compulsion to study Aristotle or Indian medicine. They already possessed perhaps the most powerful empire

on earth. Nor could turning to these sciences have been only utilita-
rian. The interest in these sciences was most of all intellectual and
spiritual and directly related to the nature of Islam as a revelation
based upon knowledge. As a way of knowing, Islam could not remain
indifferent to other ways of knowing, to philosophies and sciences
which also claimed to explain the nature of things. Moreover, since
Islam accepted the religions before it as having come from the same
source as itself, this principle being particularly emphasized in the case
of Judaism and Christianity but also accepted for Zoroastrianism and
even to some extent for the Sabaean eclecticism of Harranians, and
later Hinduism and Buddhism, the Muslims could not but engage in
theological and philosophical debates with followers of these religions
all of whom had already developed their own theologies and
philosophies. Muslims, therefore, had to confront the challenge of
modes of knowing related to both the sciences of antiquity and
philosophies and theologies of religious communities which lived
amidst them.

The answer of Muslims to their challenge was the concerted effort to translate philosophical and scientific works from Greek, Syriac,
Sanskrit, and Pahlavi into Arabic. Once they determined to carry out
this task, they had at their disposal a whole group of excellent
translators belonging to various minority religious communities, especially the Christians, some of whom like Hunayn ibn Ishaq were themselves both accomplished scholars and Arab and, therefore, knew
Arabic perfectly well. Schools and centers of translation were established, often supported by public funds as was the case with the House
of Wisdom in Baghdad. As a result, in a period of less than two centuries ranging from the end of the first/seventh to the third/ninth century, an immense corpus was translated into Arabic, making the Arabic
language the most important scientific language in the world for several
centuries and a major depository for the sciences of antiquity to this
day. There are many Greek works, especially of the Hellenistic period,
which can be found only in Arabic, the originals having been lost.[28]
Altogether, the transmission of the sciences of antiquity to Islam is a
cultural event which, from the point of view of quantity and quality as
well as its later impact upon the world at large, must be considered as
one of the major events of cultural history on a global scale.[29]

At the height of the Islamic intellectual sciences stands philosophy or "divine wisdom" and Islam has created one of the richest
philosophical traditions, one which possesses great spiritual
significance for Islam itself and which has survived as a continuous

tradition to this day.[30] Heir to Pythagoreanism, Platonism, Aristotelianism, Neopythagoreanism, Hermeticism, and Neoplatonism and aware of many branches of Stoicism and later schools of Hellenistic thought, Islam created a powerful and original philosophy within the intellectual universe of Abrahamic monotheism and the Quranic revelation while incorporating those elements of Greek philosophy which conformed to the Islamic unitarian perspective. The origin of what is characteristically medieval philosophy, whether Jewish or Christian, is to be found in Islamic philosophy.

Being traditional philosophy based on the supra-individual intellect and not individualistic opinion, Islamic philosophy developed schools and perspectives which were followed over the centuries rather than being changed and overthrown by one philosopher after another. What is called Islamic Peripatetic philosophy is itself a synthesis of the teachings of Plato, Aristotle, and Plotinus in the context of the Islamic world view. It draws from certain strands from the Platonic *Dialogues,* especially *Timaeus* and the *Laws,* the main works of Aristotle including the *Metaphysics, Physics, De Anima,* and of course the *Organon,* the synopsis of the *Enneads* of Plotinus which the Muslims had come to know as *The Theology of Aristotle,* and the writings of certain Neoplatonic commentators of Aristotle such as Themistius and Alexander Aphrodisias. The Islamic Peripatetic school was begun by al-Kindi and developed by other philosophers of this school such as al-Farabi and after him al-Amiri and Abu Yaqub al-Sijistani. This school reached the peak of its development in the fourth/tenth century with Ibn Sina, the Latin Avicenna, who became the prototype of the philosopher-scientist for all later Islamic history.[31] Criticized by such theologians as al-Ghazzali, al-Shahrastani and Fakhr al-Din al-Razi, this school was temporarily eclipsed in the eastern lands of Islam while it enjoyed a period of intense activity in Spain with Ibn Bajjah, Ibn Tufayl, and Ibn Rushd or Averroes, the foremost expositor of this school in the Islamic West (al-Maghrib). As for the East, the school of Ibn Sina was resuscitated by Nasir al-Din al Tusi in the seventh/ thirteenth century and continued henceforth as an important intellectual dimension during the centuries which followed.[32]

Parallel with the genesis of Peripatetic philosophy, there developed an Ismaili philosophy, which was closer to the Hermetic tradition than the Peripatetic but which itself developed into a distinct philosophy of great variety and richness. Growing out of the enigmatic *Mother of the Book,* this philosophy produced in the figures of such men as Abu Hatim al-Razi, Abu Sulayman al-Sijistani, Hamid al-Din al

Kirmani, Nasir-i Khusraw, many of whom wrote in Persian as well as in Arabic, a philosophy which vied with the better-known Peripatetic school. The *Rasail* of the Ikhwan al-Safa, a collection which appeared in Iraq in the fourth/tenth century and which possesses a strong Pythagorean tendency, is also related to this important school. Ismaili philosophy continued even after the eclipse of the Fatimids, producing works of significance in Persia and Yemen and finally India where Ismailism, this important branch of Shiite Islam, found its final intellectual home.[33]

In the sixth/twelfth century, while Avicennean philosophy was being criticized by the theologians, a new intellectual perspective was being established by Shaykh al-Ishraq Shihab al-Din Suhrawardi, who, because he was not directly translated into Latin, is not well known in the West. Suhrawardi, who claimed to be the resurrector of the perennial philosophy which had existed in both ancient Greece and Persia, established the School of Illumination for which knowledge is based upon illumination, and the very substance of the universe is ultimately degrees of light and shadow.[34] This school, elucidated and explained by Muhammad Shams al-Din Shahrazuri and Qutb al-Din Shirazi in the seventh/thirteenth century has also had many exponents and followers during later centuries, especially in Persia but also among the Muslims of the Indian subcontinent.

During later centuries while in most of the Arab world philosophy as a distinct discipline became integrated into either Sufism in its intellectual aspect or philosophical theology, in Persia and the adjacent areas, including not only Indian but also Iraq and Turkey, various schools of philosophy continued to flourish. At the same time the different intellectual disciplines such as Peripatetic philosophy, the School of Illumination, theology and Sufi metaphysics were drawing closer together. The ground was thus prepared for the revival of Islamic philosophy in the Safavid period in Persia with Mir Damad, the founder of the "School of Isfahan" and especially Sadr al-Din Shirazi, his student, who is perhaps the greatest of the later Islamic metaphysicians.[35] Even through the gradual decay of the teaching of the "intellectual sciences" in the Madrasahs, this later school, associated with the name of Sadr al-Din Shirazi as well as those of Ibn Sina, Suhrawardi, Ibn Arabi and their commentators, continued to function and to produce noteworthy figures, some of whom have survived to the present day.[36]

The Islamic philosophical tradition, although of great diversity and richness, is characterized by certain features which are of special significance both for the understanding of it and for an appraisal of its import for the world at large. This philosophy breathes in a religious universe in which a revealed book and prophecy loom dominant upon the horizon. It is, therefore, "prophetic philosophy" whatever might be the subject with which it is concerned. Moreover, it is a philosophy which in conformity with the Islamic perspective is based on the intellect as a supernaturally natural faculty within man which is a sacrament and which, if used correctly, leads to the same truths as revealed through prophecy. It is, therefore, concerned most of all with the One who dominates the whole message of Islam.[37] This philosophy is also concerned with the basic issue of the harmony between reason and revelation and of providing, within the context of a religious universe dominated by monotheism, a metaphysics centered around the supreme doctrine of the One but also providing keys for the understanding of the manifold in relation to the One. It is, therefore, rich not only in religious and ethical philosophy but also philosophies of nature and mathematics as well as art. In fact as far as the Islamic sciences are concerned, they were cultivated in the bosom of Islamic philosophy and almost always by men who were not only scientists but also philosophers.

Islamic philosophical texts provide not only a study of metaphysics and logic but a philosophy of nature which provides the key for the understanding of both physical nature and the soul. Although the Peripatetics treat the soul as a part of natural philosophy as seen in Ibn Sina's *Kitab al-Shifa* and the Illuminationists in metaphysics (rather than natural philosophy), there is no doubt that both schools as well as those of the Ismailis and of Sadr al-Din Shirazi and his followers all provide a general matrix wherein individual sciences pertaining to both the world of nature without and the world of the soul within can be studied in the light of the principles which belong to metaphysics, as traditionally understood, and which relate the many to the One, the points in the periphery of cosmic existence to the Divine Center.

A science which found special favor with the Muslims and which accorded well with the unitarian, aniconic, and "abstract" character of Islamic thought was mathematics in which Islamic accomplishments were many.[38] The Muslims integrated Greek and Indian mathematics and upon that basis developed the so-called Arabic numerals including the use of zero, continued the development of geometry, formulated algebra, developed plain and spherical trigonometry and number theory, expanding the definition of numbers to include irrationals.

They received the Sanskrit numerals and developed them into the form that is known as the Arabic numerals which revolutionized reckoning in medieval Europe. The name of the mathematician al-Khwarazmi whose work on arithmetic first introduced these numerals into the West, entered into European tongues as algorism while the treatise of algebra by Khayyam, along with several other Arabic works on the subject, made this area of mathematics which still preserves its Arabic name known to the West in a highly developed form. The trigonometric functions also still bear in their very names the traces of their Arabic origin. The Muslims also developed computation theory and even made computation machines as seen in the work of Ghiyath al-Din Jamshid Kashani who also discovered decimal fractions. Muslim mathematicians were, moreover, interested in problems which concerned the foundations of mathematics as seen in their study of the theory of parallel lines and the hypotheses underlying Eucledian geometry.

In astronomy Muslims began their activities early, incited by practical concerns of locating the direction of the *qiblah* and the time for the daily prayers as well as more "theoretical" and philosophical considerations. They first mastered the Indian and Iranian works of astronomy before becoming acquainted with Ptolemy whose *Almagest* still bears, in its very name in Western languages, the stamp of the influence of Islamic astronomy upon the West. The Muslim astronomers synthesized these schools upon the basis of which they established Islamic astronomy whose distinct features can be seen already in the third/ninth century. By the time al-Biruni wrote his *Masudic Canon* a century later, Islamic astronomy was the most complete and perfected astronomical science known anywhere in the world at that time.

The Muslims were interested in both observational and mathematical astronomy. They compiled numerous tables called *zij* based on their observations and discovered new stars, some of which still bear Arabic names. They founded the first full-fledged observatory in Maraghah and made numerous instruments for observation of which the astrolabe, that remarkable synthesis of science and art, is perhaps the one best known in the West. Parallel with observation of the heavens, they also refined mathematical astronomy beginning a criticism of Ptolemaic astronomy in both Persia and Spain. While the anti-Ptolemaic astronomy of Spain was mostly philosophical, that of Persia associated with Maraghah and the figures of Nasir al-Din al-Tusi and Qutb al-Din al-Shirazi was combined with a mathematical study of the

motion of two vectors, to use the modern terminology,[39] and led to a
new planetary model for Mercury and the Moon which somehow
reached the Poland of Copernicus and was most likely known by him.

In physics the contribution of Muslims is to be seen in three
distinct domains: in the study of the nature of matter, of projectile
motion, and optics. For over a millenium Muslim scientists,
philosophers, theologians, and even Sufis have studied and discussed
the nature of matter, time, space, and motion. They have developed
numerous "philosophies of nature" ranging from the atomism of the
theologians and Muhammad ibn Zakariyya al-Razi[40] to the physics of
light of Suhrawardi and the School of Illumination. In the study of
motion, such figures as Ibn Sina, al-Biruni, Abu'l-Barakat al-Baghdadi
and Ibn Bajjah criticized prevalent Aristotelian concepts and developed ideas in mechanics and dynamics which are of much importance for the history of physics in general and whose effect is to be seen
not only in the physics developed by Latin Scholastics but even in the
early Galileo.[41] As for optics, perhaps the greatest Islamic physicist,
Ibn al-Haytham, placed this discipline upon a new foundation in his
Optics in which he used the experimental method in its contemporary
sense to study the problem of vision, the *camera obscura,* reflection
and refraction, etc., and made many basic discoveries in the field of the
study of light. Upon the foundation of his work, some two centuries
later Qutb al-Din al-Shirazi and Kamal al-Din al-Farsi provided the first
correct explanation of the phenomenon of the rainbow which had
preoccupied the men of science since antiquity.

The Muslims also showed interest in mechanical devices which
they treated as a branch of applied mathematics. In fact most of the
early masters of the subject such as the Banu Musa and Ibn al-
Haytham were mathematicians. In such works, of which the most
elaborate is the *Treatise on Antomata* of al-Jazari, many machines are
described, some of which are quite complicated. It is important to
realize, however, that while Muslims had developed many forms of
technology of quite a refined nature but always closely related to the
forces and rhythms of nature, they developed these complicated machines, which among the artifacts of Islamic civilizations most resem-
ble products of modern technology, for amusement and play rather
than for economic production.

As far as medicine and pharmacology are concerned, in these and
related fields the achievements of Islamic science were no less startling
than in mathematics and astronomy. Again making use of Greek as
well as Iranian and Indian sources, the Muslim integrated the Hippo-

cratic and Galenic traditions with Iranian and Indian elements to create a distinct school of medicine which survives as a living school to this day in certain parts of Asia. The early masters of this art such as Razi became as well known in Europe and Hindu India as in the Islamic world itself, while Ibn Sina, the author of the *Canon of Medicine*,[42] became known as the "Prince of Physicians" in the West, and in certain areas he has given his name in its common Persian form of Bu Ali to Islamic medicine itself.[43] Islamic medicine combined a philosophical approach to medicine, based upon the cosmological principles which dominate over the human body, with the clinical and observational approach. Muslim physicians emphasized preventive medicine, especially diet, and made an extensive study of the rapport between psychological and physical health. But they also developed surgery as seen in the works of the Spanish master Ibn Zuhr and perfected many surgical instruments. Besides discovering the causes and distinguishing many diseases such as measles, meningitis, and whopping cough, the Muslim physicians also dealt with physiology and anatomy, Ibn Nafis having discovered the minor circulation of the blood long before Michael Servetus and William Harvey.

The cultivation of Islamic medicine has been inseparable from that of pharmacology which was usually studied by the same figures who cultivated medicine. Upon the basis of Dioscorides and the extensive pharmacological knowledge of the Iranians and Indians, Muslims developed pharmacopoeias which reflected great knowledge of both mineral and herbal drugs. As far as herbs were concerned, they were also studied from the more botanical point of view, especially in Spain where the study of the plant world reached its peak with al-Ghafiqi and Ibn al-Baytar. The study of plants, especially in relation to their medical properties, was one of the fields of Islamic science in which notable work continued in both Persia and Muslim India after the period of gradual decline of Islamic activity in the other Islamic sciences.

The study of botany by Muslims was also carried out in the context of their study of natural history and geography which were deeply impregnated by the Quranic idea of studying the wonders of creation as signs of God and His wisdom. As a result of the possibility of travel and exchange of ideas throughout the Islamic world to which the annual pilgrimage to Mecca contributed greatly, Muslim natural historians and geographers were able to assemble knowledge of flora and fauna from China to Western Europe. Al-Masudi, often called the "Arab Pliny," composed works on natural history which were related to those of the Greeks but of a more comprehensive nature and deeply integrated into the religious world view of Islam. As for geography, the Muslims such as al-Idrisi produced the first medieval maps, and Muslims gained detailed geographical knowledge of such areas as the Indian Ocean. Paradoxically enough, it was Muslim geographers and sailors who led Europeans around the Cape of Good Hope to India which in turn facilitated the destruction of the trade routes, that had been dominated by Muslims until the sixteenth century, by Portugese and later other European navigators, this event in turn preparing the ground for the colonization of much of the Islamic world in the centuries which followed.

No account of the Islamic sciences would be complete without reference to what the Muslims called "the hidden sciences" comprising such subjects as alchemy, physiognomy, and geomancy which have been relegated to the category of pseudo-sciences as a result of forgetting the symbolic language in which such subjects are described and the cosmological principles upon which they are based. As far as Islamic alchemy is concerned, it reached its peak early in Islamic history with Jabir ibn Hayyan in the second/eighth century and continued during a long tradition in which the significance of alchemy ranged from spiritual psychology and cosmology to medicine and a symbolic science of materials. From the cadaver of spiritual alchemy was also born that science of material substances which is called chemistry today.[45] The name of alchemy itself, and the spread of alchemical ideas in the Occident, attest to the great influence and significance of the Islamic alchemical tradition for the West as well as within the Islamic world itself, while many of the chemical instruments still used in the laboratory bear witness to the roots of modern chemistry in that aspect of medieval alchemy which had relinquished the task of transmuting the lead of the soul into the gold of the world of the Spirit to the making of physical gold.

From the point of view of the global history of science, the Islamic sciences stood for some seven centuries as the most developed among the sciences cultivated in different civilizations. They influenced the sciences of Hindu India and China as well as the West and were only eclipsed in the West with the advent of the Renaissance and the Scientific Revolution which made use of the material of Islamic science but within a world view diametrically opposed to that of Islam. The important question is not why Islam did not continue to devote its intellectual energies to the cultivation of an ever-changing science of nature divorced from higher orders of knowledge as has happened in the West since the seventeenth century.[46] The basic fact to note is that

Islam was able to create an educational system and a scientific tradition which produced knowledge of the world of nature and mathematics but within a world view dominated by the Transcendent and imbued with the fragrance of the Divine Presence as contained in the Quranic revelation. In a world on the verge of destruction as a result of the application of a science which is divorced from knowledge of a higher order and blind to the unity which pervades not only nature but all orders of reality leading to the One, Islamic science possesses a message which is more than of historical interest. This science is a reminder to contemporary men, whether Muslim or non-Muslim, that besides modern science, which is legitimate if only kept within the confines of its own limitations, there are other sciences of nature which unveil dimensions and aspects of nature and man's own being, dimensions and aspects that have become hidden in the modern world but for which contemporary man yearns because of what man is and who he is, wherever and whenever he happens to live.

NOTES

1. In the field of Islamic sciences, despite thousands of articles and books in different languages, so many works remain to be studied and analyzed that practically every year there are major new discoveries. Although no exhaustive treatment of present-day knowledge of the Islamic sciences is available as one would find for Western science or even Chinese science (thanks to the pioneering work of J. Needham and his collaborators), there are serveral works which provide a panoramic view of the field. As far as general works on the Islamic sciences are concerned, see A. Mieli, *La Science arabe et son rôle dans l'évolution scientifique mondiale* (Leiden: Brill, 1966); M. Ullman, *Die Natur-und Geheimwissenschaften im Islam* (Leiden: Brill, 1972); J. Vernet, *Der Islam in Europa* (Bussum, 1973); F. E. Peters, *Allah's Commonwealth* (New York: Simon and Shuster, 1973); J. M. Millás Vallicrosa, *Nuevos estudios sobre historia de la ciencia espanola* (Barcelona: Consejo Superior de Investigaciones Cientificas. Instituto Luis Vives, 1960); W. Hartner, *Oriens-Occidens* (Hildesheim: G. Olms, 1970); S. H. Nasr, *Science and Civilization in Islam* (Cambridge, U.S.A.: Harvard University Press, 1968); S. H. Nasr, *Islamic Science: An Illustrated Study* (London: World of Islam Festival Trust, 1976).

For works in particular fields, see E. G. Brown, *Arabian Medicine* (Cambridge: Cambridge University Press, 1921); D. E. H. Campbell, *Arabian Medicine and Its Influence on the Middle Ages*, 2 vols. (London: K. Paul, Trench, Trubner, 1926); C. Elgood, *A Medical History of Persia and the Eastern Caliphate* (Cambridge: Cambridge University Press, 1951); M. Clagett, *The Science of Mechanics in the Middle Ages* (Madison: University of Wisconsin Press, 1964); E. S. Kennedy, *A Survey of Islamic*

Astronomical Tables (Philadelphia: American Philosophical Society, 1956); C. A. Nallino, *Raccoltà di scritti editi e inediti,* 5 vols. (Rome: Instituto per l'Oriente, 1948); D. Pingree, *The Thousands of Abū Ma'shar* (London: Warburg Institute, 1968); A. M. Sayili, *The Observatory in Islam* (Ankara: Turk Tarih Kumuru Basimevi, 1960); H. Suter, *Die Mathetatiker und Astronpmen der Araber und ihrer Werke* (New York: Reprint Corp., 1972); A. P. Iushkevich, *Geschichte der Mathematik im Mittelalter* (Basel: Pfalz-Verlag, 1964); A. S. Saidan, *The Arithmetic of Al-Uqlīdisī* (Boston: Kluwer, 1978); A. Daffa, *The Muslim Contribution to Mathematics* (London: Humanities Press, Inc., 1977); P. Kraus, *Jābir ibn Hayyān,* 2 vols. (Cairo: Institute Français d'Archéologie Orientale, 1942–43); J. Ruska, *Tabula Smaragdina* (Heidelberg: C. Winter, 1926); and S. B. Omar, *Ibn al-Haytham's Optics* (Minneapolis: Bibliotheca Islamica, 1977).

Such general works on the history of science as G. Sarton, *An Introduction to the History of Science,* 3 vols. (Baltimore: Williams and Wilkins, 1927–48); and Ch. Gillespie, ed., *Dictionary of Scientific Biography,* 16 vols. (New York: Scribners, 1970–80), as well as studies on Arabic and Persian manuscripts, especially F. Sezgin, *Geschichte der arabischen Schrifttums* (Leiden: Brill, 1970–), likewise contain a wealth of information on the Islamic sciences. The pioneering work of Sarton still remains of great value for the general student of the subject and has in fact never been replaced by a more up-to-date work of the same scope.

As for education, there is even less available of a systematic nature which would consider the philosophy of education, its history, content of syllabi, etc., for the whole of the Islamic world. Among works which are available see, besides the already cited works, A. L. Tibawi, *Islamic Education: Its Traditions and Modernization into the Arab National Systems* (London: Luzac, 1972); idem, *Arabic and Islamic Garland* (London: Luzac, 1977); B. Dodge, *Muslim Education in Medieval Times* (Washington: Middle East Institute, 1962); al-Zarnūjī, *Ta'līm al-muta'allim,* trans. G. E. von Grunebaum and T. M. Abel (New York: King's Crown Press, 1974). See also the series on Muslim education edited by S. A. Ashraf and printed in London of which several volumes have appeared since 1978.

For a more complete bibliography containing works in European languages on both science and education, see S. H. Nasr, *An Annotated Bibliography of Islamic Science* (Tehran: Imperial Iranian Academy of Philosophy, 1975–77), of which only two of seven projected volumes have been published so far.

2. The many names of the Quran, like those of the Prophet, contain in themselves a science which, if studied carefully, reveal the many facets of that reality to which the names relate.

3. See F. Rosenthal, *Knowledge Triumphant, The Concept of Knowledge in Medieval Islam* (Leiden: Brill, 1970), where this veritable celebration of knowledge in Islam is recorded in detail.

4. See S. H. Nasr, *Knowledge and the Sacred* (New York: Crossroad, 1981), where this theme has been treated extensively on a global scale and not limited to the case of the Islamic tradition.

5. See F. Schuon, *From the Divine to the Human,* trans. G. Polit and D. Lambert (Bloomington, Ind.: World Wisdom Books, 1982); and also Schuon, *Logic and Transcendence,* trans. P. Townsend (New York: Harper and Row, 1975).

6. To this day education in official circles in most of the Arab world is called *al-talim wal-tarbiyah* while in Persia, the Persian counterpart of this term, namely *Amuzish wa parwarish,* has been used as the name for the ministry of education itself.

7.

8. The importance of this period in introducing the child to oral traditions existing within Islamic society was immense. Much of this oral tradition served later in life as the basis for the highest forms of metaphysical knowledge for those qualified to master such knowledge.

9. Before modern times, this was true of most Islamic languages whose alphabets were drawn either from Arabic directly or from Persian whose own alphabet is the same as that of Arabic except for the addition of four letters.

10. There are several miniatures of student scenes in famous medieval Islamic universities showing female students and also references in the literature.

11. As mentioned by I. Illich in his many studies on education, including *De-schooling Society* (New York: Harper and Row, 1971), which contains many ideas similar to the traditional Islamic philosophy of education, in traditional society, benefiting from a book was confined not only to the reader, but it usually encompassed many people through the fact that in most cases while one person read aloud many listened. This practice is still to be seen in certain parts of the Islamic world such as Persia where many people who have never had a formal education know not only verses of the Quran, but poems from Firdawsi's *Shah-namah* or Sadi's *Gulistan* as a result of listening to traditional story tellers who often actually recite stories and poems for them from the greatest literary masterpieces of the language.

12. It has, of course, always been known that such academic terms as chair in English and *license* in French are direct translations of Arabic terms, but in earlier works on the medieval European universities such as the classical opus of H. Rashdall, *The Universities of Europe in the Middle Ages* (Oxford: Oxford University Press, 1895), this influence has usually been deemphasized. The full import of this influence is traced with great care and scholarship by G. Makdisi in his recent work, *The Rise of Colleges: Institutions of Learning in Islam and the West* (New York: Columbia University Press, 1981).

13. See the study of B. Dodge, *Al-Azhar; a Millenium of Muslim Learning* (Washington: Middle East Institute, 1961), which provides a detailed study of the history and significance of this venerable institution.

14. On this important but little studied Madrasah see F. Jamali, "The Theological Colleges of Najaf," *Muslim World* 50 (1960): 15–22.

15. See T. Burckhardt, *The Art of Islam* (London: World of Islam Festival Trust, 1976).

16. On this division, see S. H. Nasr, *Science and Civilization in Islam* (Cambridge: Harvard Univ. Press, 1968), pp. 59–64.

17. To this day, in fact, no Madrasah in the Islamic world has been resuscitated successfully as far as encounter with modern forms and modes of knowledge are concerned despite many different types of experiments carried out in Morocco, Tunisia, Egypt, India, etc. The traditional and modern educational systems have become contending and competing forces in most of the Islamic world.

18. See Abu Bakr al-Akhwayni al-Bukhari, *Hidayat al-mutaallimin,* ed. J. Matini (Meshed: Meshed University Press, 1965), which concerns medical education whose origin can be traced to Razi and the hospital educational system of the fourth/tenth century.

19. On the observatory as a scientific and educational institution, see A. Sayili, *The Observatory in Islam* (New York: Arno, 1981).

20. See S. H. Nasr, *Knowledge and the Sacred* (New York: Crossroad, 1981), chapter four.

21. On Sufi training of the soul, see J. Nurbakhsh, *What the Sufis Say* (New York: Khanigahi Nimatullahi, 1980), part 1.

22. The arts and crafts are the same in Islam, and no distinction of a fundamental nature can be made in the context of Islamic civilization between what are called the major and minor arts in the West.

23. This could in fact be said of all traditional art but is especially evident in Islamic art with its mathematical clarity and harmony. See A. K. Coomaraswamy, *Christian and Oriental Philosophy of Art* (New York: Dover, 1956). See also Nasr, *Knowledge and the Sacred,* chapter eight.

24. The reason for the spread of this learning eastward is itself a fascinating chapter of cultural history related to the separation of the eastern Christian churches from Constantinople. See the still-valuable works of O. De Lacy O'Leary, *How Greek Science passed to the Arabs* (London: Routledge and Kegan Paul, 1949); and M. Meyerhoff, *Von Alexandrien nach Bagdad* (Berlin: Akademie der Wissenschaften, 1930).

25. On the significance of the school of Jundisapur built by the Sassanid king Shapur I on the model of the school of Antioch, see M. Mohammadi, "The University of Jundishapur in the First Centuries of the Islamic Period," *Journal of the Regional Cultural Institute* (Tehran) 2 (1969): 152–66.

26. These Sabeans are not to be confused with the present-day Sabeans of Iraq and southern Iran. See J. Pedersen, "The Sabians," *A Volume of Oriental Studies presented to E. G. Browne,* ed. T. W. Arnold and R. A. Nicholson (Cambridge: Cambridge University Press, 1922), pp. 383–91.

27. On the "Islamic nature" of the Islamic sciences, see Nasr, *Science and Civilization in Islam,* introduction; also Nasr, *An Introduction to Islamic Cosmological Doctrines* (London: Thames and Hudson, 1978), prolegomena.

28. On Greek works in Arabic, see M. Steinschneider, *Die arabischen Übersetzungen aus dem Griechischen* (Graz: Akademische Druck-und Verlagsanstalt, 1960); F. Rosenthal, *The Classical Heritage in Islam,* trans. E. and J. Marmonstein (Berkeley: University of California Press, 1975); and A. Badawi, *La Transmission de la philosphie grecque au monde arabe* (Paris: J. Vrin, 1968). See also F. Sezgin, *Geschichte,* where numerous references are made to Arabic translations of Greek texts.

29. When the works of the Greek authorities such as Aristotle were being translated into Arabic, there was still a living oral tradition known to the translators who made use of the "unwritten" text as well as the written one in their translations. Arabic translations of Greek texts, especially in philosophy, are therefore in a sense closer to the original than those made in modern European languages directly from the Greek but without a continuity of world view and an oral tradition accompanying the written word. In any case, far from being less-perfect renderings of the Greek originals, Arabic texts provide precious documents for the knowledge of antiquity independent of that type of interpretation in the modern world which is colored by Renaissance humanism and seventeenth-century rationalism, not to speak of twentieth-century irrationalism.

30. See S. H. Nasr, "The Role and Meaning of Philosophy in Islam," *Studia Islamica* (Paris: Maisonneuve et Larose, 1973) 37: pp. 57–80.

31. On Ibn Sina and the philosopher-scientists in Islam, see S. H. Nasr, *Three Muslim Sages* (Albany, N.Y.: Caravan Books, 1975), chapter one.

32. Most of the Western works on Islamic philosophy include on this school and even in this case limit their discussions to Ibn Rushd as if Islamic philosophy had ceased to exist after him. The only history of Islamic philosophy which does justice to the much richer intellectual life of Islam are M. M. Sharif, ed., *A History of Muslim Philosophy,* 2

vols. (Wiesbaden: O. Harrassowitz, 1963–66), and H. Corbin (with the collaboration of S. H. Nasr and O. Yahya), *Histoire de la philosophie islamique* (Paris: Gallimard, 1964). This volume covers only the period up to the death of Ibn Rushd, but Corbin completed the later periods of this history in "Histoire de la philosophie," *Encyclopédie de la Pléiade* (Paris: Gallimard, 1974). See also the other major studies of Corbin such as *En Islam iranien*, 4 vols. (Paris: Gallimard, 1971–72); and his *La Philosophie iranienne islamique* (Paris: Buchet-Chastel, 1981). The work of Corbin to turn the attention of the Western world to the integral tradition of Islamic philosophy has been followed by S. H. Nasr, T. Izutsu, M. Mohaghegh, and several other scholars.

On Islamic philosophy, see also M. Fakhry, *A History of Islamic Philosophy* (New York: Columbia University Press, 1970). An extensive bibliography on Ibn Sina and general works on Islamic philosophy is found in Nasr, *An Introduction to Islamic Cosmological Doctrines.*

33. The history of this school like much of Islamic philosophy remains full of unknown elements with many texts remaining to be studied and analyzed. For a summary of what is known of the history of this school, see Corbin, *Histoire*, pp. 118–51.

34. On Suhrawardi, see Nasr, *Three Muslim Sages*, chapter two; Corbin, *En Islam iranien*, vol. 2.

35. On these figures, see Corbin, *En Islam iranien*, vol. 4; the essays by Nasr in Sharif, *History of Muslim Philosophy*, vol. 2; and S. H. Nasr, *Sadr al-Dīn Shīrazī and His Transcendent Theosophy* (London: Thames and Hudson, 1978).

36. See Nasr, "Islamic Countries," in J. R. Burr, ed., *Handbook of World Philosophy* (Westport, Ct.: Greenwood Press, 1980), pp. 421–33; Nasr, "The Influence of Traditional Islamic Thought upon Contemporary Muslim Intellectual Life," in R. Klibansky, ed., *Contemporary Philosophy* (Florence: La Nuova Italia, 1971), pp. 578–83.

37. See F. Coplestone, *Religion and the One* (New York: Crossroad, 1982), chapter 5, where a leading Roman Catholic historian of Western philosophy looks upon the significance of this problem for Islamic thought in comparison with both Eastern traditions and Western thought.

38. For a general account of the contribution of Muslims to mathematics and astronomy, see E. S. Kennedy, "The Arab Heritage in the Exact Sciences," *al-Abhath* 23 (1970): 327–44; and A. I. Sabra, "The Scientific Enterprise," in B. Lewis, ed., *The World of Islam* (London: Thames and Hudson, 1976), pp. 181–200.

39. This model has been called the "Tusi couple" by its modern discoverer E. S. Kennedy. See his, "Late Medieval Planetary Theory," *Isis* 57, part 3 (1966): 365–78.

40. On Islamic atomism see the still valuable work of S. Pines, *Beiträge zur islamischen Atomenlehre* (Berlin: A. Heine, 1936).

41. See S. Pines, *Nouvelles études sur Awhad al-Zamān Abu'l Barakāt al-Baghdādī* (Paris: Durlacher, 1955); Pines, "What was original in Arabic Science?" in A. C. Crombie, ed., *Scientific Change* (New York: Basic Books, 1963), pp. 181–205. See also D. R. Hill, *The Book of Ingenious Devices by the Banū (Sons of) Mūsā bin Shākir* (Boston: Kluwer, 1979), for an analysis of a major text on mechanics which like al-Jazari's better-known work—also translated by Hill—*Al-Jazari: The Book of Knowledge of Ingenious Mechanical Devices* (Boston: Kluwer, 1974), touches upon certain problems of physics although the discipline of mechanics belongs to another category in the Islamic classification of the sciences.

42. This work is probably the most influential single book on the history of medicine.

43. On the general survey of Islamic medicine and pharmacology, see M. Ull-mann, *Islamic Medicine* (Edinburgh: University of Edinburgh Press, 1978).

44. For the historical account of the "occult sciences," see M. Ullman, *Die Natur-un Geheimwissenschaften im Islam.* But the significance of these sciences, especially alchemy, cannot be discovered save in the light of the metaphysical and cosmological principles of which alchemy is a particular application. See T. Burckhardt, *Alchemy, Science of the Cosmos, Science of the Soul,* trans. W. Stoddart (Baltimore: Penguin Books, 1971); and E. Zolla, *Le meraviglie della natura. Introduzione all' alchimia* (Milan: Bompiani, 1975).

45. See "From the Alchemy of Jābir to the Chemistry of Rāzī," in S. H. Nasr, *Islamic Life and Thought* (Albany, N.Y.: SUNY Press, 1981).

46. In fact no traditional civilization has ever sacrificed its vision of the Immutable for an ever-changing and accumulative science of nature which continues at the expense of the forgetting of that *scientia sacra* that is rooted in the very substance of intelligence.

4

$\mathcal{L}aw$ in $\mathcal{I}slam$

John L. Esposito

$\mathcal{C}$ ONTEMPORARY WRITING on the Muslim world is dominated by the Islamic resurgence with its social and political implications. In addition to increased interest in religion and religious observance (mosque attendance, fasting, almsgiving), Muslim activists have called for the implementation of more Islamically oriented states and societies. Integral to realization of this Islamization of society is the implementation of Islamic law. This stands in sharp contrast to the pattern of modern legal reform in the Muslim world by which Islamic law was progressively replaced by Western inspired legal systems. Why, then, is a call for the return of the Islamic law common to Islamic revivalism from North Africa to Southeast Asia?

If theology provides the key to Christianity's beliefs, doctrines and practice, in Islam (as in Judaism) that function is served by law.

Islam means "submission" to the will of Allah; Islamic law evolved from an attempt by Muslims to delineate in a comprehensive fashion God's will for mankind. Today, after several centuries of colonial dominance during which Western-based laws have governed much of Muslim life, Islamic laws have been implemented and religious courts reestablished in post-revolutionary Iran as well as Pakistan. Within many other Muslim countries from Egypt to Malaysia attempts are being made to introduce Islamic legislation in varying degrees.

This chapter will (1) review the sources and historical development of Islamic law in order to appreciate its nature and scope and to understand those factors which have a direct bearing on modern reform; (2) explain legal reform in the Muslim world; (3) discuss the reintroduction of Islamic law today and some of the issues and problems that underlie the process of Islamization of law.

CLASSICAL ISLAMIC LAW

At the center of Muslim life is Allah—the one, true God and His Divine Will as revealed to the Prophet Muhammad and preserved most completely and perfectly in the Quran. From the beginning of Islam, God's revelation in the Quran and the teachings of the Prophet Muhammad clearly explained that God had given this world to man as a trust (S. 33:73) and that it was the Muslim's divinely mandated vocation as God's representative or vicegerent to strive to realize God's will on earth (S. 2:30, 35:39). If Islam means submission to God's will, the Muslim is one who submits, that is, strives to bring about God's will in history. Success or failure provides the basis for divine judgment on the Last Day, eternal reward or punishment.

Both the teachings of the Quran and the example of Muhammad also made clear that the Muslim had not only an individual but a corporate identity. The primary community or society was no longer to be the tribe but rather the community of believers. Identity, allegiance, and commitment were to be vested in a universal brotherhood of believers whose individual and communal commitment was to carry out God's will.

As the early conquests and expansion of Islam are a testimony and confirmation of the religio-political nature of the Islamic community and its sense of mission to spread Islamic rule, so too the early Islamic centuries reflect Muslim concern to know, interpret, and apply God's will—His law, i.e., what it is that Muslims as individuals and as a community ought to be doing with their lives. During the earliest Islamic period, Muslims had direct access to divine guidance. The revelations which constitute the Quran were given to Muhammad over a period of twenty-two years. Muhammad himself served as the religo-political guide of the community, for he was both a prophet and the political, military, and legal head of the community. Both Quranic teaching and Prophetic example guided and governed the early Islamic state. However, it was during the early centuries following the Prophet's death (632) that Islamic law developed into a comprehensive system which encompassed and governed personal and public behaviour.[1]

THE SOURCES OF ISLAMIC LAW

According to Muslim jurisprudence, there are four sources of Islamic law: (1) the prescriptions of the Quran, (2) the example and teachings of the Prophet Muhammad, (3) analogical deduction and regulations derived from the two preceding sources and (4) the consensus of the Muslim community. This description of the sources of Islamic law is the classical formulation which came to be accepted and handed down from generation to generation. In fact, the actual development of law was a far more dynamic, creative and complex process. An awareness of the real history of legal development is critical both to understand the true nature of Islamic law and to appreciate the problems and possibilities of Islamic reform today.[2]

After the death of the Prophet Muhammad, the Muslim community was ruled by his successors, the Caliphs of Islam. Since Muhammad was the final prophet of God, the Caliph assumed political, though not prophetic leadership of the community. The first four Caliphs of Islam (Abu Bakr, Umar, Uthman and Ali) were all companions of the Prophet. So revered is this period (632–661) of Islamic history that it is remembered as the rule of the Four Rightly Guided Caliphs. This Medinan Period (622–661), when Muhammad and the Rightly Guided Caliphs led the community, has remained the ideal or normative period, that pristine exemplary time to which Islamic revivalist movements have turned throughout Muslim history.

Since the Quran includes only eighty verses that may be seen as laws in the strict sense, it does not provide a legal code. Therefore, although God is the supreme lawgiver and the Quran the revelation of His divine will, the interpretation and application of His will for society had to be worked out by Muslims in time and space. During his lifetime, Muhammad had guided the community and served as its chief judge. After his death, in cases where the Quran or the practice of Muhammad did not provide injunctions or precedence, the early Caliphs with their advisers guided and governed through *ad hoc* decisions which addressed the many new problems which the community encountered.

A new page was turned in the history of Islamic law with the founding of the Umayyad Dynasty (661–750) and the movement of Islam's capital from Medina to Damascus. The Umayyad Caliphs had to develop an administrative structure to govern what had become a rapidly expanding empire. One result was the creation of the office of judge. The judge was originally an official who was a delegate of the provincial governors; he was charged with seeing that government decrees were carried out and with settling disputes. It was during this period that legal development began to take on a more complex character. While judges consulted the Quran and the Prophetic example (as preserved in the traditions) for guidance, their individual interpretation of texts often differed. In many cases their decisions were based upon the prevailing Arab customary laws of their particular province. Since the empire was vast, the local practices varied from one geographic area to another. Thus the legacy of the Umayyad period in the area of legal developments consisted mainly of government administrative regulations and decisions of judges which were based upon their opinions formulated in light of Arab or local customary practice and the Quran. The resultant diverse, non-systematic body of laws laid the basic foundation for Islamic law.

These laws, however, were very much the product of the discretionary activity of rulers and judges, a fact that led pious Muslims toward the end of the Umayyad rule to decry this situation, desiring to have their law and life more systematically grounded in religion. In major cities, such as Medina, Mecca, Kufa, and Basra, they began systematically to review customary law/practice in light of Quranic teachings. These loosely organized endeavors were the beginning of the early Islamic schools of law.

Major developments in Islamic jurisprudence and law occurred during the second century of Islam, in particular, during the Abbasid Caliphate (750–1258). The Abbasids justified their revolution and seizure of power in the name of Islam, denouncing the Umayyads as impious rulers. While in many respects individual Caliphs were no more pious than their Umayyad predecessors, they did become patrons of Islam. During their reign Islamic thought and civilization developed and flourished, especially in the areas of language, literature, science, and law. The concensus of jurists during this period produced the binding legal formulations that were to govern Muslim life down through the centuries.

With Abbasid patronage, the law schools grew and flourished. From henceforth it was the jurists and scholars rather than the judges who interpreted and formulated Islamic law; the judges were restricted to its implementation. Islamic law did not grow out of the practice of judges and courts but through the careful study and reflection of jurists who set out a religious ideal. From 750 to 900 jurists sought to produce a comprehensive legal framework that would encompass every area of

Muslim life. Those interpretations which came to enjoy the consensus or acceptance of its members constituted the practice of a law school and were preserved in its law books.

However, it was not long before there was a reaction against this newly established system. Despite the self-conscious attempt at a systematic development of Islamic law based upon the Quran, significant differences continued to exist. Since the Quran is not a legal code, the doctrines of the law schools remained dependent in large part upon the discretionary interpretation or opinions of jurists who were, in turn, influenced by the differing customs of their respective social milieu. Reformers argued that if God is one, his divine will for mankind must be one. In this light, how could Muslims justify such diversity and human input in discovering God's revealed divine law? Was this not tantamount to making laws? They insisted that the rule of reason must be limited and that the law must be more firmly rooted in its revealed source.

Muhammad al-Shafii (+820), the Father of Islamic jurisprudence, emerged as the champion of those who sought to curb the diversity of legal practice in the Muslim world through the unification of Islamic law. Al-Shafii was responsible in great part for the formulation, which after much resistance and debate, became the classical doctrine of Islamic jurisprudence, restricting the sources of law to the Quran, the teachings and practice of the Prophet, and consensus and analogical reasoning.

Al-Shafii maintained that there were only two material (textual) sources of law, the Quran and the example of the Prophet, as preserved and collected in narrative stories or traditions. He maintained that the example of the Prophet Muhammad was divinely inspired and thus normative for the community. The measure of al-Shafii's success can be seen in that throughout Islamic history Sunnah in Islam came to be identified with the practice of Muhammad and no longer referred to tribal customary practice or consensus of the schools of law. Moreover, al-Shafii asserted that the authority for legal interpretations was not the consensus of a law school but that of the entire Muslim community. Buttressed by a saying of Muhammad, "My community will not agree upon an error," the agreed-upon practice of the Muslim community became the third infallible source of law. Fourthly, in the event of a new legal problem where no explicit revealed text or community consensus existed, jurists should resort to deductive reasoning, that is, seek a similar situation in the revealed sources (Quran and tradition) from which to derive a new regulation. Thus, al-Shafii rejected the established practice of individual interpretation based upon opinion and restricted reasoning utilized in legal matters to analogies restricted by the parameters of the revelation and prophetic precedent, thus eliminating what he considered to be the arbitrary nature of legal reasoning.

Al-Shafii's restricted definition of legal reasoning was generally accepted by later scholars. Thus, for example, while many laws were the product of the personal opinion or the independent reasoning of the early judges and the later jurists, this fact was now overlooked as previously developed doctrines were now attributed to a tradition of the Prophet or to analogy. Resistance to this process is reflected in the Hanafi and Maliki schools of law that accept subsidiary sources of law such as the public interest and juristic preference.[3]

The classical formulation of the sources of Islamic law followed al-Shafii with one major exception. Whereas he defined consensus as that of the entire community, other jurists acknowledged the consensus of the leading scholars of a generation. Al-Shafii's uniform, ideological formulation replaced the more actual, dynamic, and creative process of legal development in the mind, memory, and consciousness of the Muslim community. The historical development of the law was forgotten; the ideal replaced the real.

By the tenth century, the basic development of Islamic law was completed. Law was God's law—the divinely revealed mandated path, Shariah, which provided the blueprint for Muslim society. Islamic jurisprudence was the application of revelation of the many circumstances of Muslim life.[4] By the end of the tenth century, the general consensus of Muslim jurists was that Islamic law had been satisfactorily and comprehensively delineated in its essential regulations as preserved in the law books or legal manuals produced by the law schools. Therefore, it was no longer necessary or permissible for individuals to develop or reinterpret its implications. Personal or independent interpretation was replaced by the imitation or following of tradition, the practice of the Muslim community preserved in its law. Change or innovation was prohibited as an unwarranted deviation.

There is a danger of exaggerating the fixed nature of Islamic law. Indeed, where questions of legal practice exist, Islamic jurisprudence made provision for the use of a legal expert, a jurisconsult, whose opinions were sought and used by the courts. In this endeavor he was expected to look to the legal manuals for their guiding principles.

It should be noted that despite the general unity of Islamic law, a diversity among its various schools resulted from the role played by the independent reasoning of judges and jurists as well as the impact of varying customs of quite different social milieus. This diversity remained throughout the medieval period as the judges preserved and applied the laws of the various schools. For example, while Hanafi law restricted the grounds on which a woman could seek a divorce, Maliki law was far more liberal, allowing such grounds for divorce as failure to maintain and desertion.[5]

SCHOOLS OF LAW

The development of various schools of law helped preserve the diversity of Islamic law which was sanctioned by the reported saying of the Prophet, "Difference of opinion within my community is a sign of the bounty of Allah." These schools took their names from their founders. Although there had been many law schools by A.D. 1300, four major Sunni schools predominated. Today they predominate in the following areas: the Hanafi in the Middle East and the Indian subcontinent, the Maliki in North, Central and West Africa, the Shafii in East Africa and Southeast Asia and the Hanbali in Saudi Arabia.

In addition to Sunni law schools, there are Shiah schools such as the Jafari in Iran and Iraq. Limitations of space have necessitated a primary focusing on law in Sunni Islam, to which 90 percent of the world's Muslims belong. However, some attention to Shiah Islam is required. The Sunni-Shiah split was caused by a political/constitutional issue, the succession to leadership of the Muslim community. At the death of Muhammad, Ali's supporters maintained that as the Prophet's son-in-law and closest male relative, Ali was Muhammad's legitimate successor. However, their desires were thwarted when Abu Bakr was elected as the first Caliph. Although Ali eventually became the fourth Caliph of Islam, he was murdered only five years after his succession to power. Muawiyyah, who had challenged Ali's leadership, assumed and founded the Umayyad dynasty. The supporters or partisans of Ali refused to recognize Umayyad rule, maintaining that rightful leadership was vested in Ali's house, his descendents. Shiites divided into a number of sects, the most important of which are the Ithna Ashari (or

Twelvers) and the Ismaili (or Seveners). The former are concentrated in Iran and southern Iraq while the latter are in the Indian subcontinent and East Africa.

The fundamental political and legal difference between the Sunnis and Shiahs is the Shiah doctrine of the Imamate. For the Sunnis the Caliph is the elected successor of the Prophet, the political leader of the community/state. In contrast, the Shiah maintain that the leadership is vested in the Imam who must be a descendent of the Prophet Muhammad and the first Imam Ali. The Imam is the divinely inspired religio-political leader and serves as the final authoritative interpreter of Islamic law.

The doctrine of the Imamate resulted in fundamental differences in Islamic jurisprudence. While for both the Shiah and the Sunni the Quran and the Sunnah of the Prophet are the inspired authoritative textual sources of law, the Shiah have maintained their own collections of traditions at the same time rejecting consensus and analogy since they viewed the Imam as the supreme legal authority and interpreter. In his absence, qualified religious leaders serve as his agents or representatives. Thus, unlike Sunni Islam, for the Shiah the door of interpretation has never been closed. However, although they do not accept the Sunni doctrine of imitation Shiah Imams and interpreters of the law have also tended to consult and follow their medieval legal manuals.

ISLAMIC LAW IN MUSLIM SOCIETY: THE CONTENT OF LAW

The Shariah then was the sacred law of the Islamic community/state. The task of the ruler was to assure governance according to the Shariah. But what was the content of law and how was it applied? Law in Islam, as previously indicated, is to govern all aspects of life. It comprises a Muslim's rights and duties before God. Moreover, it differs from Western notions of law in that Islamic law encompasses both law and morality. Here law followed the Quranic prescription that the Muslim task is "urging to the good and dissuading from the bad." Therefore, jurisprudence not only categorized acts as good or evil but also classified them according to a system of "Shariah values" as recommended, permissible, obligatory, blameworthy, and forbidden or prohibited. While the law indicated the "ideal"—what a Muslim ought or ought not to do—ethical categories such as blameworthy or recommended were not subject to legal sanction.

THE JUDICIARY

Application of law was the province of Shariah courts and their judges. In general the judiciary was dependent upon the executive, for the Caliph judges were appointed by the government, paid by it, and served at the Caliph's pleasure. Although under Islamic law Shariah court decisions are final, with no system of judicial appeal, in reality all decisions could be reviewed by the political authority—the Caliph or his provincial governor.

Judges were simply to apply the law as found in legal manuals, and they were not to interpret or add to it. Thus, Islamic law does not recognize a case law system that is, there is no system of legally binding precedents. This reflects the fact that Islamic law is not judges' law but that of scholar-jurists. Other notable judicial procedures include rules of evidences which require two adult, male eyewitnesses of established moral character or, if this is lacking, an oath sworn in God's name, the exclusion of circumstantial evidence, and the absence of cross-examination of witnesses.

Although in theory the Shariah was the only legitimate norm and judges' courts the only judicial system, in practice this was not the total picture. While the Caliph as head of the community could not legislate, yet his right to enact administrative regulations within the limits of the Shariah was recognized. This practice was justified in the name of Islam since it was maintained that such ordinances enabled the ruler to fulfill his mandate to assure Shariah rule amidst changing political and social circumstances. Thus, in the name of Shariah governances the ruler had broad discretionary powers to issue ordinances or regulations,[6] as well as create their own complaint courts. Originally established for the ruler to hear complaints against his senior officials, they soon became a system of courts whose scope and function were determined by individual caliphs. While the Shariah remained the basic law, in fact the ruler had broad legislative and judicial powers, justified as administrative powers, through his issuance of ordinances and his complaint courts. As a result, two jurisdictions came to exist: the Shariah courts which dealt primarily with family laws and religious endowments and the complaint courts which dealt with public law, especially criminal law and taxation.

To conclude this section on classical Islamic law, the Shariah is the perfect and complete, divinely revealed law for Muslim society. Interpreting and applying its revealed principles and values to Muslim life entailed a complex process of legal development. By the tenth century, Muslim jurisprudence had achieved a consensus regarding the sources of law as well as its essential delineation in the legal manuals produced by the law schools. Therefore, the majority of jurists agreed that further interpretation of law was no longer necessary; the task of Muslim society was simply to conform and follow God's law.

Throughout the long centuries of Muslim rule classical Islamic law remained the established avowed law of Muslim empires. Indeed when Muslim jurists and theologians faced the question of what to do if a Muslim ruler proved to be a tyrant, the accepted conclusion was that the nature of an Islamic state was determined not by the religious or moral disposition of the ruler but by Shariah rule, that is, whether the Shariah was acknowledged as the law of the state.[7]

BEGINNINGS OF LEGAL CHANGE

Legal Reform in the Middle East

The beginnings of legal reform in the Middle East were initiated in the Ottoman Empire in the middle of the nineteenth century through the promulgation of commercial and penal codes such as the Ottoman Commercial Code (1850) and the Ottoman Penal Code (1858). These codes, both in form and substance, were largely derived from European codes as a result of the increasingly close contact with the West (especially France and Great Britain) in the nineteenth century. In addition, secular Nizamiyyah courts were established to handle civil and criminal law limiting the jurisdiction of the Shariah Courts to the area of family law. This process may best be characterized as a displacement of Islamic law by Western codes rather than one of reinterpretation and reform. It continued throughout the twentieth century in most parts of the Islamic world as modern commercial, penal, and finally civil codes were enacted.

However, material from Islamic law was still central to family law. In 1875 Muhammad Qadri Pasha, under official Ottoman government sponsorship, compiled a code based on the classical Hanafi school which included 647 articles concerning family law inheritance. Although this legal code was never officially adopted as legislation, this compendium of classical family law was used as the major reference for Shariah courts in many Middle Eastern countries. Thus, despite official legal change in the areas of civil and criminal law during the latter half of the nineteenth century and early twentieth century, Muslim family law, which had been practiced through the centuries, remained unchanged. The fact that no major legislation in family law occurred until 1920 was consistent both with the general lack of social progress and the centrality of the family in Muslim life.

Legal Reform in India-Pakistan (Anglo-Muhammadan Law)

The practice of traditional Muslim law in India-Pakistan in the early stages of British rule was unimpaired by foreign intervention. Although many changes came about in other areas of life, the judicial attitude of the British was characterized by non-interference with the prevailing legal system.

This situation remained essentially unchanged until the latter half of the nineteenth century when the application of Muslim law was narrowed by the enactment in 1862 of the India Penal Code and the Code of Criminal Procedure. Moreover, portions of the civil code were also codified. As a result of such measures, Islamic law in the Indian sub-continent, as had happened in the Middle East, came to be restricted to the domain of family law.

However, unlike the Arab experience, the first family law reforms (The Indian Evidence Act of 1872 and the Child Marriage Restraint Act of 1929 and finally The Dissolution of Muslim Marriages Act of 1929) were not enacted by the Muslim community itself but imposed upon the Muslim community by the British.

MODERN MUSLIM FAMILY LAW REFORM

In a real sense, in most Muslim countries since the nineteenth century modern legal reform has meant the progressive restriction of Islamic law to Muslim family laws. Indeed family law reform has provided the primary area for Islamic modernist reform. The early family law reform in the Middle East and the Indian subcontinent sought to accomplish two purposes: (1) improve the status of women and (2) strengthen the rights of parents and their lineal descendents, in effect, strengthen the nuclear family at the expense of more distant members of the extended family. The three major areas of family law reform are marriage, divorce, and intestate succession.

Among the more significant marriage reforms have been the elimination of child marriage and the restriction of polygamy. To accomplish the former, legislation in Muslim countries was introduced to raise the original minimum marriage ages as interpreted in traditional law. For example, in Egypt and Pakistan, the minimum ages were raised to sixteen for wives and eighteen for husbands.

Modern reform legislation regarding polygamy has had a far more complex history of development. Although Egypt was the leader among modern Muslim nations in family law reforms, early attempts to restrict the Muslim male's right of polygamy in Egypt were thwarted. Syria was the first modern Muslim state to legislate any restrictions in this area. The Syrian law of Personal Status of 1953 requires that a married Muslim male must obtain permission of the court before contracting an additional marriage. Permission is to be given only if the court is convinced that the husband is financially capable of assuming this new obligation.

In 1957 Tunisia enacted a far more radical change. President Bourguiba through legislation outlawed polygamy entirely on two grounds: (1) polygamy, like slavery, was an institution that belonged to the past—that is, it had served a purpose in the past but was now repugnant to most people; (2) following the position of Muhammad Abduh, religious validation for this change was claimed by reference to the Quranic verses on polygamy which required equal treatment of wives: "Marry women of your choice, two or three, or four; but if ye fear that ye shall not be able to deal justly (with them) then only one" (S. 4:3), and especially to S.4:129 which states: "Ye are never able to be fair and just between women even if that were your ardent desire." This last verse was interpreted as scriptural proof for the impossibility of fulfilling this ideal of equal treatment.

However, no other Muslim country has followed the Tunisian path. Rather, more modified legislation has been enacted. Thus, for example, Morocco in 1958 drafted legislation which permitted a wife to include a stipulation in the marriage contract that gave her a right to divorce should her husband take an additional wife. Even where a wife had neglected to include such a stipulation in her contract, she could still sue for divorce on the grounds that her spouse's second marriage was injurious. This right followed from the more general assertion of this legislation that polygamy was not permitted by the Quran in cases where any injustice between wives was to be feared.

Iraq provides an instructive example of the dilemma of modern Muslim legislation. The Iraqi Code of Personal Status of 1959 went further than that of any other Muslim country except Tunisia. Under Iraqi law, court permission was necessary for a Muslim desiring to take a second wife. Moreover, violation of the 1959 law would have not only resulted in criminal sanctions but also rendered the second marriage invalid. In 1963 however, this was changed so that such a union, while illicit and subject to criminal sanctions, is nevertheless valid. This approach has generally been common to all Muslim family law reforms (with the exception of Tunisia): violation of statutes renders an act illegal but it does not make the action invalid.

In addition to marriage, the second and perhaps most important area of legal reform affecting the Muslim family is divorce. Although the Quran enjoined equitable treatment for wives and called for a waiting period of three months before a final irrevocable divorce could take place, yet under traditional Muslim law a husband can divorce his wife at any time and for any reason. While Islamic jurisprudence agreed that to repudiate a wife without sufficient reason was reprehensible, nevertheless such repudiation was legally valid. Moreover, under traditional Hanafi law, which was the official law for most of the Middle East and the Indian subcontinent, Muslim wives had very limited grounds for obtaining a divorce. Therefore, a major area of divorce reform has been the broadening of the grounds upon which a wife may obtain a divorce and a restriction of the husband's unilateral right of divorce.

The first changes in the grounds for divorce occurred in the Ottoman Empire in 1915 with the promulgation of two imperial edicts granting women the right to sue for divorce in cases of desertion or where the existence of a husband's contagious disease made conjugal life dangerous.

Broader grounds for divorce were established in Egypt's Law No. 25 of 1929. This reform legislation recognized four additional situations in which a woman could sue for divorce: (1) her husband's failure to provide maintenance; (2) dangerous physical or mental disease of the husband; (3) desertion and (4) maltreatment. Most Muslim countries have followed this lead. However, in Tunisia and Pakistan reforms have gone beyond this point. Under the Tunisian Code of 1957, a wife may demand a divorce for any reason if she is willing to pay whatever financial compensation the court decrees. In Pakistan, on the other hand, a wife may obtain a divorce upon the allegation that her marriage has become intolerable, provided she return her dower.[8]

A major abuse of both the spirit and letter of the Quran was the "disapproved" divorce. This innovation circumvented the Quranically prescribed "waiting period" between pronouncements by permitting the husband to utter the divorce formula three times consecutively on the same occasion and thus immediately effect a final irrevocable divorce. Although viewed as repugnant such a divorce was valid. However, through legislation, beginning in Egypt and followed by Sudan, Jordan, Syria, Morocco and Iraq, most Muslim countries have decreed that all divorce pronouncements, regardless of the number of times indicated by word or sign, shall count as only a single and therefore revocable repudiation and not a final and irrevocable one. The main purpose of this reform has been to return to the Quranic intent providing a "waiting period" or opportunity for reconciliation of the estranged couple.

Perhaps the most contested restriction on male divorce rights has been the transfer of the right of divorce from the individual Muslim male to the jurisdiction of the courts. In Syria and Morocco if a Muslim does not obtain court permission, the courts may require a husband who has unilaterally divorced his wife to pay her compensation.

Tunisia in 1956 introduced the most radical reform in decreeing that any extra judicial repudiation is invalid. Iran in the Family Protection Act of 1967 went further than all other Muslim countries except Tunisia, legislating that a husband may not divorce his wife until he has received a "Certificate of Irreconcilability" from the Court. Pakistan has a much more modified law requiring that a pronouncement of divorce is not effective until ninety days after it has been reported or officially registered and attempts at reconciliation have failed. Both Iran's and Pakistan's requirements regarding periods for arbitration and reconciliation follow the spirit of the Quran: "if you fear a breach between the two, bring forth an arbiter from his people and from her people" (S. 4:39).

The third and final major area of Muslim family law reform is that of intestate succession (inheritance). The system of succession was clearly geared to meet the needs of traditional Muslim society.[9] The Quranic prescriptions which stipulated fixed fractional shares of inheritance emphasized the more immediate family and especially improved the status of female family members. These changes were superimposed on pre-Islamic Arabian tribal customary law. After the

Quranic heirs received their portions, the residue of the estate passed to the nearest male agnate, no matter how distant a relative he might be. This arrangement may have adequately served traditional Muslim society. However, in modern times when greater mobility has led to a lessening of extended family ties, modernists cite the problem of a parent whose child receives only a Quranic portion of his estate while the residue passes to a distant agnatic relative. Therefore, the tendency of modern reforms has clearly been to increase the rights of more immediate family members at the expense of the favored position enjoyed traditionally by more distant agnatic heirs. Rather than a direct change in the law of inheritance, most Muslim countries chose to do this indirectly through reform in the law of bequest. The general rule had been "no bequests in favor of an heir." A testator's right to bequeath up to one-third of the estate had excluded the Quranic heirs (wife, daughters, etc.) of the more immediate family. However, legislation in Egypt in 1946, followed by other Muslim states, changed this situation so that such a bequest is now possible. Thus, a parent may bequeath up to one-third of an estate in favor of a daughter or wife.

A final example of change in the law of succession reflecting a concern to protect the rights of the more nuclear family is the case of orphaned grandchildren. Under traditional Islamic law, such children were excluded from any share in their grandfather's estate (that is, from enjoying their predeceased father's share) if another son of their grandfather (their uncle) were alive. Such a regulation reflected traditional Muslim society in which family solidarity was a basic feature of the extended family and the senior member was to provide for the remainder of the family. However, the changing circumstances of the modern Muslim family necessitated protection of the rights of these children. Therefore, through a different means reforms were introduced which insured that orphaned grandchildren would receive the equivalent portion of their grandparent's estate to which their predeceased parent would have been entitled.

Despite the relative success of Islamic legal reform, many issues were skirted and remained unresolved. First, whereas classical Islamic law was the product of religious scholars, modern reforms have been accomplished through the action of parliamentary bodies. The vast majority of these legislators were laymen who lacked the traditional qualifications for an interpreter, that is, one who is knowledgeable of the Shariah and qualified to exercise his role in religious matters. In most instances the Ulema felt disenfranchised and viewed the process of modern legal reform as un-Islamic.[10] They maintain that a Western secular-oriented elite has used its political power to tamper with Islam and force unwarranted innovations (deviation from tradition) upon Muslim society. In some instances the Ulema mounted counter attacks.[11] While never totally successful, conservative religious leaders have managed to limit the scope of reform legislation. Moreover, while some Ulema have accepted reforms, the more conservative have been content to bide their time until a more favorable period when Islamic law might once more be implemented.

Perhaps the most fundamental methodological issue underlying Islamic reform in general and legal reform in particular is that of the unquestioned following and authority of tradition versus the need for reinterpretation and reform.[12] For conservative Muslims, the classical legal manuals represent the Shariah and thus provide the revealed pattern or norm to be followed. Thus, the extent to which a dichotomy exists between law and society indicates society's departure from the straight path of Islam. The remedy is not adaptation and change but a return to established norms. However, Islamic reformers maintain that the regulations in the law books represent the understanding and interpretation of early Muslim scholar-jurists who had applied the principles and values of Islam to their societies. Therefore, Muslims today must once again respond to the needs of modern society. While acknowledging the immutability of Shariah principles and regulations found in the revealed sources (Quran and the example and teaching of the Prophet), they distinguish Shariah from the corpus of classical law, emphasizing the contingency and relativity of the latter.[13] Advocating re-interpretation they call for Islamic legal reform to adapt law to the changing conditions of modern Muslim life.

ISLAMIC REVIVAL AND SHARIAH REFORM

During the 1970s the Shariah re-emerged as an issue in Muslim political and legal development. The contemporary resurgence of Islam has included a reassertion of Islamic identity both in the personal and public spheres of life.[14] Rejecting the westernization and secularization of Muslim society, revivalists seek to root social change more firmly and authentically in their indigenous, Islamic heritage. As in politics imported Western models are judged social failures, responsible for the profound socioeconomic disparities in most Muslim countries. An Islamic alternative is seen as the antidote for social ills (break up of the family, corruption, crime) and the firm foundation for social justice. Given this agenda the logical starting point for the Islamization of society has been the Shariah since it embodies the normative ideal for Muslim behaviour. Thus, from Egypt and the Sudan to Pakistan and Malaysia there is a call for more Shariah law in order to establish more Islamically oriented states/societies.[15] In Egypt, from the mid 1970s there were increased calls from the religious establishment at al-Azhar University, a major center of Islamic education, the Muslim Brotherhood, and more radical religious groups for the rejection of "imported ideas" and a return to the Shariah.[16] In Pakistan, the government of Zulfikar Ali Bhutto began to introduce Islamic regulations such as the prohibition of gambling and alcohol. After the 1977 *coup détat,* his successor General Zia ul-Haq committed his government to the establishment of an Islamic system of government and gave it formal promulgation in his "Introduction of Islamic Laws."[17] In addition to the enforcement of Islamic laws, a federal Shariah Court has been established whose jurisdiction is to determine whether or not a law is repugnant to Islam, that is, contrary to the Quran and example and teachings of the Prophet. In post-revolutionary Iran Islamic law and Islamic courts have been used to improve political, social, and legal controls over Iranian society as punishments, including execution have been meted out in the name of Islam for crimes ranging from the political to the social (prostitution and adultery).

The primary area of contention in Islamic law is family law, reflecting the centrality of the family in Islam. Conservative religious leaders tend to reject modern legal reforms. Thus, after the revolution, Iran abrogated its major family law reform, *The Family Protection Act* of 1967. Similar demands have been made by Ulema in Pakistan regarding the *Muslim Family Laws Ordinance* of 1961. Such activities frustrate Islamic reformers and confirm secularist fears that a return to the Shariah will mean a regressive enactment of classical (medieval) law.

Additional legal change has been advocated and/or enacted in other areas. In a number of countries, the traditional Islamic punishments for those offenses for which there is a fixed prescribed punishment in the revelation have been reintroduced. Thus, theft, alcohol consumption, armed robbery, apostacy, illicit sexual relations, or false allegations of unchastity are once more punishable by flogging, amputation or stoning respectively. The degree of enforcement has varied from country to country. Other legal reforms have included public observance of the Ramadan fast, taxation and the banning of usury. In fact, usury, as applied to bank interest and certain forms of insurance, has not been completely outlawed or eliminated. Instead, there has been a burgeoning of Islamic banks and insurance companies which offer an "interest free" Islamic alternative in banking transactions.[18] The principle means is profit/Loss Sharing(PLS). Under this system, the depositer and the bank (or the borrower and the bank) enter into a partnership in which both share in the profit or losses of a venture.

At the heart of the debate and conflict over the introduction of Shariah law is a fundamental question of Islamic renewal: does a "return to Islam" mean a replication of a normative past or a process of reform (reconstruction), informed by the Islamic legal tradition but not restricted to it. In Islamic terminology the question involves both the permissibility and extent of reinterpretation. Many critics of the current process of Islamization see it as simply implementing a negative Islam. They point to its use by the Ayatullah Khomeini in Iran and the martial law regime of Zia ul-Haq in Pakistan, and see their definitions of Islamic law as simply encompassing political control, social control (drinking, gambling, women's dress), taxation, and banking interest. To this, they ask "Whose Islam?" and "Why a negative Islam?"[19]

Whatever the specific developments in individual Muslim countries may be, there has been a growing recognition throughout the Islamic world of the failure to achieve a viable synthesis between Islam and modernity. The need to rediscover and reappropriate one's historical and cultural roots in defining an "Islamic modernity" is acknowledged by many Muslims, conservative and modernist, politicians and technocrats, lay and religious. However, how this will be achieved remains a topic of great controversy and diversity of opinion. Given the traditional role of Islamic law in providing the ideal, comprehensive statement of the Islamic way of life, Shariah reform will be integral to any attempt to define state and society more Islamically. In undertaking this task, conservatives and modernist reformers have a rich resource in Islamic legal history. For if correctly understood, it offers a picture of a dynamic, creative, adaptive religious tradition. The process of Islamization which characterized the early, formative period of Islam was one in which the interpretation and application of Islamic principles and values to the exigencies of modern Muslim life was accompanied by the adoption and adaptation of what was best in other cultures. To what extent this will be realized and utilized remains to be seen.

NOTES

1. For a concise history of Islamic law, see Joseph Schacht's "Pre-Islamic Background and Early Development of Jurisprudence" and "The Schools of Law and Later Developments of Jurisprudence," *Law in the Middle East* (Vol. I, *Origin and Development of Law*), ed. M. Khadduri and H. J. Liebesny (Washington, D.C.: The Middle East Institute, 1955), chapters 2–3. For a more extended treatment, see Schacht's *The Origins of Muhammadan Jurisprudence* (Oxford: Clarendon Press, 1950).

2. The best general introduction to the history of Islamic law is N. J. Coulson, *A History of Islamic Law* (Edinburgh: Edinburgh University Press, 1964). For an introduction to Islamic Law, see Joseph Schacht, *An Introduction to Islamic Law* (Oxford: Clarendon Press, 1964), A. A. A. Fyzee, *Outlines of Muhammadan Law,* 4th ed. (London: Oxford University Press, rpt. 1974), or H. J. Liebesny, ed., *The Law of the Near and Middle East* (Albany: SUNY Press, 1975).

3. Subhi Mahmasani, *Falsafat al-Tashri fi al-Islam (The Philosophy of Jurisprudence in Islam),* trans. by Farhat J. Ziadeh (Leiden: Brill, 1961).

4. See S. 2:228–229.

5. S. 65:1. For a discussion of divorce in classical family law see John L. Esposito, *Women in Muslim Family Law* (Syracuse, N. Y.: Syracuse University Press, 1982), pp. 28–39, and Fyzee, *Outline,* pp. 139–179.

6. Coulson, *History,* pp. 132–45.

7. The pioneer in the study of Muslim law reform is J. N. D. Anderson. In addition to his many articles, see *Islamic Law in the Modern World* (New York: New York University Press, 1959) and *Law Reform in the Muslim World* (London: Athlone, 1976). For a presentation of classical family law with an analysis of modern legal reform see Esposito, *Women in Muslim Family Law.*

8. The law of the Indian subcontinent is an amalgram of Islamic and British law called Anglo-Muhammadan Law. As a result, although judicial precedent was not recognized by Islamic jurisprudence, it is an accepted means for modern legal reform. In *Balquis Fatima* vs. *Najm-ul Ikram Qureshi* the Lahore High Court ruled that grounds for divorce existed where serious incompatibility made a harmonious marriage impossible. *Pakistan Legal Debates* 1959 (W. P.) Lahore 566.

9. A comprehensive discussion of inheritance in Islamic law may be found in N. J. Coulson, *Succession in the Muslim Family* (Cambridge: Cambridge University Press, 1971). See also Esposito, *Women in Muslim Family Law,* pp. 39–48, 63–66, 88.

10. Aharon Layish, "The Contribution of the Modernists to the Secularization of Islamic Law," *Middle East Studies* 14 no. 3 (October 1978): 271 ff.

11. In 1955 Pakistan created a Commission on Marriage and Family Laws consisting of five lay members and one representative of the Ulema. In 1956 the religious scholar dissented from the committee's final report. His minority report provides a succinct summary of a conservative religious critique of modern legal reform. See "The Minority Report" in *Islam in Transition: Muslim Perspectives,* ed. by John J. Donohue and John L. Esposito (New York: Oxford University Press, 1982), pp. 205–208. Compare this argument with "The Modernist Majority Report" on pp. 201–204.

12. For discussion of this problem by Muslims and suggested responses see Muhammad Nuwayhi "A Revolution in Religious Thought," pp. 160–68; Subhi Mahma-

sani "Adaptation of Islamic Jurisprudence to Modern Social Needs," pp. 181–87; and A. A. A. Fyzee "The Reinterpretation of Islam," pp. 188–93, in ibid.

13. Kemal A. Faruki, *Islamic Jurisprudence* (Karachi: Pakistan Publishing House, 1962), p. 104. See also Fyzee, *Outlines,* p. 21.

14. For an overview of the Islamic resurgence, see John O. Voll, *Islam: Continuity and Change in the Modern World* (Boulder, Col.: Westview Press, 1982), pp. 275 ff. See also Mohammad Ayoub, ed., *The Politics of Islamic Reassertion* (New York: St. Martin's, 1981); Ali E. H. Dessouki, ed., *Islamic Resurgence in the Arab World* (New York: Praeger, 1982); John L. Esposito, ed., *Islam and Development: Religion and Sociopolitical Change* (Syracuse, N.Y.: Syracuse University Press, 1981); and John L. Esposito, ed., *Voices of a Resurgent Islam* (New York: Oxford University Press, 1983).

15. Pakistan provides the most extensive contemporary experiment at Islamization of law. John L. Esposito, "Pakistan: Quest for Islamic Identity," in Esposito, ed., *Islam and Development,* pp. 152–57; William L. Richter "Pakistan," in Ayoub, ed., *The Politics of Islamic Reassertion,* ch. 9; and Esposito, "Islamization: Religion and Politics in Pakistan" *Muslim World* (January 1983).

16. M. Martin and R. Masad, "Return to Islamic Legislation in Egypt," *Islamic Law and Change in Arab Society 1976, CEMAM Reports* (Beirut: Dar El-Mashreq, 1978), pp. 47–78.

17. Esposito, "Pakistan: Quest for Islamic Identity," pp. 153 ff.

18. For a discussion of Islamic economics, see John T. Cummings *et al.,* "Islam and Modern Economic Change" in *Islam and Development,* ch. 2; K. Ahmad, ed., *Studies in Islamic Economics* (Leicester: Islamic Foundation, 1980).

19. Esposito, "Pakistan: Quest for Islamic Identity," pp. 157 ff.

5

The Experience of Muslim Women

CONSIDERATIONS OF POWER AND AUTHORITY

Jane I. Smith

WOMEN IN ISLAM has become a subject of increasing attention in the past several years, marked by the appearance of a number of treatments by Western scholars and by Muslim men and women. The topic is a difficult one to define with precision, and it is often unclear if one is viewing Muslim women as Muslims (with attention to specifically Islamic regulations and practices) or considering the various circumstances of women who happen to reside in Islamic countries. In the most general terms it might be possible to distinguish between the studies done by Western observers and the essays of Muslims on the subject of Islamic women by saying that the latter tend to describe the roles, responsibilities, and privileges of women as delineated by Islam in its ideal form, Islam as it really should be, while the former are more descriptive of actual practices and situations which may fall short of the Muslim ideal.

The dimensions of history and geography make the picture even more complex. One needs to consider that the Quran introduced reforms in the seventh century that represented a notable improvement for women over circumstances in pre-Islamic Arabia, that the passing centuries were marked by a hardening of social circumstances with resulting problems and difficulties for women (recognized by Muslims and non-Muslim students alike), and that reforms again have been introduced in the last half century. Today about 400,000,000 Muslim women inhabit countries all over the globe; some of them are highly Westernized, some are living much as their forebears lived centuries ago, and others are struggling to find ways in which to enjoy the status afforded to them by the Quran and to affirm their identity with and participation in the tradition of Islam.

89

The range of works available on the general subject of women in Islam is wide and often confusing for one coming new to the study. There are general surveys of the religion and culture of Islam, sociological studies of educational and work opportunities for women in Islamic countries, ethnographic descriptions of kinship relations and group dynamics, legal analyses of the ways in which Muslim countries are dealing with personal and family law. All of this is balanced by an increasing number of essays in English by Muslims attempting to show the high position Islam has accorded to women and their role in the maintenance of Islamic society.

Early Western studies of the role of women in Arab Muslim societies were generally done from the perspective of religion and often tended to be unduly critical or derogatory. Take, for instance, the description of a veiled Muslim woman from Charles Doughty's *Travels in Arabia Deserta:* "loathly to look upon! for the feminine face was blotted out by the sordid veil-clout; in our eyes, an heathenish Asiatic villany."[1] Western studies tended to cite Islam as the reason for whatever problems were seen in Muslim societies, without regard for political and social analyses. This evoked a response on the part of Muslims which was understandably apologetic and defensive.

Since 1960 studies have been focussed more specifically on issues such as employment, education, family planning. Scholars have come to realize that distinctions must be made among the circumstances of women in rural or pastoral, village and urban contexts. Several analysts have noted that earlier attempts to establish distinctions between the public and the subordinate private spheres in Islamic societies, the former the domain of males and the latter the domain of women, are superficial and conditioned by Western presuppositions.[2] Related to this is the distinction often made between the formal and informal aspects of Islamic religion as applying respectively to practices of males and females. This is partly a result of the relative paucity of works on Muslim women's actual religious practices. Studies now being done suggest that in fact women's religion has an organizational complexity that makes these distinctions much less obvious than was heretofore supposed.

Underlying such superficial analyses is the notion that women in Islam have no power since authority lies ultimately and by divine ordination in the hands of men. More will be said on this later; what we are now seeing, however, is that not only do women have forms of power in the domestic sphere but that in their religious practices they are able to exercise degrees of power that extend into the male domain. As Cynthia Nelson, long-time observer of Egyptian society, puts it, "there exists internal evidence that our images are incomplete, that the dynamics of power and authority are much more subtle than we have been led to believe."[3]

In addition to increasingly sophisticated means of analyzing Muslim societies so as to consider the role and circumstances of women, it is also now necessary for students of Islam to make increased efforts to listen to Muslim voices as they attempt to describe, from a variety of perspectives, their understanding of women's roles and practices. Such responses vary from apologetic to critical and are increasingly deliberate in their attempts to define an Islamic position that sets itself in conscious distinction to Western ideas of equality, justice, and liberation.

Recognizing the magnitude of the task, then, my goals in this belief overview of women in Islam are to consider the following questions: What in the legal and social understanding of Islam have been the descriptions of and the prescriptions for women? What are the realities for women in a variety of Islamic countries today (with concentration mainly on the Arab world)? How do Muslims themselves, male and female, understand the goals and ideals for which they are striving? Equally important in the analysis of the role and status of women is an effort to understand ways in which they are able to exercise power in circumstances that may upon superficial observation seem to leave them relatively powerless.

Let us look first at some of the specific issues that comprise the complex picture of legal realities, social roles, and religious practices of women in Islam. Many of these are regulated by Islamic law, and in most places are only recently coming under scrutiny and change. Of the non-Communist Islamic countries, Turkey alone has officially adopted a secular law which includes personal and family law. Most other countries have a dual system of a secular civil code and a religious family code. This means that unless clear exceptions have been recognized, the provisions of Islamic law are determined by the revelation of the Quran, the practice and teaching of the Prophet, and legal analogies still pertain.

MARRIAGE

According to the Quran (S. 2:236–37, 4:4), a woman is allowed to keep her dowry unless of her own accord she gives part of it to her husband, a clear improvement over pre-Islamic circumstances. Dowry differs from bride-wealth, which is given by the groom and his family to the bride's father. In the Islamic system the woman herself maintains her dowry, a source of both wealth and self-esteem. In general the dowry system is still maintained, although in Turkey at the present time, for example, there is growing controversy over whether or not this is an outdated custom. Many young people, especially in the cities, think that it is degrading for women, although the older people generally favor its continuity. The Turkish government, according to the *New York Times,* December 21, 1980, established a commission to study this question and concluded that the dowry system should be maintained.

Within the marriage situation, it is the issue of polygamy (or, to be precise, polygyny) that has been most difficult for Westerns to understand. The Quran (S. 4:3) permits a man to have up to four wives if he is able to treat them all equally. Co-wives must be housed in separate but equal quarters. Muslims point out, correctly, that polygyny did not originate with Islam but was a pre-Islamic practice, and that the ceiling of four wives is both an improvement on earlier circumstances and a way in which to provide for single women in periods of war. A Muslim woman convert defending polygyny stated in 1978 that in wartimes the choice for women, "bluntly stated, is between a chaste and childless old maidenhood, or becoming somebody's mistress." She concluded that "most women would not welcome either of these."[4]

In contemporary Islamic societies bigamy is probably practiced by less than 10 percent of the population and polygyny by far less than that. Only Turkey and Tunisia have officially banned multiple marriages although Syria and Iraq require the husband to receive permission of the court before taking a second wife, and Morocco and Lebanon allow the wife to stipulate in the marriage contract that she will permit no second wife for her husband. In Egypt polygyny is still legal, although the husband must now have the permission of his first wife. Even in Saudi Arabia, where all stipulations of Islamic law are valid and functional, there are relatively few polygynous unions.

An interesting element in the question of multiple marriage is the economic factor. While in many instances a husband simply cannot afford to take a second (or third) wife, the increase in the numbers of working women has in some cases changed the picture. A young husband may, in fact, find that two working wives contribute much-needed income to the maintenance of the family. Monogamy is increasingly the rule although there are exceptions such as in Kenya, where 30 percent of the married women live in polygyny. In August 1979 a marriage bill requiring the wife's consent for the husband to take another wife was shelved by the Kenyan parliament.[5]

Aside from the issue of polygyny, many Westerners find difficulty with the fact that Muslim men can marry Christians and Jews as well as women of the faith, by Quranic stipulation, while Muslim women can marry only Muslims (S. 5:6). This issue has not been addressed by legal change except in a few cases such as the 1956 Personal Status Code in Tunisia. (The proposed 1974 marriage and divorce law in Indonesia also removed the difference in religion as an impediment to marriage, a regulation which angered Muslim conservatives.) Marriage is not a religious ceremony as in the West but is a legal contract carried out between two parties; it is not strictly necessary for the wife even to be present. The contract must be signed by two witnesses, and the bride is entitled to receive and own a copy.

Also part of the marriage context are several issues currently being addressed by those who seek to raise the status of women in the Islamic world. Among these are marriage age, fertility patterns, and birth control. The traditional pattern has been for the families of the bride and groom to arrange the marriage, with the age for girls somewhere soon after puberty. Arranged marriages are still the norm in many places although in urban areas this is clearly changing. The young age of course has led to hardships, lack of educational opportunities, and a breaking with one's family ties in order to be aligned with the husband's family. Officially most Muslim countries have raised the minimum age for marriage to about eighteen for boys and between fifteen and seventeen for girls. Unfortunately these measures have not guaranteed an improvement in the situation; for example, the average age for females to marry has decreased in Algeria since World War II (16 percent of girls are married between eight and sixteen) and has gone down in Tunisia since 1965. Such statistics, however, are balanced by clear increases in the marriage age in places such as Lebanon, Syria, and Jordan.

The high fertility rate of Muslim women has obvious ramifications for their health and education. Statistics suggest an average of seven births per married Muslim woman. In Kenya the average woman has 8.1 children, a number that is increasing as health care improves. Family planning is taking place in a number of countries, despite opposition from arch-conservatives, and efforts are being made to show that fertility control is not prohibited in Islam. Only abortion and sterilization are opposed as un-Islamic (Tunisia and pre-revolutionary Iran did legalize abortion), although the incidence of induced abortion is high in some areas. Four Middle Eastern countries have adopted official population policies intended to reduce the rate of population growth: Egypt, Iran (before the revolution), Morocco and Tunisia. Other countries such as Afghanistan, Algeria, Iraq and the Sudan participate in family planning activities, while a number of others have made initial moves toward family planning.[6] The overall trend is toward lower rates of fertility, with a few exceptions such as Algeria and Kuwait. Here again one must be careful both to see that high birth rates are not necessarily linked to Islam but find their explanation in a number of social and economic factors, and to understand that like many issues in the Middle East and elsewhere, family planning has been affected by its association with the West. "In some ways the most persistent and the most ominous argument against family planning in developing countries is political," says Fazlur Rahman. "It is urged that the idea of limiting the size of population originated in and is being propagated by the West, which fears the rising population of developing countries."[7]

DIVORCE

Equally as chilling as the idea of polygamy for many Westerners has been the image of a Muslim man unilaterally and in a single moment repudiating his wife by the triple pronouncement "I divorce you." And without question this kind of repudiation has been a source of great pain for many Muslim women as well as a tool for their subjugation. It must be understood, however, that ideally divorce is a last resort and that the legal mechanisms for its execution are quite different in their entirety from that of single repudiation. Based on the injunctions of the Quran, Islamic law has designated several kinds of divorce.

1. Divorce at the man's initiative is by far the most frequent. One form of this is in accordance with the Sunna, therefore acceptable, and can be either a single pronouncement effective at the end of the mandatory three-month waiting period (to make sure the wife is not pregnant) or three statements in successive months. Another kind of male-initiated divorce is in the sinful but legal category—the saying of three pronouncements at once, amounting to immediate repudiation. It appears, unfortunately, that this form has been far overused, which gives rise to the Western stereotype of Muslim males repudiating their wives for little or no provocation.

2. Divorce may be initiated by the woman in several instances. It may be instigated by the wife to whom the husband has delegated divorce rights in the marriage contract (usually, but not always, involving return of the dowry to the husband). Or it may be a divorce sought by the woman on specific grounds such as non-maintenance, abuse, desertion, impotence, disease, or insanity. While divorce initiated by the wife has always been legally possible, the problems in actually carrying it out have been great. Wives often have not been educated to their rights, and male members of the family have sometimes made it difficult for women to act even as they are entitled. Now in most countries divorce initiated by either the wife or the husband must take place in court, and the triple repudiation at one moment has generally been banned.[8] In Tunisia and Algeria women can divorce with no grounds if they give financial compensation to their husbands; in Egypt the wife can divorce on grounds of cruelty if her husband treats her, according to the terms of the regulation, in a way intolerable to one of her social status.

It is difficult to ascertain exactly how high divorce rates are in the Muslim world; some reports indicate that they are considerably lower than in the United States and Europe while others show startlingly high rates in certain areas. What feeds into some high divorce statistics is really only the breaking of the engagement contract. Many Muslims will argue persuasively that developments in marriage and divorce regulations in Europe and the United States are actually more in conformity with the Islamic pattern, such as counseling before marriage and a speeding of the divorce process if it is necessary to be separated.[9]

In Islamic law the basic rule is that the child of a broken marriage belongs to the father and the father's family. This often has meant extreme hardships for the Muslim women who have been repudiated and have had to give up their children at a young age. Increased reforms are taking place so that in many countries such as Syria, Tunisia, Iraq and South Yemen mothers keep boys until puberty and girls until they reach marriage age.

INHERITANCE AND OWNERSHIP OF PROPERTY

According to the Quran (S. 4:11) women are entitled to inherit property although only at the rate of one half that of men. (This formula gets more complicated with special circumstances but stands as a basic rule.) The recognition of the right of women to inherit was clearly a positive reform over practices in early Arabia. While the picture has been mixed, and many women have been cheated out of their inheritance or simply have not known how to take advantage of it, it remains true that until recently the ability of a woman to own and manage property in the Islamic system represented a significant advantage for her over her sisters in Europe and the United States.

The apparent inequity of inheritance between men and women is explained and defended in the Islamic system as the proper balance due to the responsibility of the man to provide for the economic welfare of the woman and the family. Muslims argue, in effect, that what is the man's also belongs to the wife and the family while what is the woman's remains hers alone. This "one-half" rule, incidently, is paralleled by another Quranic injunction that says the testimony of two women is equal to that of one man. These stipulations have had some interesting ramifications. In 1974, for example, an Afghani life insurance company valued a woman's life as only half that of a man.[10] And from the *Wall Street Journal*, June 4, 1981, account of a similar circumstance in Saudi Arabia, "If an individual is killed intentionally or accidentally, the family is entitled to 'blood money' as an alternative to punishing the killer. The amount for a dead Muslim man is the price of 100 camels, now about $20,000. Women (and Christians) are valued at half that amount." (One relishes in this context the remark reputedly made in the summer of 1981 by the Foreign Minister of Iraq after having tangled with U.S. Ambassador to the United Nations Jeanne Kirkpatrick, that "one Kirkpatrick was equal to more than two men. Maybe three.")

Many Muslim women feel that the time has come to change the inheritance laws, that contemporary social and economic circumstances justify an equality that the ancient law does not recognize. Thus far only Turkey, Albania, and the Soviet Union have eliminated the Muslim law of inheritance. The fact of property ownership at all for women has created some notable situations in the oil rich Gulf states today. In Saudi Arabia, for example, while women can by Quranic law control their own money, they are not allowed to mingle with men in banks. Thus there are five new banks open in Riyadh and four in Jeddah exclusively for women since the Saudi Monetary Agency sanctioned the construction of separate facilities in 1980. Even more interesting is the report in the United Kingdom's *Sunday Times*, November 22, 1981, that women own just over 50 percent of the buildings and

property in Jeddah, the commercial center of Saudi Arabia, and somewhere over 25 percent in the capital of Riyadh. Clearly women in that
society which is renowned for its strict segregation of women have a
real power potential in economic terms.

VEILING AND SECLUSION

A third stumbling-block for Western understanding of Muslim family
regulations, along with polygyny and easy repudiation, is the practice
of veiling and seclusion that still persists in many quarters of the Islamic world. Here we are up against an enormously wide variety of
practices and attitudes, and it is a subject that requires some special
attention.

The Quran itself does not suggest either that women should be
veiled or that they should be kept apart from the world of men. On the
contrary, the Quran is insistent on the full participation of women in
society and in the religious practices prescribed for men. It does say (S.
24:30–31) that the wives of the Prophet were to speak to men from
behind a partition for propriety, and that women should not expose
themselves immodestly. Some scholars say that only the hands and
face should be left uncovered, others that the face should be covered.
And some say that the specific verses in the Quran relating to separation applied only to the wives of the Prophet while others assert that
they apply to all Muslim women.

The actual practice of veiling most likely came from areas captured in the initial spread of Islam such as Syria, Iraq, and Persia and
was adopted by upper-class urban women. Village and rural women
traditionally have not worn the veil, partly because it would be an
encumbrance in their work. It is certainly true that segregation of
women in the domestic sphere took place increasingly as the Islamic
centuries unfolded, with some very unfortunate consequences. Contemporary Muslims are quick to point out, and quite correctly, that the
proper understanding of woman in Islam is as a full partner with her
husband (though there are various qualifications to this which we will
consider later).

In this century, as more Muslim women have become acquainted
with the West and new ideas on liberation, there has been a steady

reversal in practices of veiling (a term used to refer to a wide variety of dress and covering), until recently when some very interesting developments have taken place. The event usually cited as the beginning of this kind of liberation is the stripping off of her veil by the Egyptian feminist Huda Sharawi in the 1920s. Since then increasing numbers of educated women have adopted Western dress and refused to wear garb which would identify them as backward or oppressed. What one finds now in the Islamic world is a somewhat changing picture. There are many different "stages" in the veiling and seclusion process, as well as greatly varying attitudes. While some women are *still* wearing traditional garb such as chadors and burkas, and while others are highly Westernized in their dress, still others are *again* putting on clothing that identifies them as Muslim women. This last phenomenon, which began only a few years ago, has manifested itself in a number of countries. It is part of the growing feeling on the part of Muslim men and women that they no longer wish to identify with the West, and that reaffirmation of their identity as Muslims requires the kind of visible sign that adoption of conservative clothing implies. For these women the issue is not that they *have* to dress conservatively but that they *choose* to. Let us look at some specific examples to see what women are wearing and why:

Egypt

Long a center for movements of female emancipation, Cairo has recently given evidence of increasing numbers of young women wearing long dresses or pantsuits with long jackets, their heads covered with scarves or wrappings not unlike the Catholic wimples.[11] This kind of dress is very different from the old-fashioned face veil that is still in evidence in a few very conservative countries. The trend began about 1973 as part of the reaction to the Arab-Israeli war and the hope that closer identification with Islam would help bring victory to God's people. Feminists were outraged, but the movement has clearly gained momentum; until a few months ago one could find Islamic clothing (called *shari* or legal dress) worn by numbers of middle- and upper middle-class university students. It remains to be seen whether or not the prohibition of legal dress by the regime of Hosni Mubarak will really eliminate this practice.

The West Bank of Palestine

Time Magazine, February 1, 1982, reported that at Bir Zeit University "student supporters of a Khomeini-type Islamic fundamentalism" are evidencing the new forms of dress—ankle-length dresses with scarves on their heads, the faces as usual uncovered.

Turkey

Before the revolution of Ataturk in the 1920s, rural and town women were not veiled, while city women were. Now there is a general reversal in which city women are unveiled and those in small towns (though not rural areas) often do wear veils. However, in a situation remarkable for the most "secular" of the Islamic countries, young women and men there too are beginning to return to visible signs of identification with Islam. The *New York Times,* December 29, 1981, reported that Turkey's military rulers, like Mubarak in Egypt, are now banning head scarves for female students and faculty as well as Islamic caps for men. In what is described as an attempt to curb Islamic fundamentalism, in the same spirit at Ataturk's ban on the veil half a century ago, the government is outlawing the "raincoat-like garb and head kerchiefs that have become the symbol of Islamic regeneration."

Saudi Arabia

Veiling is strictly enforced although Saudi women who travel abroad often choose not to wear it. Within the country the religious police are vigilant in their pursuit of women, even Western visitors, who are not properly clothed. In addition, some freedoms enjoyed not many years ago are being denied in new waves of religious conservatism. "A woman's life in Saudi Arabia has never been free and easy, but this summer the rules about what she can or cannot do have reached a new level of severity," says an August 12, 1979, article in the United Kingdom *Observer.* The real truth is that the situation in Saudi Arabia is in such extreme flux that it is difficult for the outside observer to be really up to date on what might be called advances and reversals for women. Beauty salons were closed and then reopened. By local custom women are forbidden to enter such public places as swimming pools and restaurants although private dining rooms can be reserved. Fitting rooms in dress shops are closed for the protection of women from occasional prying male eyes. Women were forbidden from accepting scholarships to study abroad for a brief time but may now do so again. Concerned over the rising divorce rate in the country, the ruling orthodoxy has decreed that women may now unveil their faces to prospective bridegrooms once the formal engagement has been set, as reported in the *New York Times,* April 20, 1981, a practice actually long observed by brides from educated families.

North Yemen

In this traditionally conservative country veiling and seclusion are the rule in San'a, the most traditional urban center, though not so much in the other cities. Modifications, however, suggest that this country is in transition between forced veiling and chosen forms of dress, either Islamic or Western, as is the case in Egypt and other places. Increasing numbers of girls have the outside veil completely lifted, keeping the inner veil through which the eyes can be seen. More are wearing the long sleeved ankle-length coat over trousers with a scarf on the head rather than a veil, dress considered acceptable by the religious leaders.[12]

United Arab Emirates

Here one finds an extremely conservative and traditional form of Islamic dress among the majority of women—black veils over the clothes or a burka covering from head to toe. Often women wear face masks and both head and face scarves. Except when travelling with their husbands they spend most of their time at home. Little wonder that they may find it perplexing to hear the President of the U.A.E. say, "What makes me most happy is to see women taking the position appropriate for them in society, with no obstacles to their progress. The highest positions are now open for them, as for men."[13]

Iran

The Islamic country that has most captured the attention of the West in the past several years is Iran. Western feminists and others have been horrified to see that many Iranian women seem to have accepted the dictates of the new regime under Imam Khomeini docilely, "going back" to the wearing of chadors seen by observers as symbols of retrogression. This issue is extremely complex, and there is no single answer to what has been happening nor a single point of view among Iranian women. Some, clearly, wish to maintain the position won many years ago when wearing of the chador was banned. Others have chosen to identify with the forces opposing the Shah and to affirm their Islamic identity by adopting again the covering cloak. Still others have used it as a handy means of hiding their real identity. "Taking to the streets in large and energetic crowds, demonstratively flaunting the *chador,* whose banishment had been one of the regime's most visible and often-cited progressive achievements, they presented an ambiguous picture to outside observers," says Cheryl Benard describing the scene at the time of the revolution. "The *chador* is not only a symbol for expressing opposition to the Shah," she says, "but also a type of camouflage for leftist and feminist women."[14]

As part of his return to fundamentalist Islam, Khomeini first insisted that women must wear the veil and chador. His often-quoted statement, as reported in the *New York Times* on March 11, 1979, that women should not go to work "naked" led both to harrassment of unveiled women and to large demonstrations by women who felt they had been betrayed after supporting the revolution. Khomeini modified his position and agreed that while the *chador* is not obligatory, modest dress is, including loose clothing and non-transparent stockings and scarves.

Veiling, whether enforced or voluntarily chosen, has not left women powerless. It has been observed that in women's society in North Yemen, the veil is not merely an obstacle for women but also a tool for manipulation, used effectively to control their own circumstances and to control their men.[15] Even seclusion has been used by women for their own ends. Women interviewed by anthropologist Jerome Barkow in a Hausa village said that they preferred to be kept secluded—it raised their prestige and lowered their work loads. It is sometimes hard to decide, he reflects, if men impose seclusion on women, or women impose it on men.[16]

The circumstances described above are not intended to suggest that all Islamic women, or even most, are veiled by force of tradition or by their own personal choice. Many are horrified at the conscious adoption by their sisters of dress that they have long since disgarded. What we would call Western dress has been the mode in their families for generations, and that apparently will not change for them. The point here has been to show that our preconceptions of the enforced nature of conservative modes of dress may be entirely too limited. To an increasing extent, women in Islamic countries over the world are finding themselves in positions where they can choose what to wear, and in that choice reflect their own needs, desires, and circumstances. As yet, as we have seen, this is not true for all Muslim women.

Two other areas of Muslim women's present experience need to be addressed, although advancement for women in these areas generally is not directly related to the fact that the countries under consideration happen to be Islamic. These are education and employment opportunities.

EDUCATION

Despite the stated goals of most Islamic countries to try to raise the educational level of both men and women, the gap between female and male literacy rates in many places is increasing, and the overall level of illiteracy is extremely high. (Afghanistan, for example, has 98 percent illiteracy among women, Iran between 70 and 95 percent, Saudi Arabia 95 percent.) But there are many encouraging indicators. In Afghanistan, since the revolution in 1978 there has been a major literacy campaign; education is no longer limited to the middle and upper classes. In Iraq the elimination of illiteracy is one of the major goals of the Arab Baath Socialist Party. Education is compulsory—men must allow their wives and daughters to go to school—and at present there are almost half as many women students in the university system as men. The president of the U.A.E. has given top priority to the education of women. In Tunisia almost one third of the university students are women. To counteract the strong opposition of the Muslim Brotherhood to girls' education the Prime Minister of North Yemen devoted a whole speech to the importance of women's education; the high dropout rate in that country is gradually being lowered. One fourth of the students in Riyadh University are women; they are taught either by female professors or by males over closed-circuit television. Since 1960 the program for education of girls in Saudi Arabia has been a government priority. Still, education for rural women is difficult, and the low marriage age means that girls often drop out after only a few years of schooling.

While raising the educational level for women is a stated goal of many governments of Islamic countries, it is clear that one of the obstacles to real equality of education with men has been the conservative Muslim view of female potential. One of the reasons given to explain the Quranic allotment of two female witnesses to equal that of one male is that women are swayed by emotion and thus have unstable judgment.[17] There are many degrees of Muslim male opinion regarding both the nature and the capacities of women, of course. And it is certainly true that men have been leaders in insisting that women be given equal educational opportunities. Nonetheless, vestiges of the notion that men are more rational and women more emotional, or are simply not the intellectual equals of men, have added to the difficulties for women in the educational area. With this has been the stress on women not appearing in public places or being in situations where they interact with men. "A woman's mission is to be a good wife and a compassionate mother . . . an ignorant rural woman is better for the nation than one thousand female lawyers or attorney generals," said the Egyptian Muhammad al-Ghazzali in 1963.[18] It is true, however, that women at the university level are often guided (or even restricted) to subjects considered more "appropriate" for them, which generally means the humanities, liberal arts, and medicine.

EMPLOYMENT OPPORTUNITIES

Related to the question of whether or not women should leave the home, be in the company of men, and in general be competitive in the world of males is the issue of employment. Statistics about numbers of women in the work force are problematic, in large part because they do not accurately reflect the role of women in rural areas, working on the land, and doing other activities that may not necessarily bring them independent salaries.

Percentages of women in the urban work force in the Middle East are among the lowest in the world, although the situation is changing.

Attitudes such as fear of promiscuity if women work alongside men are being challenged by hard economic realities. Women are simply needed for the economic support they can give by taking jobs outside the home. In Egypt increasing numbers of young educated husbands are agreeing that their wives should work in order to help support the family—there women work in factories and heavy industries as well as in the more traditionally "female" jobs such as teaching and medicine. The need for income brought in by daughters will not only mean more young women working but undoubtedly will have ramifications for raising the marriage age.

For many Muslim women work is easier than for Western women because of the support of extended families to take care of children and the availability of inexpensive domestic help. At least for women in upper-income families this means that working outside the home does not necessarily create the guilt sometimes carried by Western women who "leave" their homes and children, nor does it always mean taking on responsibilities in addition to doing all of the work at home. For others, probably the vast majority, the general disinclination of the husband to assume home responsibilities means that the task of the woman who works is doubled. In many places work outside the home is little more than an extension of their normal female routine with no opportunity to learn new skills. Women become maids or textile or food industry workers, or they assume other jobs that are really extensions of their work at home. Moroccan sociologist Fatima Mernissi speculates that with tougher economic circumstances men may find repudiation an easy way to get out of family responsibilities, an unfortunate situation that leaves women with little training responsible for the welfare of their families. Here the patriarchal attitudes still prevail: "A husband whose wife works outside is a husband who shares the wife's allegiance with another male, and this is precisely the negation of patriarchal pride," says Mernissi.[19]

Work statistics in many countries continue to show inequities for women. In Tunisia the average income for women is 30 percent lower than for men. In many rural areas of Turkey female labor does not receive recognition because men feel that non-working wives are more prestigious and thus claim that their wives do not work. Even in Egypt, where women in the work force have been recognized for many years, they constitute only 2 to 3 percent of the industrial labor force and 4 percent of the clerical and administrative group.

In other places opportunities for women to work are increasingly good. The Syrian government guarantees the jobs of all persons who are employed, providing an important element of psychological security for women as well as social security benefits.[20] In Kuwait there have been enormous changes since 1950—work participation for women is among the highest in the Middle East, with many women employed in government service as civil servants, teachers, and the like. In Indonesia, generally more liberal than Islamic countries of the Middle East, women work not isolated or separated from men; a 1971 census showed half as many women as males in the work force. And in Iraq, there have been increasing opportunities for women to work in a variety of jobs. Those who join the military are guaranteed access to equal rank with men. Favorable laws have been passed giving maternity leaves from work and providing for child care. The role of women in the work force is not considered a feminist question but a necessity for the advancement of the country, and thus a question of nationalism. Vocational training programs provide opportunities for women in all fields; women work in gas stations, are employed as technicians and engineers, sit on courts of justice. It is said that the percentage of women in the Iraqi labor force is expected to reach 28 percent by 1985.

Saudi Arabia presents a very interesting situation in relation to working women. The strict rules of dress and segregation naturally make it difficult for women to be employed outside the home, along with conservative reactions against this possibility. On the other hand, one of Saudi Arabia's more serious problems is a shortage of both skilled and unskilled labor. Political and religious leaders are thus being forced to choose between the somewhat distasteful alternatives of importing more foreign workers or adopting a more liberal policy for women in the work force. The problem, of course, is how to enact this without making basic changes in current attitudes. Aside from the issue of dress, women are not allowed to appear in public places alone except in unusual circumstances, to have their pictures taken, to ride alone or with other women in taxis, or to drive. Sheikh Abdel-Aziz Bin Baz, general chairman of the administration of IFTAA, Quranic interpretation, said in a 1981 interview reported in *Women's International Network News,* Winter 1981, that allowing women to drive cars would be "fraught with depravity, including being bare-faced, being alone with strangers, and running the risk of falling into incalculable sins." Nonetheless, it is clear that work opportunities for women in Saudi Arabia are opening up, and in the near future the economic situation of that country most probably will force some notable changes for women in the employment field, with clear ramifications for their personal and social circumstances.

Thus far we have considered the broad picture of "how things are" for women in a number of Islamic countries, looking at legal, social, and economic realities. Let us return to an earlier theme, that of power and authority, to get another perspective on the lives of women in the Islamic world.

That men are given authority over women according to Islam is quite clear in verse 4:34 of the Quran, which says, "Men are in charge [or are the protectors] of women, because God has given preference to the one over the other, and because (men) provide support for (women) from their means. Therefore righteous women are obedient. This is clearly understood by most Muslim men and women to be because of the responsibility men have to care for their wives and the other women in their families. As Abdul Rauf comments in *The Islamic View of Women and the Family* (1977), "the wife should be the one who inspires the soft, soothing gentleness: and the husband should be the protective shield, the main source of bread and butter, and the independent, dependable authority."[21]

Those who presume that women have no access to power because designated authority lies with males have failed to grasp the subtlties of Islamic society. In addition to the acquisition of the kinds of power evident from the above discussion of increased educational and economic opportunities, it is the case that women have always been able to exert a degree of control over their own circumstances, and over the men in their lives, which to a certain extent belies the more obvious historical fact of their segregation and subjugation. Fatima Mernissi in *Beyond the Veil* argues that despite their protestations, Muslim men, rather than really believing the woman to be inferior, have set up mechanisms of repression because they fear her power over them.[22]

Muslim women have been able to enjoy a particular kind of power in that they alone are childbearers in a society in which children, especially sons, are so highly valued. They maintain a strong influence over their sons throughout their lives. An observer of Moroccan society comments that a wife has a degree of power through sexuality, while the mother-in-law gets power by control of the communications network of the household and her special relationship to her son. Old women get power through manipulation of outside agencies such as witchcraft which, among other things, may make a man impotent.[23]

Rural women are often keepers of the family wealth, which they are able to invest. Their sons save money with them, consult them about getting married, and they are the power behind selection of the bride and settlement of the general marriage affairs. In Hausa society in Wurinsalla, Nigeria, one of the greatest fears a man has is the humiliation of having his wife leave him, rendering him ridiculous and impotent.[24] And in her study of North Yemeni women, Carla Maklouf observes that because of the circumstances of segregation and veiling, men are as much excluded as women are secluded. They are thus forced to rely on women to learn what is going on outside their immediate kin-groups, giving women surprising information-imparting and decision-making power.[25] Within the home women have recourse to such negative sources of power as withholding favors, seeking revenge over husbands by embarrassing them in front of guests, gossiping, sexual manipulation, and in general undermining male honor.

Clearly one of the ways in which women exert a degree of power over their own circumstances, and sometimes even over men, is in the area of their own particular religious practices. According to the Quran women are accorded full rights with men in terms of religious responsibilities and opportunities and are guaranteed equality of access to the Gardens of Paradise for lives lived in accordance with God's laws. It is also true, however, that for a variety of reasons women often have been denied access to the more public areas of worship and religious responsibility, which have come to be defined as male areas. They have thus developed systems of religious involvement that overlap with those of men, yet give them access to a space that can more clearly be defined as their own.

Both in the major religious responsibilities of Islam, often called the five pillars or duties, and in more informal practices, women have developed their own forms of response. Rather than praying in the mosques as they did in the time of the Prophet, for the most part women for centuries have conducted their prayers in their own homes. (When they do join in the Friday prayers at the mosque they normally are put in side corridors or in separate sections at the rear, so as not to go through the positions of prayer in front of males.) They participate with pleasure in the pilgrimage, as it affords them an opportunity to travel and are especially active in visiting tombs and shrines of saints. Women are diligent in observance of the fast (except when menstruating, pregnant, or nursing), perhaps in part because of the social dimension of preparing the communal meals through which the breaking of the fast is observed. While it is the responsibility of the husband to determine the exact amount of alms-tax given, the wife has often been the agent through whom monies or goods have been distributed to the poor.

Beyond this, women have played roles peculiar to them in the overall religious structure. They are much more likely than men to be involved in practices of "magic," curing, fortunetelling, and other things which, while ostensibly extra-Islamic, given them a notable degree of control over men. Women are the primary participants in *zar* ceremonies in Egypt and the Sudan, rituals designed to "cure" them of spirit possession. Lucie Wood Saunders has remarked on the power such participation gives them: a man fears to disobey the command of the spirit that his wife participate in the *zar,* and she can can exercise some monetary control by pressuring him to spend money for her to join in the ceremonies.[26] In most Muslim societies spirit possession cults are almost exclusively the province of women.

In some circumstances women are permitted to play particular leadership roles in the religious structure, as in Iraq where a woman can be a religious leader called a *molla,* a position that is usually hereditary. *Mollas* are highly regarded and receive substantial payment for such activities as holding sessions in which they read about the life of the martyred Hussayn. As with the *zar* ceremonies, these sessions provide one of the few traditionally sanctioned opportunities for women to meet together outside the home.[27] In Nubia women play an important role in the maintenance of shrines. The female shrine keeper is often the recipient of special instructions coming directly from the deceased (but believed to be still alive in the grave) saint.

Daisy Dwyer has highlighted the importance of roles payed by women in the practices of saint veneration in Morocco. Women hold positions legitimated through election, birth, or ritual transmission of power, she notes. During the childbearing years, while men are busy making money and are not particularly concerned with religion, women are religiously aware and are important decision makers in determining forms of communal religious affiliation for their sons.[28]

The picture of women in Muslim societies, then, emerges as extraordinarily complex. Rights and responsibilities are Quranically guaranteed, but in fact often have been denied. Traditional attitudes remain strongly entrenched, and yet in all facets of their lives women have made and continue to make strides toward full participation in society. Societal pressures not truly in keeping with Islam, with the message of the Quran, have served to seclude them from the world of males and from traditional formal religious practices, but women often have developed their own means of exerting power and control over their circumstances and over the males to whose authority they are entrusted. Rather than rejecting Islam as patriarchal and therefore repressive, increasing numbers of women are, by their own choice, affirming their Islamic identity and their allegiance to what they clearly see as God's religion, the only viable way of life. How are we to understand these responses?

It is crucial to see that for the Muslim the message of the Quran is eternal, divine, and absolutely authoritative. If the Quran says that men have authority over women, it is important to understand that the context is one of care and responsibility, but even more important to respect the statement as God's final word. Therefore to talk about equality in Western terms is to be out of tune with the Muslim understanding. The issue is not equality per se, but complementarity. A commonly stated interpretation is that God has created men and women with different constitutions and differing roles, and the task of each husband and wife is to work toward the kind of true cooperation that God intends. For both, this is a balance of rights and duties.

One of the themes most often stressed by contemporary Muslim writing about family life and male-female relations is that of the natural order of things. The regulations for married life in Islam are clear and are in harmony with human nature. According to this interpretation, because of the particular psychological and psyiological natures of men and women, rights and claims are equal except for the responsibility of leadership. That is seen by many Muslims to be consistent with the nature of man, who is viewed as the stronger and more rational. Referring to the Quran verse which affirms that men are a step above women (S. 2:228), Muslim apologist Fatima Heeren has this to say: "Those who want to find fault with Islamic regulations consider this detrimental to the dignity of women. But I am of the opinion that this one sentence includes all that is necessary to my happiness as a woman. . . . Does it not lie in the very nature of a woman that she wants a powerful, just, wise and considerate husband who is capable of making these decisions?"[29]

To be sure, not all Muslim women (or men) hold to this view, although it reflects a significant opinion among those writing in defense of Islam today. Lawyer Badria al-Awadhi of Kuwait is angry that she as a lawyer and Dean of the Faculty of Sharia should be expected to cover her face and accept that she is not on equal terms with men. "Half rights are very dangerous," she says, "because one never gets the other half."[30] Former Egyptian Director of Public Health Nawal al-Saadawi (removed from office because she was too outspoken in her views about women) is deeply angry about the injustices perpetrated on Muslim women daily. "If one day woman is forced to choose between her work outside the home and her work inside the house," says al-Saadawi, "she is better off, as a human being, to choose her work outside the house as a priority. Any of the sacrifices made by women to continue their work outside the home are, in my opinion, much less than the one made by staying at home and resigning herself to the same fate as that of her mother and grandmother."[31]

The range of responses of Muslim women to their own circumstances varies widely, as do the ways in which they choose to identify with Islam. What they seem to share, and with them Muslim men who seek to reaffirm the eternal validity of Islam, is a deep distrust of the West and of Western solutions. Westernization, for years a goal of many in the Islamic world, is increasingly identified with various forms of imperialism. Muslim women find the implications of Western definitions of women's liberation to be frightening; in general they do not want to forsake their femininity, to cut themselves off from the world of males, or to achieve personal freedoms at the price of sacrificing their identity with the family unit and with the larger structure of the Islamic community.

Muslim women will continue to experience many changes in the coming years with increases in educational opportunities, employment in the work force, and participation in the political process. With these changes will come increasing pressure to take a stand with regard to tradition, to society and the world of men, and to their own understanding of themselves as Muslim.

It is important for Westerners to understand that much of the contemporary Muslim reaffirmation of Islam is due to a disillusionment with the West, to the recognition that in the Muslim view, "liberation" as it is defined in Western terms has led to a breakdown of the family and a dangerous relaxation of ethical and moral strictures. In a word, many Muslims today feel that things simply "don't work" in Europe and the United States and that the Islamic system offers a relationship and a structure that can, and does, succeed.

It is also essential for those of us outside of the community of Islam to recognize that for the Muslim, critique of the words of the Quran—in regard to the relation of man and woman as in any other matter—amounts to rebellion not against a human system but against one that is considered to be divine. The traditions of men can be changed, but God's ordered plan for humanity cannot. The task of the Muslim woman will be to understand the difference, and to take her stand for self-identity within the divinely ordained structure of Islam.

NOTES

1. Charles Doughty, *Travels in Arabia Deserta* (London, 1936), I, p. 280; cited in Caroll Pastner, "Englishmen in Arabia: Encounters with Middle Eastern Women," *Signs* 4, no. 2 (1978):315.

2. James Allman, ed., *Women's Status and Fertility in the Muslim World* (New York: Praeger, 1978), p. xxxiii.

3. Cynthia Nelson, "Public and Private Politics: Women in the Middle Eastern World," *American Ethnologist* 1, no. 3 (1974):561.

4. Aisha Lemu, "Women in Islam," in F. Heeren and Aisha Lemu, *Women in Islam* (London: Islamic Council of Europe, 1978), p. 28.

5. *Women's International Network News* 4, no. 4 (Summer 1979). Only a few years ago wife beating as every husband's right was discussed in the Kenyan Parliament. *WIN News* 7, no. 2 (Spring 1981).

6. Allman, *Women's Status and Fertility,* pp. xxxix ff.

7. Fazlur Rahman, "A Survey of Modernization of Muslim Family Law," *International Journal of Middle Eastern Studies* 11 (1980):465.

8. There are, of course, exceptions. Fatima Mernissi reports that in Morocco, which has the highest divorce rates in the world, repudiation thrives. "The Patriarch in the Moroccan Family," in Allman, *Women's Status and Fertility,* pp. 312–332.

9. Lemu, *Women in Islam,* pp. 22.

10. Erika Knabe, "Women in the Social Stratification of Afghanistan," in C.A.O. van Nieuwenhuijze, ed., *Commoners, Climbers and Notables* (Leiden: Brill, 1977), p. 339.

11. John Alden Williams, "Veiling in Egypt as a Political and Social Phenomenon," in John L. Esposito, ed., *Islam and Development: Religion and Sociopolitical Change* (Syracuse, N.Y.: Syracuse University Press, 1980), pp. 71–85.

12. Carla Makhlouf and G. J. Obermeyer, "Women and Social Change in Urban North Yemen," in Allman, *Women's Status and Fertility,* pp. 333–42.

13. From "The Women's Movement in the United Arab Emirates," available from the U. A. E. Ministry of Information and Culture, cited in *WIN News* 6, no. 3 (Summer 1980).

14. Cheryl Benard, "Islam and Women: Some Reflections on the Experience of Iran," *Journal of South Asian and Middle Eastern Studies* 4, no. 2 (Winter 1980):10, 11.

15. Makhlouf and Obermeyer, "Women and Social Change" in Allman, *Women's Status and Fertility,* p. 342.

16. Jerome H. Barkow, "Hausa Women and Islam," *Canadian Journal of African Studies* 4, no. 2 (1972):323.

17. See, e.g., Gamal A. Badawi, "Women in Islam," in Kurshid Ahmad and Salem Azzam, eds., *Islam: Its Meaning and Message* (Leicester: The Islamic Foundation, 1955), p. 145.

18. *Min Huna Na'lam,* p. 204, quoted in Yvonne Haddad, "Traditional Affirmations Concerning the Role of Women as Found in Contemporary Arab Islamic Literature," in J. I. Smith, ed., *Women in Contemporary Muslim Societies* (Cranbury, N.J.: Associated University Presses, 1980), p. 81. Cf. the comment of Ayatollah Shariat Madari in Iran that women should not be judges because they do not have the requisite

intellectual faculties and because they are lacking in logic. *New York Times,* April 22, 1979.

19. Mernissi, "The Patriarch in the Moroccan Family," in Allman, *Women's Status and Fertility,* p. 231.

20. Haddad, "Traditional Affirmations Concerning the Role of Women," p. 68.

21. Abdul Rauf, *The Islamic View of Woman and the Family* (1977), p. 67. Cf. the reference of Fatima Heeren to Syed Abul A'la Mawdudi's statement that the man must "uphold the tenets of faith and his authority symbolizes that of God in the world." "Family Life in Islam," in Heeren and Lemu, *Women in Islam* (1978), pp. 36–37. Kurshid Ahmad, in a traditional valuation of the home and the importance of the woman's role in it, admits in *Family Life in Islam* (Leicester: The Islamic Foundation, 1974), p. 28, that the woman runs the world of the home with responsibility and authority.

22. Fatima Mernissi, *Beyond the Veil* (New York: John Wiley and Sons, 1975), pp. xv–xvi.

23. Amal Rassam, "Women and Domestic Power in Morrocco," *International Journal of Middle East Studies* 12 (1980): 178.

24. Barkow, "Hausa Women and Islam" (1972): 324. "Women are hardly powerless in Wurinsalla," comments Barkow.

25. *Changing Veils: Women and Modernization in North Yemen* (London: Croom Helm, 1979), pp. 34, 42. Cf. Soraya Altorki commenting on Saudi Arabian society: "The situation is paradoxical: the very segregation of the sexes that prevents women from gaining access to information and authority in the wider society creates the condition for their far-reaching control over a man's destiny to the extent that it is linked to his marriage," from "Family Organization and Women's Power in Urban Saudi Arabian Society," *Journal of Anthropological Research* 33 (1977):282.

26. "Variants in Zar Experience in an Egyptian Village," in Vincent Crapanzano and Vivien Garrison, eds., *Case Studies in Spirit Possession* (New York: Wiley, 1977), pp. 185 ff.

27. Robert A. and Elizabeth W. Fernea, "Variations in Religious Observance among Islamic Women," in Nikki Keddie, ed., *Scholars, Saints, and Sufis* (Berkeley: University of California Press, 1972), pp. 385–401.

28. "Ideologies of Sexual Inequality and Strategies for Change in Male-Female Relations," *American Ethnologist* 5(1978):598.

29. "Family Life in Islam," p. 43.

30. Interview in *The Middle East* 74 (December 1980):47.

31. Mona Mikhail, *Images of Arab Women* (Washington, D.C.: Three Continents Press, 1979), quoting Nawal al-Saadawi from the preface of *Al-Jins wa al-Mara.*

6

Aspects of Mystical Thought in Islam

Annemarie Schimmel

WESTERN SCHOLARS have defined Sufism, the mystical dimension of Islam, in a wide variety of ways. Some have seen it as an expression of the common mystical trend that can be discerned as a kind of poetical undercurrent in all religions. Others have insisted that its true character was fully developed only in the school of Ibn Arabi (d. 1240) which affirmed the unity of being in which the phenomenal world is but an expression of God. Modern Muslim fundamentalists reject these views, claiming that Sufism is unrelated to the general phenomenon of mysticism as defined by historians of religion. They see it rather as the unique contribution of Islam to spiritual life.

Sufism pervades Islamic life. It has taken a number of forms and has been expressed in a variety of beliefs, practices and expressions. Even scholars who have ventured on longer discourses have but touched on certain of its facets. One can compare Sufism to the elephant, in the famous story recounted by Sana'i (d. ca. 1131) and Rumi (d. 1273), which was touched by several blind men each providing a different definition of what the animal was like depending on their experience, the part they came in contact with. One can also, perhaps more logically, see Sufism as a large tree, a kind of Banyan tree, which grew from the root of Islam and was watered with the remembrance of God and the example and teachings of the Prophet. In the course of centuries it assimilated flavors and colors from the various cultures with which the Muslims came in contact, until some very strange birds built nests in its branches.

Sufism has grown organically from the deepest stratum of Islam. The early ascetics in Iraq and Khorasan lived in the constant meditation of the Divine word as revealed in the Quran for which they found thousands and thousands of interpretations. The "Koranization of the memory," as Pere Nwyia[1] has called the process of constant life with the Quran, is something that permeates the whole history of Sufism. It explains why Persian and Persianate mystical poetry constantly comes back to the figures mentioned in the Quran and takes them as examples, symbols, and paradigms. It also sheds light on why the allusions to Quranic sayings invariably form the texture of Sufi writings not only in Arabic but in all Islamic languages, even in the most remote corners of the Muslim world, such as Sindhi mystical folk poetry and Swahili religious texts.[2]

THE FORMATIVE PERIOD

In the early days, many of the Sufis collected hadith (traditions of the Prophet) and strove to imitate the Prophet's actions as faithfully and closely as possible. Bayezid Bistami (d. 874), known for his ecstatic flights into the Divine Presence, would not eat melons because there was no reliable tradition as to how the Prophet used to cut them. In later times, members of the mystical orders often served as transmitters of Prophetic traditions. They compiled handbooks of Sufi ethics which were filled with traditions serving as precedent and example after which the novices were supposed to model their lives.

In the later part of the eighth century, the woman mystic Rabia al-Adawiyya (d. 801) introduced the element of pure love into Sufi expression. Divine love became the means by which the seeker was empowered with the capacity to bear the affliction that God visits on the ascetic to test his intent and purify his soul. Divine love is the agent that transforms asceticism into true mysticism. Through its mediation, the Sufi attains insight and knowledge of divine mysteries. The fact that a woman played an important role at the very beginning of Sufi history seems typical. Throughout the ages we find names of pious women who pursued the mystical path, either independently or as consorts or mothers of Sufis. Many of their names are noted in the hagiographical works, and the memory of many saintly women is kept alive in small sanctuaries found in North Africa, Anatolia, and particularly in Muslim

India. (These sanctuaries are not accessible to men.) This role of women is not astonishing since in the Islamic Middle Ages women participated in various aspects of social life. We know of not only poetesses and calligraphers but also a considerable number of transmitters of the traditions of the Prophet and even ruling princesses such as Shajarat al-Durr in Egypt (d. 1249) or Raziya Sultana of Delhi (reg. 1236–1240). In the mystical life, women have played an important role to this day; even some successful leaders in the modern traditions have been women.[3]

The ninth century was the truly formative period of Sufism. Great leaders of the movement appeared in different corners of the Muslim world. In northern Iran the lonely Bayezid Bistami expressed his longing for God in strange and bewildering paradoxes, trying to approach the Divine essence by the negative way, that is, by complete depersonalization, stressing the concept of annihilation, and aiming at nothing but complete extinction of "the world."

Shortly before him, Dhu'n-Nun in Egypt (d. 859), became famous not only as a mystic but—according to legend—also as an alchemist. He focused on the Quranic statements about the constant praise of God in creation. Was not everything created in order to worship the Lord? He listened to the songs of praise proclaimed by trees, brooks, birds, and stones. He joined them to his own prayers which he expressed in sonorus, long sentences whose rhetorical beauty carries the listener away. These prayers prefigured some of the most eloquent hymns by later poets in Iran and other parts of the Islamic world: "O God, I never hearken to the voices of the beasts or the rustle of the trees, the splashing of the waters or the song of the birds, the whistling of the wind or the rumble of the thunder, but I sense in them a testimony to Thy Unity, and a proof of Thy comparability, that Thou art the All-Prevailing, the All-Knowing, the All-True."[4] At the same time, Sufis in Baghdad, most noted among them al-Muhasibi (d. 857), developed the psychological dimension of mysticism. Careful introspection and the constant education of the "lower soul" was refined and elaborated.

Junaid of Baghdad (d. 910) was the leading master of what we call the "sober" trend in Sufism. Junaid's cryptic utterances prove that he was well aware of the danger that the secrets of Sufism might be divulged to the uninitiated and thus cause difficulties for the simple believers who would barely understand the meaning of a statement such as "man has to become as he was when he was not" so that God is as alone as He always was. This is the essential and existential Sufi interpretation of the words of the Islamic Profession of Faith: "There is no deity save God." True personality belongs only to God; only He has the right to say "I." Thus, even the profession of God's unity is subtle "associationism," because it established the speaking person as something "other than God."[5]

Man has to strive to attain this knowledge by unceasing spiritual purification. True "unification" is the goal to which the methods of mystical education lead. These methods, developed in the ninth and tenth centuries, have remained practically unchanged through all later developments. The Sufis were well aware that man's *nafs*, the lower soul principle (sometimes perceived as "the flesh" in the biblical sense) is, as the Quran says, "instigating to evil" (S. 12:53). Therefore they held that their whole life should be a struggle against the lower soul by using the method of "little eating, little sleeping, and little talking," to which, later, "avoidance of people" might be added at times. By strictly following the injunctions of the Divine Law, the Sufi could proceed on the path, where he would experience various stages and stations, each of which had special aspects to it. Beginning with "repentance," he might finally reach the state of "love," and/or spiritual knowledge, gnosis. Each station and stage again had specific aspects to it according to which the Sufi had to behave. During the "Greater Holy War," as the struggle against the lower soul was called, man might reach the stage of "the blaming soul" (S. 75:2), which can be equated roughly with the concept of conscience. Finally, he attains the last stage, that of the "soul at peace" (S. 89:27), from where, as the Quran attests, he will be called back to his Lord.

Since the Quran has stated: "Verily by the remembrance of God the hearts acquire peace" (S. 13:28), the remembrance of God,[6] the *dhikr,* forms an important part of the spiritual education of the Sufi. Its focus can be one of the Divine Names, a religious formula, or the profession of faith which can be repeated up to thousands of times a day because *dhikr* varies according to the stage which the seeker has reached. It is entrusted to him by the spiritual guide who watches carefully over his progress. Since the effects of a wrong formula could affect the novice psychologically and even physiologically, the wayfarer is not permitted to use such a formula without proper initiation. He might choose a formula which could be too powerful for his present state.

The mystical path, as developed and experienced by the early Sufis, is a series of deaths. The motto was "die before ye die!" One has first to die to one's lowly qualities and replace them by positive qualities. The idea of sacrificing part of one's lower self every day, of dying to one's self and being revived on a higher spiritual level, permeated Sufism in all its shades. The secret of being reborn has been expressed by the Sufis in numerous symbols and metaphors, such as, among many others, the moth casting itself into the flame of the candle, or the rain drop that sinks into the depths of the ocean. It accounts also for the innumerable cruel images in later Sufi poetry in which the poet sings of his longing to die for the sake of the Divine Beloved or to be martyred in the battlefield of love.

THE MARTYR MYSTIC AL-HALLAJ

Some of the great Sufis have attained the rank of martyrdom, the most famous among them being al-Hallaj, popularly known by his father's name, Mansur, "The Victorious one." His affirmation: "I am the Absolute Truth *(haqq),*" is generally translated as "I am God" (for "Truth" is the central quality of God and becomes, particularly in the later tradition, the normal term for God as understood by the Sufis, i.e. "the Only Reality"). "I am the Absolute Truth" has been taken up, interpreted (and at times also criticized) by most Sufis, and has been discussed in Orientalist circles as well during the last 150 years. His "I am the Absolute Truth" refers to the experience that the uncreated Divine Spirit can, in rare moments, enfold the created human spirit and speak through him. Therefore many later Sufis have interpreted Hallaj's experience as being similar to that of God speaking through the Burning Bush on Mount Sinai. Rumi has compared it to that of red hot iron that claims with its whole being, with mute eloquence: "I am the fire," because it has assumed all the qualities of fire and yet is different in essence.[7]

For the modern scholar, Hallaj's life and his tender poetical prayers, as well as his daring interpretation of the fate of Iblis (Satan), as "the true monotheist and lover," are almost as fascinating as his "I am the Absolute Truth" which became a kind of tug-of-war for later extremist, pantheistic Sufis particularly in the Indian and Turkish tradition. They found in this the secret of the essential unity of man and God expressed very clearly.[8] Hallaj's religiosity was very personal, and he tried to infuse new life into Islam at a time when personal, warm religious feeling seemed to give place to the disputations of learned theologians and when the Divinely revealed law had become enshrined in books dealing with minutest details of legal processes. An ascetic who undertook the most difficult tasks in fasting and prayer, Hallaj wandered through the eastern lands of the caliphate (Gujarat, Sind, Kashmir, and Central Asia) to call people to God. His relations with various groups of strange people aroused the suspicion of the government, a suspicion that was strengthened by his "unorthodox" practical piety. If implemented in the common life it seemed to threaten the social fabric of Islam and the prevailing status of the government. Accusations of this kind have been made many times against Sufis whose behavior was suspected of leading to antinomianism, especially in the later Middle Ages. Hallaj's outspoken attempt to interiorize the commands of the Divine law and his sometimes eccentric behavior upset even the more "sober" Sufis of Baghdad. Hallaj spent the last nine years of his life in prison and was finally executed on March 26, 922. Attar sums up the secret of his life in the short report: "They asked him: 'What is love?' And he said: 'You will see it today and tomorrow and day after tomorrow.' And that day they cut off his hands and feet; the next day they hanged him on the gallows; and the third day they gave his ashes to the wind."⁹

The story of Hallaj's life and in a special way his death as a "martyr of Divine Love" has inspired countless numbers of Sufis all over the world, particularly in the Persianate areas. His teachings were kept alive in Shiraz by Ibn-i Khafif (d. 982) and his disciples. The stern ascetic, Ibn-i Khafif, had been one of his last visitors in prison and greatly admired him. Through him Hallaj's ideas slowly percolated into Persian mystical poetry and appeared in a sudden outburst, as it seems, in the works of Ruzbihan Baqli (d. 1209) in Shiraz. Baqli's interpretation of the "paradoxes" of the Sufis and in particular of Hallaj's works is of immense importance for our understanding of the latter's teachings.¹⁰ At almost the same time, in the second half of the twelfth century, Fariduddin Attar in Nishapur (d. ca. 1220) was spiritually initiated by Hallaj into the Sufi path. He devoted to the martyr mystic the most touching chapter in his hagiographical work, the *Tadhkirat al-auliya*. In later Sufi poetry, especially in the popular songs of the mystics in India and Turkey, Hallaj appears as the true lover who was killed for his love by the soulless theologians who knew only the letter of the law and not the spirit. As Bedil sings in India around 1700:

It is not easy to pluck the rose in the garden of Certainty;
There is still the color of Mansur's blood in that garden!¹¹

Or as Ghalib in nineteenth century Delhi said in a verse which has become proverbial:

> The secret that is hidden in the breast is not a sermon:
> you cannot utter it in the pulpit, but on the gallows.[12]

Hallaj was later perceived as the typical representative of all-embracing Unity of Being, proclaiming openly the secret of unity and therefore liable to be killed:

> Water earth stream—one cry—
> Tree and bush—one scream: I am God!
> All things have become worthy of pain,
> all have become Mansur—
> whom of them are you going to hang?
> Everywhere the Friend's word,
> the presence of the Beloved—
> all the world is Mansur:
> how many are you going to kill?[13]

Thus says Shah Abdul Latif (d. 1752) in Sind in his Sindhi *Risalo*.

Today Hallaj is praised by progressive writers as the prototype of the idealist who sacrifices everything for his ideal. His name appears often in the works of contemporary Arabic, Urdu, and Persian writers. (Salah Abdus Sabur's *Ma'sat al-Hallaj,* available in English as "Murder in Bagdad," is a fine example of the interpretation of his life from a socialist perspective.) With Hallaj's death, the first period of Sufism comes to an end.

THE PERIOD OF SYSTEMATIZATION

The following phase is one of systematization. The works written in the late tenth century by Abu Talib al-Makki, Kalabadhi, and Abu Nasr as-Sarraj show how Sufism was interpreted in conformity with the Divine law. These handbooks offer important information about the early period of Sufism and give definitions and formulations of crucial points.

Biographical dictionaries and detailed hagiographic books are known from the early eleventh century onward and become a special genre in Arabic, later in Persian, Turkish, and Urdu literatures. This process culminates in Ghazzali's (d. 111) *Ihya' ulum ad-din, "The Revival of the Sciences of Religion,"* a work in forty chapters in which the leading theologian of his time teaches the way to a loving fulfillment of personal religious duties so that one is prepared to face the Lord at the end of one's life and account for one's acts and thoughts. Only the last quarter of the work deals with truly mystical problems. It discusses the ideals of the sober Baghdadian school in which Ghazzali found his spiritual refuge after he had realized that neither jurisprudence nor speculative theology or philosophy could satisfy his quest for God.[14]

In the meantime, Sufism had taken roots in various parts of the Muslim world where new trends developed, among them the veneration of the Prophet Muhammad. The first expressions of this veneration go back to the mystical teachings of Sahl at-Tustari[15] (d. 896), from whom his disciple Hallaj learned the idea of the pre-existent "light of Muhammad." the fountainhead of everything created.[16] The Prophet, called in the Quran "a radiant lamp", is interpreted as the lamp mentioned in the so-called Light-Verse (S. 24:35) of the Quran,[17] a lamp that radiates the Divine light into the world. Thus, his birth was surrounded with miraculous events in which his light shone in the darkness. His ascension to heaven became the focal point of his career. What the Prophet had achieved in the body, namely the immediate presence before God where even Gabriel had no access, became the goal that the saint might achieve in the spirit. Only the absolutely purified *spirit* of the mystic can be compared to the luminous *body* of the Prophet.

Such definitions show that even during the formative period of Sufism some of its adherents had begun to determine the grades of sanctity a human being could achieve. Around the year 900, several works were written dealing with the problem of the hierarchy of the Sufi saints, a hierarchy that culminates in the "Pole" or "Axis" or "Spiritual Help," the highest guiding principle of earth. The saints—invisible as they are to others—are never separated from God. Through Him they work for the amelioration of the world, and it is due to their blessings that things happen the way they should. The theories of saintship form an important part of mystical theology. However, the claims of some Sufis are placed in perspective when the modern reader sees the numerous poems and prose pieces in which Sufi leaders constantly claim to have reached the status of the "Pole" and to possess all kinds of spiritual powers, especially when such claims are made by several individuals at the same time and in the same place.[18]

The earliest hagiographical writings note the miracles of Sufis. These miracles are known as the "charismata" in contrast to those wrought by a prophet. By the strong concentration of his spiritual energy, the Sufi is able to exert enormous influence over his disciples. The "miracles" of bilocation, thoughtreading, of constant presence in the heart of the disciple, anasthesia against pain and wounds, fire-walking, among others, are well attested even in our time. Many other miracles belong to the sphere of folklore. The same event is often ascribed to saints in various areas. Frequently miracles aim at the conversion of infidels or heretics. The great masters, however, were always aware that miracles might prove an obstacle on the path toward perfection; they could be a ruse of God to hinder the Sufi from further progress because he might take pride in his power and thus fall again a prey to his lower soul for: "the *nafs* [lower soul] has a rosary and a Koran in her right hand, and a dagger in the sleeve,"[19] as Rumi says. Yet from as early as the tenth century we read reports about contests in miracle-working between two Sufis through which each tried to prove his superiority or verify his claims to spiritual authority over a certain area.

It is certain that the earliest Sufis had contacts with Christian hermits in Egypt and Lebanon and probably that they were aware of some remnants of Buddhism in northern Afghanistan where monasticism once flourished. Foreign influences soon penetrated Sufism and began to color it slowly and almost invisibly. The growing acquaintance with Hellenistic and Neoplatonic thoughts, which began in the ninth century, inspired some thinkers to apply certain philosophical concepts to their mystical theories. This tendency was associated first with al-Hakim at-Tirmidhi (d. 892), whose surname "al-Hakim" seems to point to his "philosophical" interest. In the course of time a more "theosophical" [in its classical meaning] approach to the Ultimate Being became current among the mystics. Since works from this later school of thought were the first to become known in Europe, the general tendency of earlier Western scholars was to explain all of Sufism merely as arabicized Neoplatonism, which is certainly not correct. To be sure great similarities were there. They appear more and more distinctly in the works of thinkers in the eleventh and twelfth centuries. But the exact steps that led to the growth of these influences have not yet been completely discovered. It is certainly more an assimilation of kindred ideas, as they were in the air in the Near East, than a conscious borrowing.

One of the most interesting figures in this process is Shihabuddin Suhrawardi "The Master of Illumination," often called *maqtul*, "the one who was killed," because he was executed in Aleppo in 1191 at the age of thirty-eight. However, he is not acknowledged as a true mystical martyr, as was Hallaj. His Arabic and Persian works, which have only recently been studied in more detail due to the efforts of Henry Corbin and his disciples, display an ingenious metaphysics of light.[20] Suhrawardi has gathered traditions from Egypt and Greece, from ancient Iran as well as Islamic sources to construct a fascinating system of illuminations that emanate from the first, Divine light. They reach man through reflecting and reflected ranges of angels. Even a reader who is puzzled by his sophisticated mystical speculations can enjoy Suhrawardi's little stories in which he translates high mystical experience into a simple, poetical language.

ORDERS AND FRATERNITIES

Suhrawardi Maqtul must not be confused with his two namesakes Abu Najib (d. 1164) and the latter's nephew Abu Hafs Umar as-Suhrawardi (d. 1234) who are noted as authors of handbooks of instruction into the Sufi path. In sober clear language, they delineated the proper attitude of a seeker in every moment of life.[21] It is largely due to these two individuals that Sufi orders in the proper meaning of the word came into existence. But we have to beware of comparing the Sufi "order" to the Christian monastic order. Sufism does not espouse celibacy, for, as the Prophet said, "There is no monkery in Islam," and "Marriage is my way." Thus, the leaders and the members of the orders were generally married, and the Sufi master was often succeeded by his son. Moreover, the orders tended to spread abroad and did not limit their membership and activity to a single "monastic" retreat or cloister, even though the founder's seat (or, in many cases, the founder's tomb) always remained the center of piety where those affiliated with the order sought help in worldly and otherworldly matters.[22]

The Suhrawardiyya is one of the earliest of the larger congregations in which pious souls could find inspiration and guidance. In earlier times the disciples of a master were a small elite group while the master himself might have been a man of any normal profession. A consolidation of fraternities began on a larger scale from the mid-twelfth century onward. People of all classes were attracted to the meetings where they hoped to find some spiritual uplifting and an outlet for their emotions in congregational prayer, remembrance of God, and perhaps also in listening to music.

A contemporary of Suhrawardi, Abdul Qadir al-Gilani died in Baghdad (1166). This stern representative of the Hanbalite School of law (noted for its criticism of Sufi excesses) had gathered a great number of disciples and followers who formed the nucleus of an order that was to extend its activities from West Africa to Indonesia. The Qadiriyya is to this day the most widespread Sufi fraternity. The question as to why and how the demanding preacher Abdul Qadir was transformed into a veritable saint to whom innumerable miracles are ascribed and "whose foot is on the neck of every saint," is still not answered.

The growth of orders or fraternities is a most important phenomenon in the history of Sufism. It was largely due to their efforts that the message of mystical Islam was brought to the masses. The members of Sufi orders were in the forefront of those who preached Islam in the ever expanding border provinces of the empire. Around a small nucleus of dervishes who lived close to the Master, the majority of members formed what one may call a "third order" (tertians). Their relation to the order may consist of attendance at the annual festivities connected with the anniversary of the founder's death, seeking spiritual enlightenment or consolation from the Master or requesting an amulet from the members of the cloisters or making vows at the tomb of the saint. From the thirteenth century onward, the Muslim world from Africa to India became covered with a network of Sufi cloisters in which the tired wayfarer could find rest for a day or two, and the hungry traveller might find some food (the free kitchen is still part of larger establishments). It may be assumed that the nondiscriminating hospitality of the Sufi cloisters contributed significantly to conversions, especially in India with its strict food taboos among the Hindus. From these places a simple kind of basic Islam was brought to the masses—a process in which the utilization of poetry in the regional languages played an important role, as we shall see.

While the process of the formation of orders continued throughout the thirteenth century and later, one can observe a general upsurge of mystical ideas during the whole thirteenth century. This coincided exactly with the time when the Mongols overran Central Asia and Iran and finally destroyed the caliphate in Baghdad (1258). It was a period in which the entire political and social fabric of the Middle East was destroyed, and in which, later, new political constellations emerged. As though they were to counterbalance the powers of political destruction, a large number of Sufis appeared in this age everywhere in the Muslim world. Among them were those who decisively influenced the later development of Sufism.

THEOSOPHICAL SUFISM

The central figure in this regard is undoubtedly the Spanish-born Ibn Arabi (d. 1240). Initially he was introduced to Sufism by two women saints. Later on in life, while on pilgrimage to Mecca he was inspired by his meeting with a young Persian lady to write his mystical love poetry, the *Tarjuman al-ashwaq,* "Interpreter of Longing."[23] Despite his numerous journeys, which took him to Egypt, Syria and Anatolia, Ibn Arabi was a most prolific writer who claimed to write under inspiration. His most frequently cited works, which shaped the whole thought system of Sufism after 1300, are the *Futuhat al-Makkiyya,* "The Meccan Revelations," and the *Fusus al-hikam,* "Bezels of Wisdom."[24] The first is an enormous compendium of his "theosophy" while the second is a small but weighty introduction to the mystical aspects of the prophets mentioned in the Quran. Both works have received extensive attention and commentary; their terminology has influenced even those who disagreed with Ibn Arabi, the "Magister Magnus," as he soon was called by his admirers.

His system, usually referred to as "Unity of Being," has often been interpreted as sheer pantheism or monism by Orientalists who wrote during the nineteenth and early twentieth centuries. But true assessment of Ibn Arabi's work has proved to be extremely difficult. Henry Corbin, Sayyid Hussein Nasr, and lately a number of Western devotees of Ibn Arabi have shown that indeed, for the "Magister Magnus," the Divine Essence always remains transcendent; it is the Divine Names that work on the level of creation. Basing his system on a famous extra-Quranic Divine saying, Ibn Arabi conceived God as "a hidden treasure." In the loneliness of pre-eternity the Divine Names longed to be known; therefore, the world was created as a mirror for God, and God in turn is its mirror. The world stands in relation to God like ice to water, being part of it, but in a different aggregate. The highest experience of man is to lift the veils of ignorance in order to realize the essential unity of everything, beyond which the Essence of the Creator remains eternally unknowable and unattainable. The world is created afresh every moment in the movement of the Divine breathing, which is reflected, as it were, in the human attestation that there is "no deity save God." "There is no deity," means that the world emerges from the Divine breath and is taken back with the attestation of "save God" to fall back into the unfathomab!e depth of Unity. It is, of course, easy to sum up the whole system in the simple Persian phrase which translates as "Everything is He," a phrase that came into vogue prior to Ibn Arabi and became the main theme of mystical bards all over the Persianate world. But this blurs the sophisticated distinctions of Ibn Arabi's system.[25]

All these ideas were taken up, though often diluted, by the Sufi orders. Consequently, the utterances of poets from Morocco to India and from Turkey to East Africa bear a distinct similarity. All of the Sufis hope to transgress the stages of the various prophets and to reach union with the "archetypal Muhammad," striving to become the "pole," the true leader of their community. The feeling of all-pervading unity is likewise typical of their songs. This explains the aversion of Muslim modernists to Sufi poetry in which the borders between Islam and infidelity, between mosque and idol temple, or between the Muslim and the Hindu prayer beads are blurred, if not completely wiped out. The dispute as to whether Ibn Arabi can be regarded a true Muslim or is to be dismissed as a heretic has continued for centuries, and as late as 1979 his works were once again banned in Egypt.

SUFISM IN THE PERSIAN WORLD

The leading mystical poet in the Arab world is Ibn al-Farid (d. 1235). His refined verses are as beautiful as they are difficult to disentangle.[26] The Persian and Persianate world on the other hand, produced a large number of mystical poets. Some Persian poets had started to use their mother tongue for literary purposes in the latter part of the tenth century. By the late eleventh century, the first mystical works in Persian were composed by Hujwiri,[27] who died in Lahore around 1071. He wrote his important theoretical work *Kashf al-mahjub* (which has be-

come popular in the West thanks to R. A. Nicholson's excellent translation). Others include Abdullah-i Ansari[28] (d. 1089) who composed his
touching and tender short prayers in rhymed prose with interspersed
poetry—a form that became normative for many small mystical and
ethical treatises in Persian. Ansari also translated Sulami's hagiographical work, *Tabaqat as-sufiyya*, from the Arabic into the Persian dialect
of Herat. Somewhat later, around 1100, the former court poet Sana'i
(d. ca. 1131) in Ghazna used for the first time the form of rhyming
couplets, *mathnawi*, for mystico-didactic purposes. Along with his
small *mathnawi* "The Journey of the Servants to the Place of Return,"[29]
his poem "The Garden of Truth" has formed the model for innumerable
later works by other poets. His lyrical poetry abounds in grand
eulogies for the Prophet.

The style of Sana'i was later perfected by another master from
the eastern parts of Iran, Fariduddin Attar (d. ca. 1220), "the druggist"
of Nishapur, whose epics are perhaps the most perfect allegories of the
constant journey of the soul toward God. His poetical description of
the difficult Sufi path is given in the famous *Mantiq ut-tair*, "The Birds'
Conversation" in which thirty select birds perform the pilgrimage
through seven valleys and mountains in search of the divine bird, the
Simurgh, who lives at the end of the world. Finally, they come to
recognize that they, being *si murgh*, "thirty birds," are the *Simurgh;*
the individual souls discover their identity with the Divine. Attar's
Musibatnama[30] externalizes the experiences of the novice in the *chilla,*
a place where he has to spend forty days of seclusion in prayer and
meditation, constantly supervised by his master. The poet, searching
for God, asks everything created how to reach Him. The various answers of angels and of wind, of sun and of plants, of stones and of stars,
are translated and interpreted for him by the master. Finally he reaches
the Prophet, who advises him to enter the ocean of his own soul and
lose himself there in order to find God. Does not the Quran state that
God is closer to man than his jugular vein? (S. 50:16)

Attar's stories, from which he teaches the mystical truth, are
usually sad, sometimes ironical, and critical of the society. Social criticism, often put in the mouths of mentally deranged people without
inhibition, accuse God of having strange ways of dealing with the world
and rebel against Him. Sometimes Attar's verse becomes very bitter;
at other times he indulges in endless pages of ecstatic anaphora in
which he tries to circumambulate the secret of God and to praise Him
in ever new images. Attar certainly is, as he says of himself, "the voice
of longing."

RUMI

Legend tells that toward the end of his life, Attar was visited by a young boy whom he blessed. That was Jalaluddin from Balkh who was to settle in Anatolia *(Rum)* and became therefore known as Rumi.[31] In Rumi's work, composed between 1245 and 1273, mystical poetry reached its apex. His some 36,000 verses sing of his divine love, his longing, his joy and grief, and his relation with his mystical beloved Shams-i Tabriz. He takes his inspiration from even the most mundane events and views. Just as, according to Oriental Love, the sun can transform pebbles into rubies, virtually everything Rumi saw or heard could trigger off the process of poetical inspiration so that he was able to transform it into a symbol of a higher truth. He knew that poetry was flowing from his tongue without his own effort:

> I think of rhymes, but my beloved says:
> "Don't think of anything but of my face!"[32]

During the years of burning pain after Shams had disappeared, in which Rumi learned the lover's task is:

> To become blood, to drink one's own blood,
> to sit with the dogs at the door of faithfulness,[33]

and during which "Love took a mace and beat Intellect's head,"[34] he poured out his verse almost under a hypnotic spell. Then followed a period of calming down in the company of his quiet friend, the goldsmith Salahuddin Zarkub about whom he sang:

> He who came in a red frock in years past,
> he came this year in a brown garb.
> The Turk about whom you had heard that time
> Appeared as an Arab this year . . .
> The wine is one, only the bottles are different—
> How beautifully does this wine intoxicate us![35]

Rumi composed for his favorite disciple, Husemuddin Chelebi, who later succeeded him as leader of the Sufi order, the nearly 26,000 verses of his *Mathnawi,* which is a kind of an encyclopedia of mystical thought, folklore, and legend. No other mystical work has been commented upon as often and has inspired as many poets in the whole Persianate world as the *Mathnawi,* which was called by Jami (d. 1492) "the Koran in the Persian tongue." Rumi's free-roving thoughts should be understood as something born out of a very personal experience, in which the whole culture of medieval Islam is reflected, and which, by spiritual alchemy, leads the reader or listener inevitably into the world of eternal Love. As he sings in the *Mathnawi:*

> From Love, bitter things become sweet,
> From Love, copper becomes gold,
> From Love, the dregs become pure,
> From Love, pains become medicine.
> From Love, the dead are made alive,
> From Love, kings are made slaves. . . .[36]

Rumi is the most dynamic of all Sufi poets and teachers, and it is this very dynamism and the depth of his divine love which has endeared him to millions. His poetry, born out of the whirling dance, therefore has a strong rhythmical quality and a musical sound. The mystical order of the Mevlevis which was organized by his son has become known in the West as the Whirling Dervishes.

At the time that Rumi sang his immortal songs, the first attempts were being made to produce mystical verse in simple Turkish forms. The development of poetry in the various regional languages of the Islamic world is a feature that becomes more and more obvious in the history of post-thirteenth century Sufism. The Sufis did not win the hearts of the masses by theoretical discussions about the Unity of Being or prophetology in a technical vocabulary which only the elite could understand. Rather, they utilized the words and images of simple villagers, of fishermen and spinning women, which served to express the secrets of Divine love, of love for the Prophet, and the necessity of patience and gratitude. Thanks to them, those who were excluded from education in theological Arabic or Persian, the literary language of the elite, understood that God's love can be expressed in every language, and that they too, although unaware of hairsplitting theological problems, could reach proximity to the Lord. The kind of Islam they thus imbibed was often considered by the stern urban theologians as too "folkish" and "primitive." Yet this living faith provided them with the capacity to endure the vicissitudes of fate by interpreting them as

God's wise acts; it has largely colored the beliefs of rural communities in Anatolia, India, and other parts of the Muslim world.

While Arabic literature produced its most important works in prose, such as the superbly beautiful *Hikam* "maxims" of the Egyptian Shadhili Sufi, Ibn Ata Allah[37] (d. 1309), who was able to harmoniously blend purity of thought and purity of language, Persian poetry, on the other hand, was largely tinged by Sufi vocabulary and Sufi thought. Even poets who were not mystics used mystical allusions most skillfully; for the Sufis had developed, in the course of time, a special way of hiding their thoughts behind a colorful veil of symbols. Many of them had discovered that Divine beauty could reveal itself in the beauty of created things, particularly in a human being. This experience (which could also give way, in the lower orders, to crude homosexuality) offered them a multifacted set of images. The object of this poetry is at the same time the charming cupbearer at the age of fourteen (which is the most perfect number, also reminiscent of the full moon) and the Divine beloved. The black tresses of the friend are real and yet, at the same time, are the manifestations which hide the radiant light of God's eternal beauty, or the Prophet's luminous face. The winehouse is actually there, but it is also the abyss of the Divine Essence where the souls quaff the wine of mystical love. It is not necessary to explain these equations in technical terminology as was done by Sufi theoreticians (such as Abdul Ghani an-Nabulusi and Muhsin Faid Kashani in the late seventeenth century); rather, the constant oscillation between the two levels of understanding constitutes the special charm of Persian and Persianate poetry, for the Sufis knew that "the metaphor is the bridge toward Reality." Thus worldly love— called "metaphorical" love—could lead to the experience of Real, Divine Love. In this poetry, the highest truths could be revealed under the simplest images. The true meaning of a good Persian poem, by Hafiz for instance, can therefore be grasped only by those who are patient enough to disentangle the numerous artistic devices which are essential to create a successful verse. Only then can they enjoy the worldly and at the same time the religious meaning conveyed by a seemingly simple line of poetry.

LATER DEVELOPMENTS

Scholars tend to regard the development of Sufism after 1300 as rather uninteresting. Sometimes the names of some great poets in the Persianate world are mentioned while founders and main representatives of orders are discussed in passing. But on the whole the later development of Sufism is considered to be rather monotonous. That is certainly not the case. It is true that Ibn Arabi's thought and terminology permeated most of the later utterances of the Sufis, and the development of the growing Sufi *tariqas* (the "path" on which mystics walk, sometimes understood as "order" or "fraternity") seems rather uniform. Yet the various aspects of mystical poetry in the languages of India or Africa form an essential contribution of Sufism to the general culture of Islam during the last seven centuries. Furthermore, the "sober" order of the Naqshbandiyya developed in central Asia where its leaders played a remarkably active role in politics during the late fifteenth century. During the days of Akbar, the Moghul emperor (1556–1605) and his son Jahangir, it was transformed by Ahmad Sirhindi[38] (d. 1624) into an instrument to counteract the all too lax tendencies of Indian Sufism which had been fostered by Akbar's policy of integration. This policy was then tried more intensely (though less successfully) by Akbar's great-grandson, the unlucky crown prince Dara Shikoh (executed 1659).[39] Sirhindi's stress on the "Unity of Vision" as contrasted to Ibn Arabi's "Unity of Being" has been singled out as his important contribution to Sufi thought. It is, however, nothing but a new formulation of the view of the "sober" Sufis that the experience of absolute unity in ecstasy is a subjective state, not an objective reality, and that the Sufi returns from this state into a world which seems to be completely changed by the light of Divine Unity, in which he then should perform his duties.

Ahmad Sirhindi, hailed by his admirers as "the reformator of the second millenium" because he appeared at the very beginning of the second millenium after the hegira (corresponding to 1592), claimed for himself the highest possible mystical rank that of *qayyum* upon whom the movement of the world relies. His successors followed him in the attempt to purify Indian Islam, particularly popular mystical Islam, from its "pollution" by Hindu customs and thoughts.

The mystics of the reformist Naqshbandiyya tried to revive Indian Muslims during their deepest depression in the eighteenth century. At the time, the northwest of the Subcontinent was not only a battlefield for Sikhs, Maratha, and Jat, but also for the Muslim co-religionists of the Moghul emperors, namely the Persians and the Afghans who repeatedly plundered the cities along the Indus, in the Panjab, and the capital Delhi. Shah Waliullah (d. 1762), the reformer whose vast work still awaits a full interpretation, his friend Mazhar Janjanan (d. 1781), the "sunnicizer" and successful mystical leader, and Mir Dard (d. 1785), the Urdu poet and propagator of "the Muhammadan Path" which is mystically deepened orthodox Islam—all three remained in Delhi during the time of destruction. Their fundamentalism steeped in mysticism gave some consolation to at least a segment of the inhabitants of the unlucky city "where now tears flow instead of rivers." At the same time the mystical bards in the plains of Sind and of the Panjab used their native idioms to sing in unforgettable verses about the painful journey of the soul and the final union in love, thus reviving mystical love in the hearts of their illiterate listeners. In their songs, the heroines of Sindhi and Panjabi folk tales are transformed into symbols of the soul who lovingly takes upon herself all hardship in the hope of reaching the far-away beloved. Shah Abdul Latif in Sind (d. 1752), Bullhe Shah (d. 1754) in the Panjab, and Rahman Baba (d. 1711) in the Pashto speaking areas are the authors of heart rending and yet consoling mystical poetry in the time of political destruction of the once so powerful Moghul empire.[40]

SUFISM AND ISLAMIC CIVILIZATION

One could go farther and ask: what was the general influence of Sufism on Islamic life? Although it organically grew out of the deep meditation of the Quran and the faithful observation of the Prophetic tradition, yet certain later developments inside some of the Sufi fraternities, such as theories of mystical union looked like "foreign plants" to many observers. Many modern critics both inside and outside Islam have perceived the danger of mystical quietism which rendered the Muslims unable to cope with the changing times and to participate in the progress of the so-called "civilized" nations. Particularly the teachings of Ibn Arabi have been held responsible for much of the decline in Islamic culture. The so-called "Pirism," the almost unlimited power of the mystical leader over his generally illiterate, poor followers has been severely criticized, not only by European scholars like J. K. Birge in his study on the Bektashi order in Turkey,[41] but even more by the Indo-Muslim modernist philosopher-poet Iqbal[42] (d. 1938). Iqbal—"the spiritual father of Pakistan"—considered the traditional sweet mystical poetry as more dangerous to the souls of the Muslims than the hordes of Jinghiz Khan and Attila. Two hundred years before him, Shah Waliullah had claimed that the books of the Sufis, even though they may contain elixir for the elite, are deadly poison for the masses, and he condemned those who go on pilgrimage to Ajmer or Salar Masud's tomb in Bahraich, two of the most sacred places of mystical Islam in India. A similar aversion to popular customs in "lower" Sufism is typical of most reformers in Islam (as it was typical of Protestant movements inside Christianity). The eccentricities of wandering dervishes, of Sufis who disregarded the religious law, were conspicuous to the Western visitor who presumed them to be typical of Sufism, for the silent masters who quietly followed the Path in devotion and love remained hidden from him. Likewise the mystical music and dance, as it was known among the Sufis from the middle of the ninth century, appeared to many to be the very essence of Sufism. Even as early as the eleventh century Hujwiri complained about those for whom Sufism is nothing but dance and music, an attitude which, unfortunately, also prevails in some modern Western Sufi movements. In the classical time, however, mystical music and dance was not a duty but rather an occupation of the Sufis in their rare moments of leisure. It was here that they could relax from the extremely hard spiritual discipline to which they were accustomed. Mystical music and dance is not at all a goal in itself; rather, it was always considered very dangerous for beginners, and is therefore rejected by a number of orders.[43]

These aspects of Sufism cannot be taken as more than externals. Sufism, as a truly Islamic form of piety, has contributed to the Islamic consciousness by giving a deeper dimension to life. Its teachings place primary importance not on the letter of the law but rather in the spirit of the revelation and the spirit of the beloved Prophet, to whom all Sufis are connected by the chain of initiation. It has refined the ethics of Islam. The fine manners among Muslims, which are so similar in most Islamic countries, are largely shaped by the teachings of medieval Sufi masters who tried to imitate the example of the Prophet and taught their followers how to behave properly in every moment of life, how to honor their fellow beings, extending tender love even to animals. This education influenced villagers and princes alike.

Of particular importance is the contribution of Sufism to the development of languages and literatures. Thanks to their experiences, new nuances of "the language of love" developed in Arabic.[44] Persian is unthinkable without the Sufi flavor even in very worldly parts of its literature; Turkish, Urdu, Sindhi, Panjabi and Pashto were all used as literary media first by the Sufis in order to preach to the people in an idiom which they could easily understand. (One may think here of the role of medieval German, Dutch, Italian, or English nuns or recluses for the development of their respective languages.) On this religious basis, the different languages began to develop profane literatures as well.

Other aspects of Sufism need more investigation. Only a fragment of the Sufi texts have been properly edited; hundreds of thousands of texts are still found only in manuscript, many of them not even catalogued, while new discoveries are likely to occur any moment. The practical aspects of life in the convents such as organization, financial support, landholding, etc. are being at present investigated by a number of young American scholars.[45] Sufi psychology deserves more interest. The role of the Sufi master as psychotherapist, who was able to heal the souls by leading the seekers to the Divine source of love, is highly important. The role of the Sufis as missionaries is well attested, but one still needs more studies about their contribution to political thought. Some orders, like the Chishtiyya, refused any dealings with the government while the Suhrawardiyya, following the example of their founder, cooperated with the rulers. The Naqshbandiyya, on the other hand, had a highly political program which contributes even now to their success in several Islamic countries. There are rebel Sufis who led their followers against the establishment and were slain in the strife for what one may call "social justice" or "religious communism," and there are heroes of the faith who paid with their lives for their missionary efforts. Others tried to do what Dara Shikoh hoped to achieve under the heading of "the merging of two oceans," (S. 18:56) by adopting ideas and spiritual techniques from their Hindu neighbors into the fabric of Sufi life, without, however, losing the deeprooted relation with the basic truths of Islamic life.

One can indeed say that the history of Sufism reflects the general history of Islam. The central quest, however, for all Sufis was one. Whether they were ecstatics or sober thinkers, poets or philosophers, dreamers or practical organizers, they all hoped to attain to the secret of the profession of faith, that "there is no deity save God," and to realize this mystery in their own lives as true witnesses of the Divine unity.

NOTES

1. Paul Nwyia, *Ibn Ata-Allāh et la naissance de la confrèrie sadilite* (Beirut: Dar el-Machreq, 1972), p. 46.
2. Annemarie Schimmel, *As through a Veil* (New York: Columbia University

Press, 1982), chap. 4; Jan Knappert, *Swahili Religious Poetry,* 3 vols. (Leiden: Brill, 1971).

3. See Margaret Smith, *Rabia the Mystic and Her Fellow-Saints in Islam* (Cambridge: Cambridge University Press, 1928); Annemarie Schimmel, *Mystical Dimensions of Islam* (Chapel Hill: University of North Carolina Press, 1975), Appendix 2.

4. Abu Nu'aym al-Isfahani, *Hilyat al-auliya* (Cairo, 1932), vol. 9, p. 342.

5. A. H. Abdel Kader, *The Life, Personality and Writings of al-Junayd,* Gibb Memorial Series N. S. 22 (London: Luzac, 1962). A fine analysis of Junayd's thought is found in *Hindu and Muslim Mysticism,* edited by R. C. Zaehner (London: University of London, Athlone Press, 1960); cf. also Paul Nwyia, *Exégèse coranique et langage mystique* (Beirut: Dar el-Machreq, 1970), p. 249.

6. Schimmel, *Mystical Dimensions,* pp. 167–78.

7. Rumi, *Mathnawi,* vol. 2, line 2523; vol. 5, line 2035.

8. Peter Awn, *Iblis in Sufi Psychology* (Leiden: Brill, 1983); Annemarie Schimmel, "The Martyr-mystic Ḥallāj in Sindhi Folk Poetry," *Numen* 9 (1962):9.

9. Fariduddin Attar, *Tadhkirat al-auliya,* ed. Reynold A. Nicholson, 2 vols. (Leiden: Brill; London: Luzac, 1905–1907; reprint, 1959) 2:142.

10. ad-Daylami, Ali ibn Ahmad, *Sirat-i Ibn al-Hafif ash-Shirazi,* in the Persian trans. of Junayd-i Shirazi, ed. Annemarie Schimmel (Ankara: Ilâhiyat Fakültesi, 1955); Henry Corbin, ed., Ruzbihan Baqli, *Sharh-i shathiyāt, Les Paradoxes des Soufis* (Tehran and Paris: Maisonneuve, 1966).

11. Mirza Asadullah Ghalib, *Kulliyat-i Farsi,* 17 vols. (Lahore: University, 1969), "Ghazaliyyati Farsi," no. 83, p. 114.

12. Shah Abdul Latif Bhitai, *Shah jo Risalo,* Sur Sohni 9:1–2.

13. K. J. Semaan, *Murder in Baghdad* (Leiden: Brill, 1972); for the tradition in various languages see also Annemarie Schimmel, *Al-Halladsch, Märtyrer der Gottesliebe* (Cologne: Hegner, 1967), and Annemarie Schimmel, "Mystische Motive in der modernen islamischen Dichtung," in *Weg in die Zukunft, Festschrift für Anton Antweiler* (Leiden: Brill, 1976), pp. 216–28.

14. G. H. Bousquet, *Ihyā ouloum ad-dīn, ou vivifaction des sciences de la foi* (Paris: Besson, 1955). Numerous parts of the Ihya' have been translated into English, German, French, and Dutch.

15. See Gerhard Böwering, *The Mystical Vision of Existence in Classical Islam: The Qur'anic Hermeneutics of the Sufi Sahl at-Tustarī* (d. 283/896) (Berlin: de Gruyter, 1979).

16. Al-Hallaj, *Kitab at-tawasin,* ed. and trans. Louis Massignon (Paris: Geuthner, 1913), pp. 16 ff.

17. The best introduction into the development of the mystical veneration of the Prophet is still Tor Andrae, *Die person Muhammads in glaube und lehre seiner gemeinde* (Stockholm: P. A. Vorstedt og söner, 1918). See also Annemarie Schimmel, *Und Muhammad ist Sein Prophet. Die Verehrung des Propheten in der islamischen Frömmigkeit* (Cologne: Diederichs, 1981) [English enlarged version in preparation], and Annemarie Schimmel, *As through a Veil,* chap. 5.

18. al Hakim al-Tirmidhi, *Khatm al-auliya,* ed. Othman Yahya (Beirut: Dar el-Machreq, 1965). About Tirmidhi see also: Berndt Radtke, *Al-Hakīm at-Tirmidī. Ein islamischer Theosoph des 3./9. Jahrhunderts* (Freiburg: Klaus Schwarz Verlag, 1981).

19. Rumi, *Mathnawi,* vol. 3, line 2554.

20. Henry Corbin, *Sohrawardi d'Alep, fondateur de la doctrine illuminative* (ishraq) (Paris: Librarie orientale et américaine, 1939); ed. *Opera metaphysica et mystica,*

vol. 1 (Istanbul: Devlet Matbaasn, 1945); vol. 2 (Tehran and Paris, 1952); ed., *Oeuvres en Persan* (Paris: Maisonneuve, 1970).

21. Examples are Abu 1-Najib as-Suhrawardi, *Kitab Adab al-muridin,* ed. Menahem Milson (Jerusalem, 1978), and *A Sufi Rule for Novices,* trans. Menahem Milson (Cambridge, Mass.: Harvard University Press, 1975), and the more extensive work of his nephew, Abu Hafs Umar as Suhrawardi, *Awarif al-maarif,* trans. Richard Gramlich (Wiesbaden: Steiner, 1980).

22. The development of the orders and their varieties are best described in J. Spencer Trimingham, *The Sufi Orders in Islam* (Oxford: Oxford University Press, 1971).

23. Ibn Arabi, *The Tarjumān al-ashwāq: A Collection of Mystical Odes.* ed. and trans. Reynold A. Nicholson (London: Royal Asiatic Society, 1911); reprint with foreword by Martin Lings (London: Theosophical Publishing House, 1978).

24. Ibn Arabi, *Fusus al-hikam,* ed. A. A. Affifi (Cairo, 1945); trans. R. W. J. Austin, *The Bezels of Wisdom* (New York: Paulist Press, 1980).

25. The different interpretations of his work can be studied in the following works: Hendrik Samuel Nyberg, *Kleinere Schriften des ibn al-'Arabi* (Leiden: Brill, 1919); A. A. Affifi, *The Mystical Philosophy of Muhyid-Din Ibnul-'Arabi* (Cambridge: Cambridge University Press, 1936); and Henry Corbin, *Creative Imagination in the Sufism of Ibn Arabi,* trans. Ralph Manheim, Bollingen Series (Princeton, N.J.: Princeton University Press, 1969); Reynold A. Nicholson, *Studies in Islamic Mysticism* (Cambridge: Cambridge University Press, 1921), chap. 2.

26. Nicholson, *Studies in Islamic Mysticism.* Chapter 3 sums up the work of Ibn al-Farid in a masterly fashion.

27. Ali ibn Uthman Hujwiri, *The "Kashf al-Mahjūb," the Oldest Persian Treatise on Sufism,* trans. Reynold A. Nicholson, Gibb Memorial Series, no. 17 (London: Luzac; Leiden: Brill, 1911).

28. The most recent English translation is Wheeler N. Thackston, Jr., *Khwaja Abdullah Ansari, Intimate Conversations* (New York: Paulist Press, 1978).

29. E. E. Berthels, "Grundlinien der Entwicklungsgeschichte des sufischen Lehrgedichtes," *Islamica* 3, no. 1(1929): 1–31; Reynold A. Nicholson, *A Persian Forerunner of Dante* (Towyne-on-Sea, North Wales: J. W. Williams, 1944).

30. Hellmut Ritter, *Das Meer der Seele* (Leiden: Brill, 1959), reprint, 1978; Isabelle de Gastines, *Le Livre de l'Epreuve* (Paris: Fayard, 1981); the *Ilahiname* has been translated by John A. Boyle, *The Ilāhīnāme, "Book of God" of Farīduddin 'Attar* (Manchester: University Press, 1976); Attar, *Mantiq ut-tayr,* ed. M. Javad Shakur (Tehran: Kitab-furush-i Tehran, 1962), p. 287.

31. Annemarie Schimmel, *The Triumphal Sun* (London and The Hague: East-West Publications, 1978), gives a survey of Maulana Rumi's life and poetry.

32. Rumi, *Mathnawi,* vol. 1, line 1727.

33. Rumi, *Diwan-i Kabir,* ed. Baduzzaman Furuzanfor (Tehran: Tehran University, 1957), Nr. 2102.

34. Rumi, *Diwan-i Kabir,* Nr. 1276.

35. Rumi, *Diwan-i Kabir,* N. 639.

36. Rumi, *Mathnawi,* vol. 2, lines 1529–32.

37. Nwyia, *Ibn Ata Allah,* gives an excellent introduction; English translation by Victor Danner, *The Book of Wisdom* (New York: Paulist Press, 1978).

38. His work has been studied by Yohanan Friedmann, *Shaykh Ahmad Sirhindi. An Outline of His Thought and a Study of His Image in the Eyes of Posterity* (Montreal and London: Montreal University Press, 1971).

39. For Dara Shikoh see Bikrama Jit Hasrat, *Dara Shikuh: Life and Work* (Calcutta: Santinitekam, 1953). His personality has often been discussed by art historians as he was a major patron of paintings and calligraphy.

40. Annemarie Schimmel, *Islam in the Indian Subcontinent* (Leiden: Brill, 1981), pp. 153–64.

41. John K. Birge, *The Bektashi Order of Dervishes* (London: Luzac, 1937).

42. For Iqbal's religious ideas see Annemarie Schimmel, *Gabriel's Wing* (Leiden: Brill, 1963).

42. See Fritz Meier, "Der Derwischtanz," *Asiastische Studien* 8 (1954), and Marijan Molé, "La Dance Ecstatique en Islam," *Sources Orientales: La Danse Sacrée* (Paris: Editions du Seuil, 1963).

44. Nwyia, *Exégèse coranique,* p. 87.

45. A good example is Richard M. Eaton's study of the *Sufis of Bijapur* (Princeton, N.J.: Princeton University Press, 1978).

Contradiction and Consistency in Islamic Art

Walter Denny

HE HISTORY of art is a mirror of the history of society and culture. Certainly the study of Islamic art as a reflection of Islamic history, social order, and cultural achievements provides a vantage point for the understanding of these entities that is useful, reliable, and even at times entertaining. It gives us a record not only of historical facts but of feelings as well. However, when we compare the history of Islamic art to that of the art of Western societies, we encounter a number of structural differences that have led in the history of Islamic art to a series of deep contradictions and conflicts between the needs of Islamic civilization, in all of its richness and diversity, and the artistic limitations defined by a revealed Islamic religion, with strict and demanding rules imposed by God upon man.

A great deal has been written on the question of the prohibition of the figural image in Islamic art, and the attitudes of Islamic theologians toward this question over time.[1] The matter is still one of theological interest in modern Islam, and the role of such images in the era of photography, television, and cinema continues to raise questions and provoke controversy in the Islamic world.[2] This tenuous position of figural art in Islam is but one aspect of a much wider ambiguity composed of a set of contradictory needs in Islamic civilization, needs that have profoundly affected the role of the Islamic artist and the product of his work.

In addition to the structural conflict of a puritanical and anti-

137

sensual religion with the often luxurious and always sensual nature of visual art, the enormous differences across the Islamic world in ethnicity and theological orthodoxy, and the embracing matrix of inherited non-Islamic or even anti-Islamic cultures, have created doubt in the minds of some scholars about the existence of an entity called "Islamic art," at least to the extent that such an entity can be defined in traditional art-historical stylistic terms. The debate over this definition is frequently as lively as that surrounding the meaning of the terms "Arab" or "Muslim."[3]

Under such circumstances, the individual who sets out to characterize and define Islamic art in broad terms must tread somewhat warily; he or she is, after all, working in a field where a commonly accepted textbook has not even appeared, and where many general works on the subject sidestep important matters of definition by resorting to watertight compartmentalization of art by medium, by dynasty, or by geographical area; this same compartmentalization is frequently reflected in the organization of museums of Islamic art. The present discussion will focus on Islamic art as a distinctive complex of contradictions and consistencies in an attempt both to relate its distinctiveness and development to other aspects of Islam and to understand its common bonds of style, genre, and meaning.

ART AND ARTIST IN ISLAM

Historians of art often forget that art history begins with the act of creation by an artist. The essential first step in examining the progress of Islamic art through time is to define the role and freedom of the artist in the creative process, as that process relates to the artist's recruitment, training, evaluation, and compensation. The notion of the artist current in the West since the time of Vasari in the sixteenth century is not altogether absent in the history of Islamic art. The stereotype of the artist as highly individual in behavior, often divinely inspired, and frequently on the fringe of society is dependent on knowledge about the artist's life as it relates to art. Such knowledge is largely lacking in the history of Islamic art, just as it is in the art of Europe until the artist's role begins to emerge quite strongly at the time of the Renaissance.[4] Islamic artists are for the most part anonymous, and outside of a small circle of cognoscenti, even the art of "famous" artists, and to a lesser extent their names, have been generally unknown. Because of the *de jure* restrictions on artists imposed by the conflict between religious austerity and secular luxury in Islamic culture, artists remained largely anonymous; and because their artistic energies were in large part directed toward genres with a limited viewership, there was little attempt to build public images of artists. Thus, despite the popularity of a few magical "big names," the association of a work of art with a particular name seems to have affected its value as a commodity to a relatively meager degree. In 1311, the entire town of Siena took a holiday to celebrate the completion of Duccio's great *Maestá* altarpiece for the Siena cathedral; little more than two decades later, another great artist painted for the ruler of Persia a depiction of the funeral of Alexander the Great that in raw emotional power has rarely been exceeded in any tradition. Not only was the work limited in fame due to its inclusion as an illustration in a royal manuscript, but until the present century the work itself, not to mention its date, its patron, place of creation, and even the name of the artist himself, were completely unknown to historians of art. We now know the first three bits of information, but as to the name of the artist we have only a bare hint from a literary source penned over two centuries after the creation of the painting.[5]

For the study of art in the West, the role of the artist as hero has demanded a focus on heroic personalities, which in the absence of written sources was created by inference from the art itself. In the Islamic tradition, until quite recently, the techniques and the level of connoisseurship necessary for the creation of such heroes remained undeveloped, giving us an art not only without artists' names, but virtually without artists altogether. One might argue that when Eric Schroeder stated, in his famous metaphor, that "to eschew the sacred wafer of Genius is no hardship to a man who chews the beefsteak of honest performance" he believed himself to be characterising the nature of Islamic art; he was in fact commenting on the state of Islamic art scholarship itself.[6] With the exception of a few artists who worked in the media of the book—painting, illuminating, and calligraphy[7]—and always with the exception of architects,[8] we are confronted in the Islamic tradition with works of art largely without known creators. This situation severs us from the rich mine of psychological interpretation, biographical approach to an oeuvre, and the web of personal influences, which in Western scholarship has so often revealed glistening lodes of publishable platinum. In a culture where a Picasso lithograph signed with pencil brings ten times the price of an identical but

Figure 7.1. The Bier of the Great Iskandar. From a *Shah-nameh* manuscript, colors on paper. Tabriz, Iran, 1332–36. *Courtesy of the Smithsonian Institution, Freer Gallery of Art, No. 38.8.*

unsigned example, and where the "Fine Arts" of painting and sculpture reign supreme, anonymous works are approached and understood with difficulty. In Islamic civilization itself, only when works of art began in a limited way to be understood as saleable commodities with a relation to well-known creators, "signatures" of a few great names such as Behzad and Riza-yi Abbasi appeared with the same frequency as the name of Raphael was scribbled on works of questionable merit in the great galleries of Europe. While connoisseurship developed in the West in part as a response to the needs of a market in artistic goods that depended on the direct association of the object with the artist, in Islamic art only painting and calligraphy saw sufficient role differentiation in their creators, and sufficient marketability, to permit it. Therefore in much of Islamic art we are both spared and denied an artist, and we are forced to interpret the work of art in a broader social, cultural, or religious context instead.

CONFLICTS BETWEEN RELIGION AND ART

The Quran, or Islamic scripture, is to Muslims the literal word of God, recited in Arabic by the Messenger Muhammad as dictated by the Archangel Gabriel. Calligraphy is the one art form in Islam explicitly and positively sanctioned by God and by the actions, traditions, and derived laws related to the life of the Messenger himself. Islamic calligraphy is eloquent not only in message but in medium, and the beauty of letters and words itself serves as symbolic affirmation of a faith made explicit in the meaning of letters and words.[9]

Islamic script evolved into a multitude of forms: the stately, rectilinear Kufic of early Arab scriptures spreads expansively across broad parchment pages; the Kufic script of the East sent lofty shoots up to floriated or foliated termini in the vertical paper pages of Iranian codices. In the Maghreb and Spain, a more cursive form with long, scimitar-like strokes below the baseline evolved. Script covered holy buildings, decorated banners and flags, protected the bearer of clothing and weapons, invoked good wishes on the owners of pottery and metalwork, and kept the evil eye from threshholds and hearths as it continues today to protect taxis, buses, and motor-scooters. The mastery of the basic cursive styles of script was the subject of learned treatises and its acquisition was as arduous as its teaching was demanding.[10]

Figure 7.2. *Mashq* or demonstration of calligraphic styles. From a workshop album, ink on paper. Iran (?), 15th century. Istanbul, *Topkapi Palace Museum*, *Hazine* 2152.

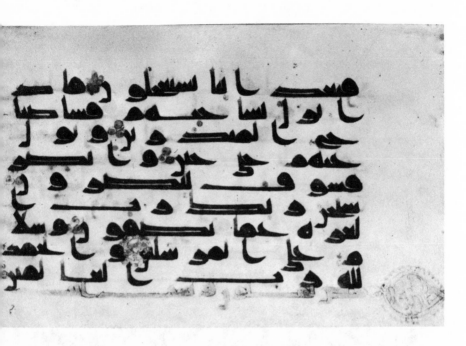

Figure 7.3. Parchment page with kufic writing. From a Quran manuscript, ink on parchment. Iraq, 10th century. Springfield, Massachusetts, *Museum of Fine Arts,* No. 59 Ms 66.

The generalized qualities of holiness and the popular apotropaic functions of Islamic script led to styles in which the meanings of words are completely submerged in the broader meanings of forms; Islamic script attained abstract heights as varied as the woven rectilinearity of a repeated holy name in a fourteenth-century album page, or the scattered and almost illegible textures of an eighteenth-century page of Iranian "broken" script (see frontispiece). The arts of margining, illuminating, gilding, binding, and the associated genres of découpage, lacquer-painting, and embossing on leather and paper developed originally as handmaidens to calligraphy, and their practitioners frequently went through training as calligraphers. Book illumination and architectural surface decoration contributed to the emergence of various geometric and vegetal pattern genres in Islamic art known collectively as "arabesque."[11] The proscription of figural images rendered the arabesque along with calligraphy as the preferred form of decoration of

Figure 7.4. Calligraphic composition. From a workshop album, ink and colors on paper. Iran (?), 15th century. Istanbul, *Topkapi Palace Museum, Hazine* 2152.

religious objects such as books and buildings including their furnishings.

This does not mean that the major Islamic religious structures, those community halls of prayer known as *masjids* or mosques ("places of prostration") were devoid of representations. To the contrary, the mosque is in many quite orthodox Islamic societies full of representations of not only the divinity, but of those men who established his Message on earth. The lamp decorating the niche indicating the direction to be faced during prayer reflects the Quran's famous metaphor "God is the Light of the heavens and the earth." It can be said that there is an Islamic iconography of inscriptions; to the right of the niche appears the name of God; to the left, that of the Messenger. In other parts of the building the names of the first four Caliphs and the two grandsons of the Prophet or other historical leaders of the Muslim community can be found. Invocations to the deity, or to saintly personages, may appear on the walls. There may be a lengthy inscription to the ruler/patron on the lintel above the main doorway, and the pulpit may also be used to invoke God's blessing on the secular power. Donors to the building are represented by other useful objects and furnishings, sometimes bearing the donors' names or blazons, and protected in perpetuity by the laws of religious endowment. Representational art is sanctioned by Islam, as long as the representation is figurative rather than figural—that is, expressed literarily (as metaphors and calligraphy) rather than literally (as depictions of the human figure).

But what of the Islamic sovereign whose name, styles, titles, and royal geneology are inscribed in majestic letters above the door of the house of God? In terms of the popular Islamic slogan appearing on numerous works of art, "Power is to God." But in practical terms throughout Islamic history, power resides in the hands of a dynastic monarch who, although styling himself, in the manner of all monarchs, as "the servant of God," often exercises that power to personal ends in profound conflict with the strict and literal interpretation of either the Quran, the traditions, or the canon law.[12] These ambiguities developed early in Islamic history; for example, we find the puritanical caliph Umar forced to reprimand some of his nomadic Arab troops bedecked in the luxurious finery of those they had just conquered. Puritanical Islam with its abstract and undefinable God burst out of Arabia to conquer civilizations with rich artistic traditions in which the definition and depiction of God was seen as an act of religious piety, where luxury was viewed as an essential adjunct to kingly power, and where

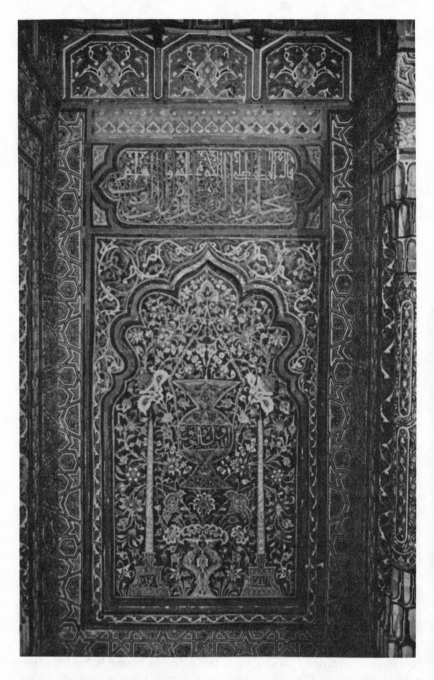

Figure 7.5. Tiled *mihrab* with a depiction of a hanging lamp. From the tomb of the Sultan Mehmed I. Turkey, Bursa, ca. 1421.

Figure 7.6. Calligraphic composition with the names of God, the Prophet, and the first Imams, in rectangular kufic script. From a wooden *minbar* or pulpit, in the mosque of Eshref Oghlu. Turkey, Beyshehir, late 13th century.

Figure 7.7. Glass lamp with cursive design incriptions and a blazon. Syria, 14th century. *Metropolitan Museum of Art,* No. 17.190.985.

the expressive aspects of the human figure in art were seen not only as the epitome of what art was and should be, but as essential aspects of an art enlisted in the service of kingship and its propagation on a popular level.

The Messenger of God had been buried in Medina less than a century before the Islamic rulers of the Middle East built great palace complexes in the Syrian desert in which fresco and mosaic artists recruited from the old regime created figural art on a large scale depicting dancing, hunting, bathing, eating and drinking, often with veiled or unveiled sexual allusions.[13] The Abbasids, thundering against the dissoluteness of the early Umayyads, replaced the caliphate of Damascus with one in Baghdad, but figural art continued to flourish. The fragmentary remains of Abbasid Baghdad and Samarra indicate a lavish figural art filled with traditional kingly images. At the other end of the Islamic world, a small casket created in Cordoba for a tenth-century Arab prince shows falconry, music, wrestling, horsemanship, and other pleasures of the urban court, while God's presence is invoked in a subsidiary manner in the inscription.

While ceramic wares created for middle-class patrons in Eastern Iran continued to rely upon the medium of beautiful script and the message of middle-class exhortations to the benefits of frugality, education, moderation, and a trust in God, the Buyyid princes of Iran and the Umayyad princes of Spain dressed in elaborate figural silks, seemingly oblivious of the Messenger's injunction that "he who wears silk in this world will forego it in the next."[14] Moreover, theological exegesis in the service of kingship created, if not a revolution in scriptural interpretation, then a sufficiently grey area in which the artist and patron had some room to maneuver without being scorched either by hell-fire or by the preached promise of it.

The dialectic between puritanical religion and luxurious kingship was productive as well as destructive—just as the conflicting demands of a jealous and all-powerful God and a dynastic-minded political order led to innovation as well as vandalism in the history of Islamic art. The social forces that often embodied these conflicting forces lead us to yet another series of contradictions in the history of Islamic art.

THE CITY-COUNTRY TENSION AND ISLAMIC ART

A recitation of the litany of Islamic dynasties in any part of the Islamic world, as well as a reading of Islamic and political history, gives an

Figure 7.8. Ivory casket with carved designs, made for the prince al-Mughira. Cordoba, 10th century. *Louvre Museum,* No. 4068.

interesting picture of the restless, hungry groups of tribal nomads or villagers constantly in conflict with settled, well-to-do urban civilizations. In the classical pattern, the former groups represented militant and puritanical Islam, while the latter represented tolerance and an appreciation of the enjoyment to be gained from worldly goods. Each change-over in political power inevitably saw the hungry newcomers settling into the same patterns they had condemned in their predecessors, until another human wave washed over the ramparts bringing both destruction and innovation in the arts as it brought dynastic, if not economic, social, or cultural change.

One of the most striking aspects of the history of Islamic art is the degree to which drastic political change often did *not* affect in profound terms the evolution of style. In certain places and times this can be traced to a commonly held belief in the economic worth of artisanry, in which talented artists were viewed as war booty to be conserved rather than as accoutrements of a vanquished regime to be erased from history. Thus we can see the development of Iranian painting from the early fourteenth century onward as an unbroken stream, despite waves of nomadic or tribal invaders who made political continuity impossible. Manuscript illustrators from conquered Arab Baghdad moved to Tabriz under the Il-Khanids and served their successors, the Jalayrids in Baghdad and Tabriz. The style moved to Timurid Shiraz under the patronage of Timur's grandson Iskandar after 1410, and thence to Herat after Iskandar's shortlived revolt ended in his defeat and blinding. The style flourished in Herat until the painters were hauled off as Özbek captives to Bukhara in the early sixteenth century, finally ending up in Safavid Tabriz under the patronage of Shah Ismail.[15] Here, dynastic, religious and country/city conflicts seem to have resulted in a coloring and enriching of continuity.

In medieval Morocco, the successive waves of rural religious reformers—Almoravids, Almohads, Merinids, Saadians, and Alawis, who looted, burned, and rebuilt the great Moroccan imperial cities— left layer upon layer of rich artistic legacy, regardless of the intensity of their initial puritanism and hatred for the city-dwellers who preceded them.[16] This particular dialectic helps to explain the apparent paradox of such monuments as the richly-decorated minarets of the great Almoravid and Almohad mosques of Seville, Rabat, and Marrakech, for the victories of these puritanical reformers demanded artistic symbols of their triumph with an inexorable logic that no amount of theological "hair-shirtery" seemed able to allay.

Figure 7.9. Minaret. From the mosque of Hasan. Rabat, Morocco, late 12th century.

RELIGIOUS ARCHITECTURE

The extension of basic principles of conduct for Muslims into the realm of artistic patronage gave rise in Islam to complex genres of architecture, housing institutions at once religious and social in their purpose. These vary widely in Islamic countries, from the Madrasah or school of orthodox religious studies, found all over the orthodox Muslim world, to a combination of water fountain and reading-room, which saw its greatest development in late Mamluk and post-Mamluk Egypt. These buildings, constructed with at least nominally pious intentions, and placed under the protection of religious endowment, constitute in fact the visible expression of what today's social historians refer to as infrastructure.[17]

In Islam, the responsibility of the ruler for the economic well-being of his subjects gave rise to such architectural genres as the Egyptian urban hotel/warehouses, the Seljuk-Ottoman rural caravansaray, and the many bridges and causeways that mark the commercial routes of the past in Islamic countries. In the realm of social services, endowed hospitals form an important architectural genre, with special distinctions made from early on between a hospital devoted to diseases of the body and one that specialized in mental disorders. Also found in Islamic cities is the alms-kitchen, a central distribution point for free food for needy people. Serving the population at large were public latrines and various types of fountains providing water for livestock and human consumption and for cleaning streets. Other endowed buildings made services available at nominal fees. Such were the public baths, some endowed for single-sex use and others either with separate facilities or with scheduled hours for men and for women. Such also were the public drinking-fountains, which served various beverages in addition to water.

Nowhere is the intermixture of social and religious structures and principles more visible in Islam than in the educational systems of Muslim countries. As in the medieval West, institutions of learning were closely controlled by the religious establishment. The buildings that housed educational functions, and the beautifully written, bound, and illustrated books that were found in the libraries of these institutions reflected their religious purposes to a high degree. Monumental inscriptions in Madrasah colleges were primarily religious in nature although the founder's name might be given some prominence and often became the name of the building or the institution as well. In the

Figure 7.10. *Hammam* of Princess Mihrimah. Turkey, Istanbul, 16th century.

Islamic world, the Madrasah thus served a dual role, legitimizing the
ruling dynasty while at the same time establishing orthodoxy on an
institutional basis.[18]

The linkage between dynastic propaganda and religious architecture, present in all genres of religious architecture in Islam, is nowhere
more noticeable than in the mosque itself. Every great city had one
mosque nominally designated as the Great Mosque or Congregational
Mosque where the entire populace could be concentrated. But just as
Rome was adorned with far more churches than her populace needed,
so most Islamic capitals show a surplus of mosques—largely the result
of dynastic patronage—the purpose of which was highly symbolic and
often only marginally practical. The great mosque/madrasah of Sultan
Hasan in Cairo, for example, was constructed at a time when the
population of that city had been severely reduced by the Black Death.
While the imperial mosques that crown many of the high hills of Ottoman Istanbul did function, along with their attached social-service
buildings, as community centers for particular quarters of the city,

Figure 7.11. Mosque/Madrasa of Sultan Hasan. Egypt, Cairo, 14th century.

their names, inscriptions, and even their architectural symbolism often served to glorify the member of the Ottoman family who was responsible for the foundation. This comfortable symbiosis of religion and secular patronage is one of the underlying dynamics of Islamic religious architecture in almost all Islamic lands.

PALACES, PRAETORIANS, AND PATRONAGE

The secular power in Islam achieved its first visual artistic manifestations in ways both visible and invisible. It seems that the desert pleasure-palaces constructed for the early Umayyad rulers of the Levant were deliberately built in places where their luxury and their irreligious figural art would not offend pious city-dwellers. The administrative headquarters within the Islamic city was often placed close to the mosque, profiting from its proximity to religion in the same way that the ruler profited from having his name mentioned from the pulpit during the Friday sermon.[19]

The practice of using foreign regiments to protect the ruler led, in the case of ninth-century Baghdad, to conflicts with the local populace severe enough to force the building of a palace city in Samarra, at some distance from the Abbasid capital itself. This Near Eastern and Mediterranean concept of a palace city, to which the element of a garrison quarter was then added, forms the basic idea of the Islamic palace enduring in our own day in such monuments as the palace of the Alawi dynasty in Rabat, and some of the Hashemite residences in Jordan. In the palace city—a world set apart, whether at a distance as in Samarra, or at a height as in Nasrid Granada—a royal art and imagery could develop without the oppressive strictures of strict religious interpretation, and the result has been a figural art of wondrous beauty, technical virtuosity, and expense, often housed in an architectural setting approximating an earthly paradise.

In the two earliest Islamic palace-cities coming down to us in a relatively intact form—the Alhambra or Red Palace of Granada, and the Topkapi or Cannon-gate Palace of Istanbul—the physical arrangement of small buildings set around courtyards, and pleasure-pavilions set in gardens, draws its lineage from the Sasanian formal garden of Iran and from late Classical Mediterranean palace complexes.[20] In these early palace-cities religious buildings are of secondary impor-

Figure 7.12. Court of the Lions, Alhambra palace. Spain, Granada, 14th century.

tance. The mosques are for the most part small and subservient structures. The important architectural elements include gateways and towers or reception halls, serving as settings for ceremonies. Just as the mosque is most emphatically *not* a setting for formalised ritual in Islam, so is the Islamic palace-city, apart from its practical functions as military and administrative center, the ceremonial setting *par excellence*. The ceremonies involving foreign ambassadors, the rituals of installation of high state officials, the observance of religious holidays, the dynastic rites of passage such as investiture of power, circumcision, and funerals, and the obligatory procession of the ruler to the mosque for the noonday prayers on Friday, all focused on the palace. In addition to these formal or public functions, however, Islamic palaces housed a hidden world as well. While the royal harem has been for many centuries the subject of repeated and rather inaccurate romanticizing on the part of Western artists, writers, and musical librettists, there is no question that the luxurious earthly paradise created for the comfort of the Islamic ruler has a firm basis in fact.[21]

The public ceremonial of court required elaborate and beautiful gifts, vestments symbolic of wealth, rank, or social position, and various sorts of ritual objects. The sword, as the symbol of the secular power, was carried near the ruler at all times, and the well-known pre-eminence of the Islamic armourer's art, which so strongly influenced the medieval West, led to the creation of beautiful ceremonial weapons and armor. Other royal symbols, such as the wine-cup, or the curious vessel descended from an animal-skin bag which carried water for the Ottoman Sultan, were manifested in elaborately decorated and beautiful objects in all media. Such objects often displayed figural images, such as those on the small casket from Cordoba illustrated above, which summarized the pleasures of the palace.[22]

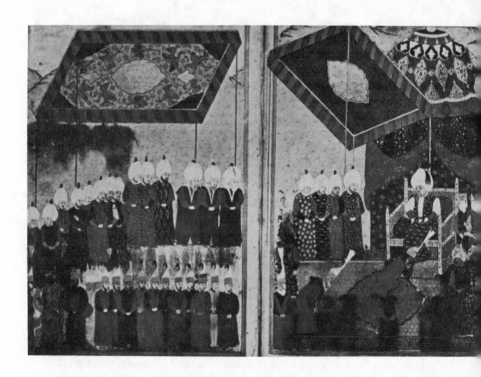

Figure 7.13. Court officials paying obeisance to Sultan Selim II. From a manuscript entitled *The Szigetvar Campaign,* colors on paper. Ottoman Turkey, 16th century. Istanbul, *Topkapi Palace Museum, Hazine* 1339.

Figure 7.14. Rock-crystal replica of a water-skin. Istanbul, 16th century, Istanbul, *Topkapi Palace Museum*.

How were these royal objects created? There appear to have been various systems through which royal artistic patronage worked in different periods and places. At some times, royal commissions in effect went to pre-eminent practitioners of a particular art form in the bazaar or urban commercial center. For other types of royal patronage, institutions were specifically set up to provide certain types of luxury goods. The royal weaving establishments, which among other things provided ceremonial robes the giving of which formed an important part of court ritual, are perhaps the best-known of such institutions in Islam. The epigraphical evidence provided by early inscriptions on textiles has proven a boon to the historian in numerous ways.[23]

The number and type of royal establishments and the degree of royal control vary from place to place in Islamic history. Perhaps the most elaborate of the royal ateliers were those which in the reign of Shah Abbas I of Iran produced the silk and metallic-thread carpets once known as "Polonaise" rugs, which were given as royal gifts to foreign notables. Another relationship between the court and commercial establishments is seen in the Ottoman empire, where royal commissions were often found in competition with a vigorous free market, and the pressures of demand led to curious economic stresses within the production system of luxury art. The passion for ivory containers at the Umayyad court of Cordoba led to the creation of a workshop within the confines of the nearby palace-city of Medina al-Zahra itself.[24]

But the most important court artistic institution in the history of Islamic art is the royal library in which the various arts of the book were practiced.[25] Because of the holy nature of calligraphy, book art always occupied a position in close orbit around religious respectability in Islam, an orbit that widened with the prominence of mystical poetry and prose and the tendency of Islamic mystics to give double interpretations even to pursuits apparently quite secular or even anti-religious (such as the drinking of wine). The tradition in which the Prophet is reported to have said that on Judgment Day painters would be required either to breathe life into their creations or to suffer eternal damnation, if not forgotten, could be conveniently placed to one side of the patrons' consciousness. It is for this reason that we see in the royal libraries of Herat, Istanbul, Tabriz, Isfahan, Delhi and Shiraz the emergence of artists of repute whose social and cultural roles most closely approximated those of the Western hero-artist, and who became the subject of biographies and whose works were avidly sought after by collectors.[26]

The phenomenon of collecting art in Islamic civilization again

Figure 7.15. So-called "Polonaise" or "presentation" rug, silk and metal thread. Iran, 17th century. Boston, *Museum of Fine Arts*, gift of Denman Ross, No. 17.603.

centers around the court, but is not simply a result of the fact that the "name" artists were concentrated in the court ateliers. While we cannot perhaps characterize the beautiful objects made for court ceremonial, conspicious consumption, and the private use of Islamic princes as constituting collections in a strict sense, the phenomenon of collecting does exist on several levels. The first is as a manifestation of historical continuity and dynastic permanence, perhaps best seen in the Ottoman Turkish court. There, costumes belonging to the sovereigns of the dynasty were kept and catalogued in the royal treasury, just as illustrated histories of the regime were jealously guarded in the royal libraries, and served as reminders of the great historical past and as relics or ikons of earlier rulers.[27]

The second kind of collecting resulted from the emergence of named artists and an almost simultaneous lessening of royal patronage in the arts of the book. This was the collecting of individual examples of calligraphy, illumination, drawing, and finished miniature painting, which were bound in albums by wealthy collectors. The practice of binding miscellaneous examples of the art of the book into albums was first a workshop practice, used by artists for their own benefit, but later became popular among royal courtiers. This type of collecting was prompted by the rising reputation of individual artists and by the development of paintings that did not serve to illustrate texts but in effect stood on their own merits. A relatively unimportant phenomenon in Timurid and early Safavid Iran, it reached great heights beginning in the late sixteenth century, when sovereigns and their courtiers alike assembled important albums, and princes such as Bahram Mirza from the Safavid court, Sultan Murad III of the Ottoman court, and the Emperor Jahangir of India assembled albums of miscellany including not only paintings, drawings, and bits of calligraphy but even texts about the history of art itself.[28]

A third type of art collecting found at the later Islamic courts has very close parallels in Europe of the same time; this is the collecting of Chinese porcelain. The well-known collecting mania of such Western princes as Augustus the Strong of Saxony was also found at the Ottoman and Safavid courts. Shah Abbas built himself a large Chini Khaneh to house his royal collection in Isfahan, while the great collections of the Topkapi Palace in Istanbul, assembled by many Ottoman sovereigns over the centuries, today rank after those in China as the greatest in the world.[29] The interest in foreign art sometimes extended even further. Various royal albums from fifteenth-century Islamic workshop collections include Chinese works of art, and in later Islamic times there is evidence that some Islamic rulers collected European paintings and prints.[30]

ART AND COMMERCE
ART OF THE CITIES AND MIDDLE CLASSES

The prosperous urban centers that flourished throughout the history of Islamic culture provide us with yet another aspect of the history of the visual arts in Islam, one in which we may encounter more problems in defining art itself. As we have noted, before the differentiation of the artists' role from that of other types of workers, a phenomenon that occurred in the West in the later Middle Ages and early Renaissance, the distinction between art and craft was relatively unimportant; the status of works of art themselves depended not upon that of their creator but often rather upon the expense and scale of the object, or the holiness of its subject in a hierarchy of ecclesiastical or theological values. By contrast, for a series of unconnected reasons, the study of such media as ceramics has assumed major importance in the history of Islamic art. Ceramics, after all, despite their tendency to break, survive the depredations of history far better than other important middle-class media such as woven textiles and embroidery, and, after architecture, ceramics not only form the major category of archaeological finds, but serve the archaeologist as a means of dating and establishing stratification. In addition, ceramics, whether as vessels or as building decoration, were always more affordable than metal, wood, and the like and thus appear to have served a wider spectrum of economic and social class, giving us a broader picture of the aesthetic tastes and practical needs of Islamic society.

To the extent that we can compare ceramics to the arts of the book—that is, to the extent that we regard ceramics as vehicles for propagating the decoration applied to their surfaces—we find in ceramic art striking parallels with the arts of the book. Calligraphy, for example, is one of the major forms of ceramic decoration, carrying both aesthetic meanings and moral messages. The famous epigraphic pottery of Khurasan, providing an epigraphic and artistic record of the prosperous city dwellers of Samanid Nishapur and Samarkand, is not only widely acknowledged to be of surpassing beauty, but also reveals a picture of the maxims by which the properous, hard-working

Figure 7.16. Pottery plate bearing calligraphic inscription. Eastern Iran, 10th century. *Louvre Museum,* No. AA96.

bourgeois of this period lived and labored.[31] A dish from the Louvre bears the inscription: "Knowledge: At the beginning its taste is bitter, but at the end it is sweeter than honey." Another, from the Freer, is inscribed: "It is said that he who is content with his own opinion runs into danger. Blessing to the owner."

Pottery made for middle-class patrons also seems to have partaken fully of the same sorts of royal and literary imagery found in the art of the court. The polychrome minai pottery made in Iran in the thirteenth century, for example, frequently contains identifiable scenes from the *Shah-nameh* and other narrative poetry; it is also quite common to find on fairly humble pottery depictions of the standard royal pursuits of hunting, music, dancing, battles, and even throne scenes.

Aside from pottery, the other great art forms associated with the urban middle class in Islam, such as textiles, have not survived in large numbers of examples from earlier times. We do, however, have all sorts of written sources which give us a picture of the rich panoply of urban craft activity from earlier times; documents from the Cairo Geniza, for example, that storehouse of bits and pieces of paper from everyday life of the Jewish urban communities, give us a wide range of insights into economic activity and the importance of crafts of all kinds not only within the urban economy of Islam itself but as items of trade around the Mediterranean basin.[32]

Recent examples of embroidery, the Islamic middle-class art form *par excellence,* are available in abundance from virtually all Islamic countries. The Suzani embroideries of Central Asia, the elaborate Mosaif from Iran, the variety of stitchery from the far-flung Ottoman realms represented by the so-called "Turkish towels" and other domestic embroideries, and the lovely embroidery of the Maghreb cities, attest both to the widespread use of the craft in the socialization of young women to a domestic role and to the love of beautiful textiles in urban middle-class Islamic societies from one end of the world to the other.[33] Only recently, however, has any serious attention been paid to this art form, due to the scarcity of older examples, the lack of reliable criteria for establishing dating and provenance, and the complexity and diversity of styles of an art form centered not in the court or bazaar but in the home.

THE ART OF NOMADIC PEOPLES

The role played in the history of Islam by nomadic peoples has been enormous, but the art of these peoples has been largely ignored until recent times. Because of the lack of written documentation, and the lack of demonstrably ancient examples of the carpets, textiles, jewelry, and other art forms found in nomadic societies, there has been little in the way of historic tradition to describe and catalogue. We now recognize that there are many links between nomadic and urban art traditions, and that many of the designs and motifs we find in the urban and

Figure 7.17. Detail, embroidered towel end. Turkey, 18th-19th century. *Private Collection.*

village art of the Middle East, not to mention social customs, are deeply rooted in a nomadic past. Moreover, these designs and motifs often appear to have meanings in which survivals of pre-Islamic and non-Islamic religious and tribal practice are observable.[34]

The limited artistic legacy surviving from the turbulent history of nomadic peoples presents us with traditions of great beauty and sensual appeal, traditions embedded in the social, cultural, and economic lives of their creators. Of the many nomadic artistic traditions, none has been better studied than that of the Turkmen tribes of Central Asia, which may serve us here as an example of the genre. Turkmen nomadic peoples were divided into major tribal groups and smaller clans and families. Their social customs and even their religion were a mixture of Islamic and pre-Islamic Turkic practices. Their major artistic forms were two—the oral epic romance—the province of men, and weaving—the province of women. In the many genres of Turkmen rug weaving, including furnishings for the tent, containers serving various

Figure 7.18. Fragment of silk vestment with cursive inscriptions. Spain, 14th-15th century. Washington, *The Textile Museum,* No. 84.29

Figure 7.19 Detail, *gul*, from a Tekke Turkmen carpet. Central Asia, 19th century. *Private Collection.*

needs of everyday life, special decorations for festivals and rites of passage, and items the sole purpose of which seems to have been advertisement of wealth and power, we find the mixture of practicality and beauty that characterizes so much of Islamic art in both city and encampment.

The repetitive medallions that grace the large Turkmen carpets and certain weavings of smaller formats appear to be symbolic emblems of the tribes themselves, tribal blazons that in some cases have apparently been living symbols for many centuries. These symbolic motifs, which occur over a wide geographic and historical span, show more clearly than any court examples the crucial role of Islamic art as a means of affirming cultural identity. The tribal symbols of some of those Turkmen who settled in Anatolia in the twelfth century later appear on commercial Turkish carpets of the fifteenth century, while they endure on nomadic carpets in Central Asia up to the end of the nineteenth century.[35] The persistence of such symbols in nomadic art has recently resulted in a great deal more attention being paid to art forms that, in their directness, their love of color and texture, and their ability to delight viewers of all cultures and all degrees of sophistication, are without parallel in any culture or time.

MEANING AND ISLAMIC ART: CONTRADICTIONS AND CONSISTENCIES

As we stated at the outset, the anonymity of much of Islamic art has meant that scholarship has turned to interpretation of that art in a number of extrinsic ways. Among these are archaeological perspectives—in which artifacts are seen as documents of bygone cultures— and cosmological perspectives—in which art is seen as the reflection of an overall religious or mystical world view. It is to be expected that the search for meaning in Islamic art should range beyond the sensual nature of art itself into an attempt to reconcile with religion itself forms that might at first appear to be anti-religious or a-religious. It is apparent that much of Islamic figural art partakes of mystical religious meanings. Fables and stories, set out in lyrical poetry and illustrated in miniature paintings, may seek to elucidate moral principles or reflect religious ideals.[36] The great Safavid figural carpets have been shown to contain amazingly complex pictorial iconography in which layer after layer of meaning—with literary allusions, visual or linguistic puns, and a combination of earthly literalism and divine metaphor—is combined into an expensive and technically prodigious marriage of the designer's imagination and the weaver's skill.[37]

In this broader context, even an act or condition expressly forbidden by the Messenger, such as drunkenness, may be viewed as an ecstatic state approaching union with God himself; thus we see in Islamic figural art the depiction of the act of wine drinking is an indication not only of actual court practice but of ritualistic religious practice as well. In a similar vein, the attraction of elderly men to comely youths, almost a cliché of later Safavid album painting, may be seen in both a literal and a metaphorical sense. Once the door is open to metaphor, the range of subjects that may be depicted expands immensely. How much of this interpretation is exegesis—the work of

Figure 7.20. Allegory of Heavenly and Earthly Drunkenness by Sultan-Muhammad. From a manuscript of the *Divan* of Hafiz, colors on paper. Iran, 16th century. *Private Collection.*

historical hindsight—and how much is a demonstrable fact of the artists' intent is still the subject of argument.

The ultimate contradiction in Islamic art, that of opposing meanings, may be seen from many different perspectives. We may favor the view of Titus Burckhardt who wrote: "the study of Islamic art . . . can lead, when it is undertaken with a certain open-mindedness, to a more or less profound understanding of the spiritual realities that lie at the root of a whole cosmic and human world."[38] We may prefer to view Islamic art as social documentation, as the record of dynastic and economic interests, or as the record of stylistic influences and geographical and historical spread of techniques. We may prefer to probe the process of artistic creation itself, the re-creation of which is for many the ultimate essence of meaning in the history of art. In common with all artistic traditions, Islamic art lends itself to many interpretations, and its meanings are as wide and diverse as is the range of those who created it and those who view it. The simplicity of aesthetic message and the complexity of iconography and imagery present a contradiction to be found in any artistic tradition; in the art that visually reflects the rich culture of Islamic peoples, such contrasts and contradictions only indicate the accuracy of the reflections of society and culture which we see in the mirror of Islamic art.

NOTES

1. Thomas W. Arnold, *Painting in Islam: A Study of the Place of Pictorial Art in Muslim Culture* (London: Dover Books, 1958); and Oleg Grabar, *The Formation of Islamic Art* (New Haven: Yale University Press, 1973), pp. 75–96.

2. Ahmad Muhammad Isa, "Muslims and Taswir," in *Fine Arts in Islamic Civilization*, ed. Muhammad Beg (Kuala Lumpur: National University of Malaysia, 1981), pp. 41–68.

3. Grabar, *Formation of Islamic Art*, pp. 1–18.

4. For example, Martin Wackernagel, *Der Lebensraum des Kunstlers in der Fiorentinischen Renaissance* (Leipzig: E. A. Seemann, 1938).

5. Eric Schroeder, "Ahmad Musa and Shams al-Din," in *Ars Islamica* 6 (1939): 113–42.

6. Quoted by Basil W. Robinson in his *Persian Miniature Painting* (London: Her Majesty's Stationery Office, 1967), p. 17.

7. The major sources for Persian painting are summed up by Stuart C. Welch and Martin Bernard Dickson in their *The Houghton Shahnameh* (Cambridge, Mass.: Harvard University Press, 1981), vol. I.

8. See, for example, L. A. Mayer, *Islamic Architects and Their Works* (Geneva: Kundig, 1956).

9. See Richard Ettinghausen, "Arabic Epigraphy: Communication or Symbolic Affirmation," in *Near Eastern Numismatics, Iconography, Epigraphy and History,* ed. Dickren Kouymjian (Beirut: American University Press, 1974), pp. 297–317.

10. Annemarie Schimmel, *Islamic Calligraphy* (Leiden: Brill, 1970), and Anthony Welch, *Calligraphy in the Arts of the Muslim World* (New York: Asia House, and Austin: University of Texas Press, 1979).

11. Ernst Kuehnel, *The Arabesque: Meaning and Transformation of an Ornament* (Graz: Akademicher Druck Verlag, 1976), and Keith Critchlow, *Islamic Patterns: An Analytical and Cosmological Approach* (London: Thames and Hudson, 1976).

12. Grabar, *Formation of Islamic Art,* pp. 141–78.

13. Ibid.

14. See the article *Harīr* (silk-weaving) *in Encyclopedia of Islam,* 2nd ed. (Leiden: Brill, 1971).

15. The schema is shown in graphic form in Robinson, *Persian Miniature Painting,* p. 34.

16. George Marçais, *L'architecture musulmane d'occident* (Paris: Arts et Métiers Graphiques, 1955).

17. On religious endowments, see the article *Waqf* in *Encyclopedia of Islam,* and Claude Cahen, "Reflexions sur le waqf ancien," *Studia Islamica* 6 (1961): 37–56.

18. On the Madrasa, see James Dickie, "Mosques, Madrasas and Tombs," in *Architecture of the Islamic World,* ed. George Michell (New York: Morrow, 1978), pp. 15–47.

19. Oleg Grabar, "The Architecture of Power," in *Architecture of the Islamic World,* ed. Michell pp. 48–79.

20. Oleg Grabar, *The Alhambra* (London: Allen Lane, 1978), pp. 99–157.

21. See, for example, Norman Penzer, *The Harem* (London: Spring Books, 1966), and Grabar, "The Architecture of Power."

22. Grabar, *The Formation of Islamic Art,* chap. 6.

23. On tiraz, see the numerous references in Maurice Lombard, *Les textiles dans le monde musulman VIIᵉ–XIIᵉ siècle* (Paris: Mouton, 1978), and A. Grohmann, *Tiraz* in *Encyclopedia of Islam.*

24. John Beckwith, *Caskets from Cordoba* (London: Victoria and Albert Museum, 1960).

25. On the organization of the royal library, see Stuart C. Welch, *A King's Book of Kings* (New York: Metropolitan Museum of Art, 1972), pp. 15–76.

26. The emergence of artists' reputations in Islamic painting is best seen in the lengthy analyses of artists and their works in Welch and Dickson, *The Houghton Shahnameh,* vol. I.

27. On the collections of the Ottoman sultans, see Tahsin Oz, *Turkish Textiles and Velvets,* vol. 1 (Ankara: Turkish Press, Broadcasting and Tourism Department, 1950), and Zeki V. Togan, *On the Miniatures in Istanbul Libraries* (Istanbul: Istanbul University Press, 1963).

28. Dost Muhammad's history of Persian painting, found in an Istanbul album, is translated in part in Lawrence Binyon, J. V. S. Wilkinson, and Basil Gray, *Persian Miniature Painting* (New York: Dover, 1971), pp. 183–88.

29. See the two works on John Alexander Pope, *Chinese Porcelains from the Ardebil Shrine* (Washington: Freer Gallery of Art, 1956), and *Fourteenth-Century Blue-and-White* (Washington: Freer Gallery of Art, 1969).

30. Among the many instances of Islamic interest in Western art, see Julian Raby, "A Sultan of Paradox: Mehmed the Conqueror as a Patron of the Arts," *Oxford Art Journal* 5 no. 1 (1982): 3–8.

31. On Samanid epigraphic pottery, see Lisa Volow, "Plaited Kufic," *Ars Orientalis* 6 (1966): 107–34.

32. Shlomo D. Goïtein, *A Mediterranean Society,* vol. I, *Economic Foundations* (Berkeley and Los Angeles: University of California Press, 1967).

33. Lombard, *Les Textiles;* on more recent embroideries, see, for example, Walter Denny, "Textiles" in *Tulips, Arabesques & Turbans,* ed. Yanni Petsopoulos (London: Alexandria Press, 1982), pp. 121–68.

34. Walter Denny, "Türkmen Rugs in Historical Perspective," in *Yörük: The Nomadic Weaving Tradition of the Middle East,* ed. Anthony Landreau (Pittsburgh: Carnegie Museum of Art, 1968), pp. 55–59.

35. Walter Denny, "Turkoman Rugs and the Origins of Rug Weaving in the Western Islamic World, *Hali* 4, no. 4 (1982): 329–37.

36. William L. Hanaway, Jr., "The Concept of the Hunt in Persian Literature," *Boston Museum Bulletin* 69 (1971): 21–69.

37. Schuyler Cammann, "Cosmic Symbolism on Carpets in the Sanguszko Group," in *Studies in Art and Literature of the Near East,* ed. Peter J. Chelkowski (New York: New York University Press, and Middle East Center of University of Utah, 1974), pp. 181–208.

38. Titus Burckhardt, *Art of Islam: Language and Meaning* (London: World of Islam Festival Trust, 1976), p. 1.

8

~~~~~~

Unity and Variety in the Music of Islamic Culture

Lois Ibsen al Faruqi

*T*HE ISLAMIC IDEOLOGY or world view is commonly referred to as
tawhid.[1] This term connotes a monotheistic creator deity who
is powerful over man and the universe but never immanent or substan-
tiated in either of them. He is beyond precise or exhaustive definition
and completely other than His creation. Yet He has benevolently dis-
closed His guidance and will to mankind in a series of revelations, the
last of which was dictated as the verbatim words of the Quran to the
Prophet Muhammad early in the seventh century.

Allah, or the Transcendent, therefore retains in the mind of the
Muslim a position above and beyond nature. He can never be represented anthropomorphically or zoomorphically. Neither is He symbol-
ically representable by any object or shape in nature.

Tawhid has been the basic ideology for a vast number of people
from various ethnic backgrounds who are dispersed in a geographic
expanse reaching from the Atlantic coast of Africa to southeast Asia.
Despite the factors of geography, race, language, climatic conditions,
economic pursuits, and national organization, which would tend to
divide and differentiate the creative contributions of these diverse peoples, an outstanding and conspicuous degree of cultural unity is apparent in all fields. This unity is the consequence of that permeating
religio-ideological core—tawhid.

One of the cultural aspects significantly influenced by that core is
the music of the Muslim peoples. In fact, music of the Muslim world

175

cannot be properly understood without reference to certain religiously based facts which have played a powerful role in shaping the essence and use of the musical arts. Two of these facts need clarification before we can show the influence of tawhid on the musical characteristics per se.

First, there has been an ongoing controversy in Muslim society over the nature and legitimacy of music. Regardless of the eventual outcome of this controversy (and it has not to this day been settled to everyone's satisfaction), it cannot be ignored that Islamic society has sought, through social pressure, religious directives, and juridical pronouncements, to control the vocal and instrumental arts in order that they contribute toward producing and sustaining a moral community. Thus the music which leads the listener to be more obedient to God has been encouraged; that which leads away from God and His directives has been avoided. The chanting of the Quran, therefore, has become the most important example of pitched sound-art in the whole of the Muslim world, and it has been used in a wide variety of religious and secular situations. Other genres of musical art have been appreciated, tolerated, or frowned upon according to their position on a continuum reaching from Quranic chant as perfect model toward the other extremity of that continuum, represented by music which is considered to be artistically divergent from Quranic chanting as well as morally debilitating. This latter type of sound-art was considered undesirable for the Muslim whether he participated in it as performer or listener. The most conservative members of the society have confined their sound-art participation and enjoyment to the chanting of the Quran and religious poetry. More liberal segments of the populace have accorded legitimacy to those vocal and instrumental improvisations and compositions that have not led to or been associated with prohibited practices such as drinking, gambling, and fornication. In addition to accepting the unquestionably approved musical types, the latter group have found pleasure and enjoyment in the music of weddings and private social gatherings, as well as in that of the military bands which have played an important role in public life of villages and towns. Probably this group has always been the one that included the largest segment of the populace, but the cultural ambiguity and even stigma against some forms of music has never been completely eliminated in the culture. For this reason, performers of the less legitimate forms have often suffered societal disregard and even disdain.

The pro- and anti-music protagonists in this cultural debate both sought substantiation for their beliefs in the Quran and in the anecdotes and sayings from the life of the Prophet Muhammad. The Quran is silent on the matter, and only by reading into the lines the desired meanings was Quranic evidence utilizable by either side. The literature recording the practice and teachings of the Prophet is richer in materials dealing with the issue; but unfortunately for the satisfactory conclusion of the debate, both pro- and anti-music anecdotes are to be found there. It is evident that the Prophet was considering the type of music and the circumstances in which music was performed rather than just the use of music itself.

A second issue deals with terminology. Because the Muslims have used no general term which includes all forms of music or sound-art, the Arabic word *musiqa* should not be considered an equivalent for the English "music." Musiqa, a Greek term borrowed and used widely by Arabic speakers, has had various connotations.[2] Sometimes it has been applied to the theoretical as opposed to the practical art of music. More generally it has been a designation for those forms of the musical art that are regarded as strictly secular, while other names identified scriptural chant and the music performed for non-ritual, religious occasions. Some forms of musical art came to be judged by the culture as legitimate and advantageous (e.g., Quranic chant, the call to prayer, chanting of poetry with noble themes, military band music), and others commonly designated as musiqa were thought to be questionable in their benefit, or even deleterious (e.g., instrumental improvisations, music related to pre-Islamic or non-Islamic origins, sensuous music). Not only the musical characteristics have determined for a particular type of music its position on the continuum between encouraged and discouraged. Each genre of music has also been judged by its contextual conformance to a proper Islamic environment; that is, the time, the place and the associates involved in the performance were equally crucial to its acceptance or rejection.[3] The charges, therefore, which are sometimes made that Islamic culture has no religious music, or that Islam proscribed all music, are gross misrepresentations. Islamic culture has actually put great support and effort into its religious music and has invested the musical rendering of the Quran with such care and esteem that it has acted as a prototype for all other musical expression in the culture throughout the centuries. Islam neither proscribed all musical art, nor did it dictate an unquestionable acceptance of all forms of music. Instead, it directed its condemnation or disapproval against certain forms of musical art which were felt to be harmful for aesthetic and/or moral reasons.[4] These, and not all music, have been known as "musiqa." The condemnations were never understood, even by the most conservative writers,[5] as including all forms of sound-art.

It is obvious therefore that Islam as a religious ideology has had a considerable effect on the very use and definition of musical art. As the following paragraphs will show, it has been no less determinant of the aesthetic and technical characteristics of the art.

AESTHETIC CHARACTERISTICS

Content

Abstract Quality

The music of Islamic culture falls into two broad categories which give evidence of rhythmic characteristics and creative process. One of these types is designated here as unmetered improvisation. That expression applies to all improvisatory vocal or instrumental performances which have a free rhythm, i.e., a melodic line not based on the regular recurrence of a rhythmic pattern (see Figure 8.1). The second category will apply to all musical performances of a composed or traditional origin that are marked by a regularly recurring rhythmic pattern or meter (see Figure 8.2). Labels for both types are known to have existed at least as early as the fifteenth century,[6] and the presence of both categories is documentable throughout the Islamic period.[7]

Tawhid, the Islamic ideology, has influenced the aesthetic characteristics of both categories of musical performance. This influence has pervaded the message as well as the organization of that message— in other words, both the content and the structure of these musical works. The Muslim artist and the Muslim spectator have demanded an art that would turn attention to a divine Being who is neither human nor part of nature. This has necessitated the rejection of figural art, while encouraging abstraction and the creation of a vast vocabulary of nonrepresentational or stylized motifs. This development in the arts was the direct result of the positive demands of the ideology of the culture, not, as has often been argued, a reaction to subsequent historical condemnations or to prohibitions by the Prophet. Such negative

Figure 8.1. Unmetered Improvisation. Quranic chant.

pronouncements were themselves consequents of the same ideological message rather than original causes for the unique quality of Islamic art.

In the musical arts, which by their very nature are far less descriptive and specific in their symbolic message-carrying than the visual arts, an analogous abstract quality is maintained. Whether metered or unmetered, improvised or composed, the musical genres of Islamic culture display little if any attempt to be musically imitative of beings, events, objects or moods. Performances proceed without drastic

Figure 8.2. Rhythmic meter. Muwashshah.

change of tempo, volume, or style, despite the constantly varying verbal material to which those elements are a musical setting. Pitch levels and melodic modes may change, but investigations have proven that these changes show little or no correspondence to junctures in literary meaning.[8] Compositions or improvisations, therefore, are commonly designated by the name of their melodic mode rather than by a descriptive title. Since a musical setting is not irrevocably bound to a single set of words, different tunes for setting a single poem or different lyrics for a single tune have been acceptable and frequent practices.[9]

Infinite Patterning

The Islamic musical arts, like their counterparts of the visual arts, should not be defined merely by their avoidance of nature as subject matter. Much more important than this negative predilection is their positive contribution to finding a new aesthetic stimulus for intuiting the divine without the use of literal symbolism or representation of nature. An explicit connection with nature would compromise the Islamic expression of tawhid. The breakthrough of the Muslims was to embody an exhaustive repertoire of tonal and durational patterns which give the impression of infinite continuity. It is these musical patterns, rather than extended melodies of varying moods, which could draw the human mind to the contemplation of God.

The infinite pattern was, therefore, the unique Islamic contribution. It involved a number of formal characteristics which were combined to insure the aesthetic impression of infinity. These structural characteristics exist in an inexhaustible variety of musical as well as visual instantiations.

Form

Divisions

One requisite for the aesthetic impression of infinite pattern is the division of the work of art into units or "modules" which can serve as the basic building blocks of the composition. In music, these modules combining tonal and durational motifs are synonymous with the independent phrases separated by periods of silence which are found in the chanting of the Quran or any poetic passage. They are equally recognizable in the distinctly separated passages of an instrumental improvisation.

Not only do such unmetered improvisations embody structures emphasizing segmentation but the metered musical examples are equally illustrative of additive organization. Although in metered performances the modules or units are not generally separated by pauses of silence, half or full cadences provide the culturally demanded closures. Short instrumental motifs or interjections are often added to emphasize endings of units (see Figure 8.3).

Modular Combinations

A second structural characteristic of the Islamic infinite pattern is its combination of modules to create successively larger entities internal to the overall design. As we have noted above, tonal and durational motifs are combined into individual unmetered improvisational or metered phrase modules. These in turn combine to form larger multi-

Figure 8.3. Sample *Lazimah* motifs.

phrase segments corresponding, in the former, to a portion of improvisation on a particular segment of the melodic mode in use or, in the latter, to a musical period, i.e., a composed vocal or instrumental sentence comprising an antecedent and a consequent phrase.

Such combinations of modules become the units of still larger organizations when, for example, they join solo verse to choral refrain, instrumental improvisation to orchestral interlude, or free rhythmed improvisation to metered refrain. In turn, these parts are combined with other pieces to create suite-like structures that are known by various names in different parts of the Muslim World.[10]

Never-Ending Quality

In order to convey an aesthetic impression of infinite pattern, the Islamic musical art product must embody never-ending continuity. The repeated succession of units sets up that demanded impression in the mind of the percipient. Not only are the modules repeated in seemingly never-ending fashion, but modular combinations proliferate in succession for as long as performer inspiration and audience interest demand. No segment closing is decisively more final than another, no mini-climax within a segment more crucial than its neighbor. These musical patterns, therefore, have no precise beginning, no single dominant climax, and no definite conclusion. Such characteristics have caused outsiders to complain of repetitiveness in the music of the Muslim peoples or to bemoan its lack of unity. But non-repetition and overall unity are characteristics which are antagonistic to the impression of infinite patterning and to the creation of an abstract art expressive of the Islamic ideology. They may be expected and admired in another art tradition, but they are not apropos of Islamic art.

Intricacy

The fourth structural characteristic of music which insures its fulfilling the aesthetic goals of Islamic culture is an intricacy of tonal and rhythmic movement. This arises, in part, through the use of a larger vocabulary of interval sizes than Western ears—attuned to half or whole tone intervals only—are accustomed. Several sizes of whole tones and semitones are used in the modal scales of the Muslim peoples in addition to the one-and-a-half tone interval which has become so typical of Muslim world scales that it conjures up impressions of "the East" in Hollywood-style musical backgrounds.

This wider tonal vocabulary is used in a great variety of combinations which form scalar segments of three, four, or five tones. Similar or different segments of higher or lower pitch are combined to form a vast number of one or two octave scales on which the improvisation or composed melody is based. We should consider these combinations as being theoretically understood rather than always practically experienced in a section of musical performance since the smaller scalar units usually retain their autonomy and are used successively rather than being absorbed in the larger entity of the octave or double octave scale.

The rhythmic base is no less complicated and fertile. Rather than a series of easily recognizable two-, three-, four-, or six-beat measures with which Western ears are familiar, the Muslims have preferred the unmetered improvisatory performance or the complicated meters of their rhythmic modes. These modes not only combine various internal combinations of durations in a prescribed sequence but determine different strengths and timbres for the beats within the cycle as well (see Figure 8.4).

A great variety of grace notes, trills, turns, mordents, glissandos, and other embellishments add further tonal and durational complication to any vocal or instrumental line. Short notes of varying lengths

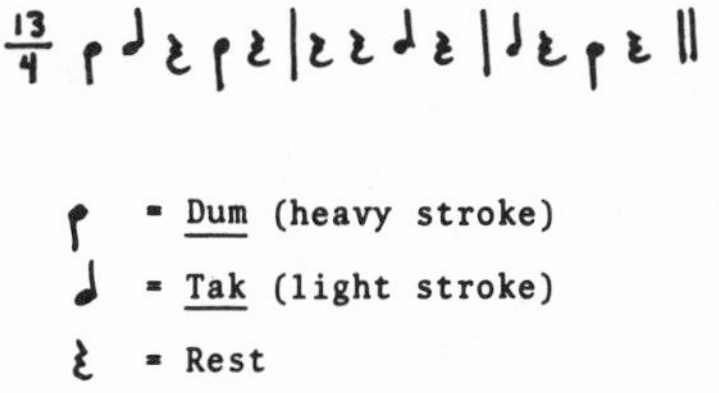

Figure 8.4. Rhythmic mode *(Iqa)* used in Muwashshah of Figure 8.2.

are the rule in all performances. The complication and variety of these durations often make transcription of the performance extremely difficult if not impossible. Long, sustained tones are rare. Instead, performers repeat the tones in rapid succession or ornament them to increase the impression of intricacy.

TECHNICAL CHARACTERISTICS

Islam the religion has also been important in determining the technical characteristics of music in Islamic culture—that is, those characteristics that pertain specifically to the practice or execution of music. Here is found a different level of religious influence, one which is less direct than that already described. Instead of moving from ideological premise to consequent aesthetic characteristic, the religious core is seen here as having first determined the chanted rendition of the Quran according to the aesthetic principles outlined above. Then that art became the model on which other musical expression was patterned.

How could this be accomplished? One reason for the permeating influence of Quranic chant is the fact that, as the word of God, this art has commanded special interest and reverence. Secondly, the Quran has been an almost ubiquitous accompaniment of life. It has not only been recited in the daily prayers and the special rituals held during Ramadan (the month of fasting), but also at the public meeting, the festive celebration, and the social events commemorating births, circumcisions, weddings, and funerals. It has formed a part of each day's radio and television broadcast time. Its technical characteristics have become, thereby, so much a part of the daily experience of the Muslim peoples that it has affected all other genres of music in Islamic culture. At least four technical characteristics can be cited as evidencing this permeating influence of Quranic chant on the other genres of musical art.

Monophonic

The first of these characteristics is the monophonic or single line melodic texture of Quranic chant. This feature has pervaded all the musical genres, whether of unmetered improvisational or metered musical variety. Solo performance, as in the chanted recitations of the Quran, is the rule. Even when accompaniments support the vocal or instrumental soloist, or when a number of vocalists or instrumentalists perform together, the musicans follow more or less faithfully the single melodic line. Even orchestral music resembles the monophonic prototype. When two or more performers are involved, the "slightly or elaborately modified versions of the same melody" constitute what is known as heterophony.[11] Harmony[12] has never been an important feature of this music.

Modal

The recitation of the Quran is based on the use of modal scale segments of three, four, or more contiguous tones. The improvisation makes use of this segment of the modal scale for as long as inspiration dictates. Then another segment, beginning from the same base note but with a different combination of intervals, or one beginning on a higher or lower tone, is utilized for subsequent phrases. No sequence of modal segments or extent of their use is predetermined. Even the same reciter will vary these features in different recitations of the same Quranic passage. This segmental use of modal materials is also common in the unmetered improvisation and metered music performances of the non-Quranic sound-art of the Muslims. Any instrumental or vocal improvisation falls under similar modal usage. In the secular art forms, conformance to certain prescribed rules for the use of modal scales and rules is more likely to be observed than in the scriptural chant. This is a result of the greater influence of music theory on the secular musicians.

Improvisatory

Quranic chant is an improvisatory art. A chanted "reading" is never performed in exactly the same way in subsequent versions, even when done by the same chanter. The insistence on the improvisatory quality of the chant has militated against any written notation of the Quran.[13] To prescribe in musical notation what actual sounds should accompany the verses would be to fossilize them and destroy their uniquely improvisatory quality.

In the other genres of unmetered music, improvisation is equally important. Though metered genres are based on composed or traditional tunes, they also evidence a high level of improvisatory skill in the rendering. Vocalists and instrumentalists display their musical expertise and skill by improvising subtle changes of embellishment or structure into the musical line. No performer of any musical passage would wish to render a repetition in exactly the same way it was previously performed.

It is for this reason that notation among the Muslims was not widely used as a prescriptive aid to performance. The improvisatory nature of the music precluded the recording with accuracy of what the performer would sing or play. Systems for rhythmic or melodic notation were invented and used for theoretical purposes from the earliest centuries, but the specificity of those systems was never developed to the degree which became necessary for the successful performance of the multi-line contrapuntal and harmonic music of the European tradition.

Vocal Importance

The Quranic prototype is a vocal and solo musical art. In many parts of the Muslim world it is generally performed by a male chanter, but in southeast Asia (Indonesia, Malaysia and the Philippines) female reciters have also achieved great proficiency in this art.

The importance of the human voice carries from the Quranic model to the rest of musical performance in Islamic culture. The human voice is indeed the most important "instrument" throughout the Muslim world. Vocal performances are often heard without, or with only minimal, accompaniment. Sometimes that accompaniment may be simple hand clapping or foot stamping. At other times a percussion instrument, a melodic instrument, or even a small orchestral ensemble furnishes support for the voice. These additions to the vocal line "shadow" the soloist faithfully or may repeat the line after its solo rendition. At other times, the instrument provides rhythmic underlay for the soloist or adds the interludes and interjections which mark the separations between modules or phrase segments.

Vocal music not only statistically dominates the musical genres of the Muslim world, but is even determinant of instrumental styles of performance. When instruments do take over the prerogatives of the

soloist, they remain faithful to the monophonic and declamatory texture and style of the vocal art.

In order, then, to understand the music of the Muslim peoples, it
is necessary to be aware of two levels of influence from the religious
core of the culture (tawhid) on that musical art. One level involves
direct influence of the ideology on the aesthetic content and form of the
art. The other level of influence is a circuitous one, which first affected
Quranic chant, and then, in turn, the other forms of sound-art modeled
on that prototype.

VARIETY IN THE MUSIC OF THE MUSLIM PEOPLES

The two levels of influence described above have resulted in many
elements of unity in the music of Islamic culture. It should also be
noted that there are other elements of the musical art of the Muslims
which have provided scope for variety and change. It is in such elements that the pre-Islamic and indigenous musical styles had their
influence on the music of Islamic culture. It is in these elements that
regional variety is revealed and tolerated.

Intervals

While the vocabulary of interval sizes used in various regions of
the Muslim world has been uniformly wide, each region has held preferences for certain interval sizes which another region may not have
emphasized. Variety of interval use is an important feature distinguishing the music of one region from that of another. It is a feature
that is recognized by even the most musically uninformed of listeners,
though those persons often do not understand the reason for their
ability to differentiate between the music of various localities.

Tonal and Durational Motifs

The favored motifs combined to produce musical phrases have
varied from century to century, from region to region, from village to

village, and even from performer to performer. Often a particular region will reveal the influence of a particular performer, or school of performers, by the consistent use of a corpus of such motifs. Familiarity with these motifs makes performances utilizing them particularly pleasurable to the initiated listener. Providing an aspect of unity in the performance literature of a particular time or place, such regionally significant melodic or rhythmic patterns, at the same time, are factors differentiating musical sub-cultures within the Islamic world.

Melodic and Rhythmic Modes

Melodic and rhythmic modes have been another source of variety and change in the music of the Muslim peoples over the centuries. The modal combinations used by their contemporaries and described by al-Kindi, al-Farabi, Ibn Sina and the later theorists of the pre-modern period, though based on common principles, have displayed a great deal of variety in their names and composition. Twentieth century theorists in the Muslim world describe still other variants of the general modal schemes. Indeed, we find not one group of modes popular in the contemporary Muslim world; instead, each region favors its own set of melodic and rhythmic modes which may be used less consistently or not at all in another region.

Instruments

Though Islamic culture has been described as one in which the vocal tradition was dominant, the Muslim peoples have developed a great variety of instruments for performing music. Certain instruments have been favored for some performance contexts while others have been used in other situations. These instruments have varied as to construction details and names from region to region and from century to century. Yet there are discernible archetypes which are found to have had continuing significance. Instruments, therefore, continue the theme of reciprocal factors of unity and variety in the musical contribution of Islamic culture.

Figure 8.5. Plucked lute.

Chordophones

Three types of instruments which sound by the vibration of strings have been consistently important among the Muslims. The most widely used of these has been the plucked lute (both short and long necked varieties). Many sizes, shapes of sound box, materials, number of strings, and tunings have been used for these instruments.

Certainly the most important instrument of the Muslims for solo and ensemble performance as well as theoretical illustration has been a variety of plucked lute with wide body, deeply rounded back, short neck, and bent back pegbox (see Figure 8.5). It has been used both as a solo and as an accompaniment instrument. A second important type of stringed instrument used by the Muslims is the bowed chordophone, made with varying dimensions, shapes, and materials. It has been known from the earliest centuries as an instrument for accompanying the vocal soloist, and it has also been used as a solo and orchestral instrument (see Figure 8.6). Variants of this "fiddle" have been used

Figure 8.6. Viol.

Figure 8.7. Psaltery.

from the Atlantic to the Philippines. Most of the lutes and viols have been unfretted in order to facilitate performance of the wide variety of intervals and melodic modes demanded in the music of the culture.

A third important chordophone which has been only slightly less important for the Muslims is that designated as a psaltery by Western musicologists. It comprises a flat wooden sound box overlaid with a varying number of strings, sometimes tuned singly, but more often with three strings tuned to each pitch (see Figure 8.7). This instrument has usually been plucked with plectra fastened to the fingers. In some parts of the Muslim world a similar instrument played with mallets (that is the dulcimer) has also been used (e.g., the santur of contemporary Turkey, Iraq, and Iran). Harp- or lyre-type instruments have also had exemplifications in many regions of the Muslim world.

Aerophones

Instruments in which sound is produced by setting a column of air in motion have also been used in many varieties by the Muslim peoples. Instruments that could be compared to the horn or trumpet, with either a cylindrical or conical bore, have been particularly popular for military ensembles. More widespread in significance, however, have been the various types of woodwind instruments. The two most important of these aerophones have been the end-blown flute (see Figure 8.8) and the double-reed, or oboe-type instruments (see Figure 8.9).[14] The former is a simple instrument, most often made of reed cane with finger holes bored to produce the tones of a particular melodic mode. The player blows across the top end of the cane without aid of sounding reed or mouthpiece. Single reed (clarinet-type) and whistle mouthpiece

Figure 8.8. End-blown flute.

Figure 8.9. Double-reed aerophone.

(recorder-type) wind instruments have also had many exemplifications and varieties.

Membranophones

Membranophones are instruments on which the tone is produced by the vibration of a stretched membrane or skin. Those used by the Muslims include cylindrical drums, barrel drums, waisted drums, kettle drums, goblet drums and frame drums (i.e., tambourines). If any of these could be regarded as more important or widely used than the others, it would probably be either the single-headed goblet drum (see

Figure 8.10. Goblet drum.

Figure 8.10) or the tambourine. These two percussion instruments have been used for a wide variety of genres and performance situations by Muslims of every continent and century.

Idiophones

Idiophones, that is, those instruments made of a sonorous material which produce their own sound, are also represented among the instruments of the Muslims. Some of these are sounded by shaking (e.g., jingles and rattles), others by percussion techniques (bells, gongs, and rhythm sticks), and still others by concussion (cymbals). These instruments have generally been avoided in religious and serious music but have been regularly employed in the military bands which have been prominent as performance groups both during war and peace time in Muslim lands.

This discussion summarizes the common aesthetic and technical characteristics in the musical arts of the Islamic world. In addition, it outlines those elements that evidence variety in that musical art. Such a description of music is certainly necessary for the non-Muslim who wishes to understand the people and the culture of the Islamic world, but it is also crucial for the contemporary Muslim. The latter, standing in today's world of rapid change and wholesale acculturation trends, is often set culturally adrift by the alien aesthetic, social, and economic bombardment to which he is subjected. An understanding of his own aesthetic traditions—of what is essential and what is variable—could help provide the bedrock of stability which is necessary if the future is to bring about the preservation and a new flowering of the Islamic spirit. That new flowering must be one that is produced in the light of new influences and developments, but it must be in keeping with the core ideology which has molded the Islamic musical tradition for the past fourteen centuries. It must, therefore, find new techniques and methods for building on that unity which is so prominently represented in the aesthetic and technical characteristics of the music of the past. At the same time, it must create new expressions of those elements of variety which have provided the necessary flexibility in a musical tradition which has proven acceptable and meaningful over such a wide expanse of time and space.

NOTES

1. *Tawhid* is the active intensive verbal noun from the root *wahada*. Literally, it implies "intensive unification."

2. See *"MUSIQA"* entry in Lois Ibsen al Faruqi, *An Annotated Glossary of Arabic Music Terms* (Westport, Conn.: Greenwood Press, 1981), p. 209; and Lois al Faruqi, "The Shari'ah on Music and Musicians," *Islamic Thought and Culture,* ed. Ismail R. al Faruqi (Washington, D.C.: International Institute of Islamic Thought, 1982), pp. 27–37.

3. These three environmental elements (time, place, and associates) were discussed by the famous writer and philosopher, Abu Hamid al Ghazali (d. 1111) in his defense of that music which is utilized in an Islamically acceptable way. See al Ghazali, *Ihya' 'Ulum al-Din,* trans. Duncan B. Macdonald as "Emotional Religion in Islam as Affected by Music and Singing," *Journal of the Royal Asiatic Society.* (1901): 195–252, 705–748; (1902): 1–28.

4. See al Faruqi, "The Shari'ah on Music and Musicians," for a more detailed analysis and a grid developing a hierarchy of the various musical genres.

5. See Taqi al-Din Ibn Taymiyyah, "Kitab al-Sama' wal-Raqs," *Majmuah al-Rasail al-Kubra* (Cairo: Matbaah Muhammad Ali Subayh, 1966), 2:295–330, where we read that there are various kinds of sound art, "some of which are forbidden, [while others are] unfavored, indifferent, recommended, or commendable."

6. Evidence for this can be found in a fifteenth-century anonymous treatise, translated into French in Baron Rodolphe d'Erlanger, *La musique arabe* (Paris: Librairie Orientaliste Paul Geuthner, 1939), 4:232–35. See also Michael Allawerdi, *Falsafah al-Musiqa al-Sharqiyyah* (Damascus: Ibn Zaydun, 1949), p. 548; al Faruqi, *An Annotated Glossary,* pp. 233, 239.

7. Henry George Farmer, *A History of Arabian Music to the XIIIth Century* (London: Luzac, 1967), pp. 18, 49–51.

8. Lois Ibsen al Faruqi, "The Nature of the Musical Art of Islamic Culture: A Theoretical and Empirical Study of Arabian Music," Ph.D. diss. (Syracuse: Syracuse University, 1974), pp. 281–90; Lois Ibsen al Faruqi, "Muwashshah: A Vocal Form in Islamic Culture," *Ethnomusicology* 19, no. 1 (1975):6–10.

9. This results in phenomena similar to the "contrafacta" of medieval Europe. See Gustave Reese, *Music in the Middle Ages* (New York: Norton, 1940), p. 218. Such adaptations of pre-existent tunes to new lyrics were used by the troubadors as well as by the earlier Arab minstrels of Spain.

10. See Lois Ibsen al Faruqi, "The Suite in Islamic Culture and History," *The Concept of a Suite in the Islamic Near East,* ed. J. Pacholczyk (Tucson, Ariz.: Pachart, forthcoming).

11. Don M. Randel, *Harvard Concise Dictionary of Music* (Cambridge, Mass.: Harvard University Press, 1978), p. 220.

12. Harmony is defined by Randel, ibid., p. 211, as "the simultaneous sounding of pitches (i.e., chords) as opposed to simultaneously sounded melodies or lines, the latter termed counterpoint."

13. Salih Amin, an Egyptian musician, is reported by Labib al-Said, *Al-Jam' al-Sawti al-Awwal lil-Quran al-Karim* or *al-Mushaf al-Murattal* (Cairo: Dar al-Katib al-'Arabi lil-Tibaah wal-Nashr, 1967), pp. 342–43, to have engaged himself in notating the

Quran, a pursuit condemned by al Said. Another Egyptian, Abd al Wahhab, proposed to make a complete notated version of the cantillated Quran. The scholars at al Azhar University made such a show of opposition that the man was forced to give up his project. Si Hamza Boubakeur, "Psalmodie coranique," *Encyclopédie de musiques sacrées,* ed. Jacques Porte (Paris: Editions Labergerie, 1968), 1:389.

14. See al Faruqi, *An Annotated Glossary,* Index of English Musical Terms, "Flute" and "Oboe," for various names which have been given to these two instruments.

9

~~~~~~

Muslims in the United States

AN OVERVIEW OF ORGANIZATIONS, DOCTRINES, AND PROBLEMS

Akbar Muhammad

*A*NY GENERAL ACCOUNT of the Muslim presence in America is necessarily one of economic, social, and cultural struggle. American Muslims are a disparate group of people searching for an acceptable *modus vivendi* in a world of appealing materialism, customs, ideals, and ideologies which offend their sensibilities and conflict with the traditions of their faith. In times past, the West, in arenas across the seas and oceans, challenged their co-religionists and forefathers on military and religious grounds. Now the descendants, whether willing immigrants to the West or brought to this country against their will as slaves, are determined simply to fare well here, economically, socially, and religiously.[1]

The ethnic groups that form the American Muslim population are mainly of Asian and African origin. There are a number of Muslims of specific East European heritage and thousands of European-American (white American) converts to Islam who are by and large descendants of early Christian settlers and later emigrants from western Europe. As one would expect, they manifest no particular European cultural tradition. They are similar to African-Americans (black Americans) who generally do not exhibit and have not adopted specific African traditions.

The number of Muslims in America is unknown. Several writers and organizations have attempted to render reliable estimates using various statistical methods and demographic data. These estimates range roughly between one and a half and three million.[2] In view of the fact that immigration, naturalization, and organizational membership figures are unreliable, and other relevant factors have not been studied sufficiently, none of the estimates seem very convincing. Perhaps the largest group are Arabic-speakers, followed by Iranians, Turks, and African-Americans.

It is almost impossible to document the first Muslim arrival in America. Given the fact that Muslims have been a seafaring people since the seventh century, one wonders whether they risked the long voyage across the Atlantic Ocean, centuries before Christopher Columbus sailed from Italy. Indeed, there is a report of an attempt to reach the Americas by early fourteenth-century sailors of the West African kingdom of Mali; some writers believe that they made the journey.[3] More plausible information about early Muslim arrivals in the "New World" is to be found in the literature concerning the companions of European explorers. They included persons of Northwest and West African ancestry who were residents of southern Spain, modern Portugal, and Italy. However, we have little indication that these early visitors remained long on the North American continent.[4]

Undoubtedly, the Atlantic slave trade was the single most important vehicle for the pre-nineteenth century transportation of Muslims to the Americas. The peak of this economic enterprise was reached in the mid-eighteenth century, but sources indicate that there was a small but continuous flow of African Muslim captives into the American colonies well into the nineteenth century. Unfortunately, we do not have enough information to estimate the number of Muslims enslaved in the United States. However, the known biographies, autobiographies, and the material concerning their attempts to gain freedom seem to suggest that perhaps they numbered in the thousands. Given the general tendency of slave masters to record the *noble* or *royal* background of slaves, it is not surprising that we do not have accounts for more than a few Muslim captives who appear to have been recruited from lower social ranks. Therefore, one should be cautious in estimating their numbers, as the slave merchant's area of operations was sufficiently large and in the interior of West Africa to ensure the victimization of Mande, Wolof, Tuareg, Hausa, Yoruba and other *ordinary* Islamized peoples. Contemporary research indicates that the majority of them were transported to Brazil; nevertheless, significant numbers, though small in proportion, existed in the Caribbean and the United States.[5]

EMERGENCE OF THE COMMUNITY

The period from the mid-nineteenth century to the present was a turning point in the chronology of the Muslim presence in America as it marked the voluntary immigration of Muslims from various lands. They came from such modern states as Syria, Jordan, Iraq, Egypt, India, the Soviet Union, Turkey, Yugoslavia and Albania. The early immigrants settled in different areas of the United States, depending upon economic opportunities and the localities in which they had relatives and friends. Although many of them were from rural and small-town communities, they tended to make their homes in and near the commercial and industrial centers in New York, Pennsylvania, Illinois, New Jersey, Massachusetts, Ohio, California, and Michigan. With little education and lack of proficiency in English, they remained on the periphery of American society, peddling their wares or seeking employment as low-level industrial and agricultural laborers. Generally, they socialized with members of their own linguistic and religious groups, familial cohesion being socially and economically important. The life of the Muslim immigrant was a difficult one relative to that of his or her Christian countryman who often was aided by American missionary organizations, churches, and individuals. Neither Islam nor the Ottoman (Turkish) Empire, which officially ruled much of the Arabic-speaking and Eastern European lands, had been endeared to the American heart.

The first immigrants were understandably more concerned with finding a comfortable economic niche in America than with propagating their faith. Therefore, their early organizations consisted of prayerplaces or small mosques located in rental residential premises. They served the dual purpose of religious and cultural preservation. If believers did proselytize, it was on a very small scale, limited to the meager number of Americans with whom they had constant contact.

It is widely believed that historically the first Muslims of American birth were the product of immigrant Arab proselytization among poor African-Americans. That is not true. On the contrary, the first recorded American convert to Islam seems to have been a rather obscure European-American, the Reverend Norman, a Methodist missionary in Turkey who embraced Islam in the 1870s.[6] He was followed in the next decade by another European-American, Muhammad Alexander Russell Webb, about whom much is now known.[7]

The earliest organization to attempt directly the conversion of Americans to Islam seems to have been the American Islamic Propaganda movement. Founded in 1893, it was headed by the erudite and imposing Muhammad Webb. The son of a newspaper editor and publisher in Hudson, Columbia County in Upstate New York, Webb was educated in private schools and colleges in his home state and in Massachusetts. As a young man he worked for well known jewelry houses in New York, Chicago, and St. Louis. The jewelry profession, however, quickly gave way to journalism and politics. Either as publisher or editor, Webb worked for more than seven newspapers in various cities in Missouri, New York, and New Jersey. Intellectually, he became an avid reader of Indian or "Oriental" philosophy and joined the spiritual and philosophical movement known as the Theosophical Society. His esoteric interests and the support he received from various prominent businessmen and Democratic politicians gained for him in 1887 the diplomatic post of American Consul General in the Philippines.

From Manila he corresponded with Badruddin Abdullah Kur, a prominent Indian official of the Municipal Council of Bombay. This correspondence led to a visit to Manila of two Indian Muslims, Webb's conversion to Islam, his resignation from the diplomatic service, and a two-month tour of India, during which he lectured on Islam and met several of India's leading Muslim thinkers. With their financial support, he returned to New York as a "missionary" in early 1893, founded a publication, *The Moslem World,* for the propagation of Islam, and lectured in several American cities. In 1892, responding to a query about his conversion to Islam, Webb said:

> I adopted this religion because I found, after protracted study, that it was the best and only system adapted to the spiritual needs of humanity. . . . About eleven years ago I became interested in the study of Oriental religions. . . I saw Mill and Locke, Kant, Hegel, Fichte, Huxley, and many other more or less learned writers discoursing with a great show of wisdom concerning protoplasm and monads, and yet not one of them could tell me what the soul was or what became of it after death . . . my adoption of Islam was not the result of misguided sentiment, blind credulity, or sudden emotional impulse, but it was born of earnest, honest, persistent, unprejudiced study and investigation and an intense desire to know the truth. The essence of the true faith of Islam is resignation to the will of God and its corner stone is prayer. It teaches universal benevolence, and requires purity of mind, purity of action,

purity of speech and perfect physical cleanliness. It, beyond doubt, is the simplest and most elevating form of religion known to man.[8]

Webb became an ebullient critic of "Church-Christians" and of Christian missionary activity in the Muslim world and the most prominent contemporary defender of Islam. He wrote three books on Islam, including an illustrated prayer manual. When financial support from India became irregular, an association with the Ottoman Sultan Abdul Hamid II gained for Webb not only an alternative source of aid but also a permanent honorary Turkish consulship in New York.

By the time of his death in 1916, he had spoken to audiences which included some of America's most prominent religious and social thinkers, including Mark Twain. He established some seven branches, called "circles," of the Moslem Brotherhood or the American Islamic Propaganda in various East Coast and Midwestern cities. Although Webb's organization died prematurely, there can be little doubt that he and other members of his organization influenced subsequent efforts to establish Islam in the United States. At least two memorial meetings have been organized in his honor, the last being as late as 1943.

Before Webb's death, Islam began to emerge as a religious and nationalistic phenomenon amongst African-Americans. The most significant of these early movements was the Moorish-American Science Temple, inaugurated in 1913 in Newark, New Jersey. Like Webb, its founder, Noble Drew Ali (born Timothy Drew) of North Carolina, had been introduced to Oriental philosophy. Having received little formal education, he worked at menial jobs including one as a pullman porter. The most striking precepts of his movement may be summarized as follows: Buddha, Confucius, Zoroaster, Jesus, and Muhammad were prophets, and Drew Ali was spiritually related to them. African-Americans were considered "Asiatics" (Asians), and descendants of the Moabites and Canaanites; Islam is the natural religion of all Asiatics, and Christianity is the religion of Europeans; African-Americans should avoid unnecessry contact with the "palefaces" (European-Americans); Hell does not exist, and Heaven is a state of mind. The small sacred book of the movement, *The Holy Koran of the Moorish Science Temple of America,* was compiled by the founder and contains separate pictures of himself and King Ibn Saud of Saudi Arabia; the organization's charter was granted by Egypt. It is apparent that the Moorish-American Science Temple doctrines were reflective not only of Eastern philosophical thought, but also heterodox Christi-

anity, spiritualism, and reverse racial ideas espoused by some of the
reputed African-American writers of the early twentieth century.[9]

"The Moors" or Moorish-Americans, as Noble Drew Ali's followers were known, established branches in several American cities,
and appealed to thousands of African-Americans. Noble Drew Ali died
either in 1929 or 1930. Although considerably reduced in numbers, a
modified version of the Moorish-American movement still exists in
some American cities.

While Drew Ali was preaching his ideas, the doctrines of the well-
known Indian reformist movement, the Ahmadiyya, were being dis-
seminated by its missionaries who arrived in the United States in 1920
and later. The founder, Ghulam Ahmad (d. 1908), was believed to be a
reincarnation of Buddha, Jesus, and Prophet Muhammad. He sought to
present a religio-social set of beliefs which would appeal to Muslims,
Hindus, and Christians.[10]

The Ahmadiyya's emphasis on what they called "scientific" and
"rational" precepts, and certain points of convergence between their
doctrines and Protestant Christianity and Western popular philosophy,
are amongst the primary reasons for their appeal in America. Unlike
the Moorish-American Science Temple organization, the proselytizers
of the Ahmadiyya Movement attempted to convert European-
Americans and African-Americans; however, African-Americans were
far more responsive. Their most active centers were in Chicago, Washington, Detroit, St. Louis, and New York.

An influential but obscure Muslim organization appeared in the
1920s in Brooklyn, New York. The Islamic Mission of America, Inc.,
was founded by Shaikh Daoud Ahmed Faisal who is said to have been
born in Granada (the West Indies) in 1892, of a Moroccan father and a
Syrian mother. Several individuals, however, believe that his parents
were Afro-Caribbeans. In about 1924, he began teaching Sunni ("orthodox") Islam and Arabic amongst African-Americans, thousands of
whom embraced the religion. Twenty years later he is reported to have
"established the Islamic Mission of America as a non-governmental
member of the United Nations and attended UN sessions on a regular
basis trying to insure that Islam was represented in a correct manner."[11]
Undoubtedly, his followers were amongst the Harlem Muslims described by Roi Ottley in 1943:

> Harlem's Moslems run into several thousand. Unlike Hindus, Moslems
> hold an annual religious festival, I'd-ul-duha [sic., Idul Adha] (Day of
> Sacrifice). Since they have no mosque, the faithful worship in private

homes and hired halls, where on Saturday mornings their children study the Koran. They lived quietly in Harlem, but during their festivals they don rich robes, shawls, turbans, and fezzes of their native land, and the women wear gorgeous brocades and heavy decorative jewelry. Ordinarily Moslems wear American dress, for most of them have lived in the United States more than twenty years. By occupation they are students, bellboys, waiters, garage mechanics, janitors, factory workers, and insurance agents. As a group, they have little of the nationalistic fervor that characterizes the Hindus—at least such is not apparent. But they possess a religious fervor that is expressed in much missionary work among American Negroes. . . . Whether they are Africans, Arabs, Tarters or American Negroes, Moors, Persians, or whites, Moslems intermarry. The racial flow back and forth defies classification.[12]

Shaikh Faisal, who seems to have had little or no academic training in Islam, was a passionate defender of orthodox Islam. He felt obliged to correct, in person or through his writings, the divergent doctrines of other leaders, including Elijah Muhammad. He provided living and prayer facilities to foreign Muslim students and delegates to the United Nations, and maintained good relations with Muslim religious and political leaders abroad. During a conversation with the writer in Cairo in 1966, he expressed great admiration for Saudi and Egyptian interest in spreading Islam in America and their efforts to educate American Muslims. His death in 1980 was mourned by many Muslims in New York.

The most prominent organization, the Nation of Islam (also known as "The Black Muslims") was founded by an immigrant in 1931. Variously known as Wallace D. Fard, Wallace Fard Muhammad and W. F. Muhammad, he is said to have been born in Mecca, Saudi Arabia, of a European mother and an Arabian father. Allegedly, the latter was a member of a god-producing family. His marriage to a European woman was consummated in order to produce a son who would be physically acceptable to African- and European-Americans. His mission would be to liberate the former from their "mental bondage" and to reunite them with their brothers in the Muslim world. Fard Muhammad is reputed to have been fluent in several European and Middle Eastern languages, and very learned. Briefly, according to this author's research he was probably of Turco-Persian parentage, somewhat versed in medieval Islamic astrology and a deviant form of Protestantism, and held a number of Bahai and Shiah views.

The ascription of divinity to W. F. Muhammad was a gradual

process. Initially, he represented himself to his Detroit followers as a brother and an emissary of the Muslim world. He assured them that "racially" he was one of them, and that all belonged to the first inhabitants of earth, the "Original Black Man." Subsequently, he was known as the Mahdi, Prophet and the Son of Man, who had been expected for two thousand years. Finally, it is alleged that he upgraded his status and announced that he was the Supreme Ruler, Allah or God in person.

The main tenets of the embryonic Nation of Islam showed some similarities with the earlier sects, but there were also acute differences. These teachings were particular to the Nation of Islam and did not reflect the normative doctrines of the Islamic religion. Apart from prophethood, God was reduced to a human being. European-Americans were considered Satan, individually and collectively, and were produced by the "Original Asiatic Black Man." All other peoples were likewise created by the Black "Asiatics"; African-Americans belong to a higher order of humanity but were oppressed providentially by the European-Americans. The Day of Judgment will be an event of the late twentieth century and will mark the destruction of American international, political, and economic hegemony. Heaven, thought to be in Mecca or the Muslim world, was said to be a human state of material and spiritual peace; Hell was supposed to be in America, which would be consumed by fire. The Quran is the sacred book, but it has been misinterpreted by most Muslim scholars and will be superceded by another revelation. Fard Muhammad profited from his superior knowledge amongst his Detroit following and sought to build a rival movement against his erstwhile associates in the splinter Moorish-American movement, some of whom had joined him.

In 1934, he disappeared mysteriously but was said to have maintained spiritual contact with his former associate and successor, Elijah Muhammad (born Elijah Poole). The son of a Baptist preacher in Georgia, he moved to Detroit in 1923 in search of a better material life. With little formal education and no particular skill, he was an unemployed father of six children when he became acquainted with Fard Muhammad in 1931. Under his leadership the deification of W. F. Muhammad was reinforced, Elijah Muhammad being raised to the status of a divine messenger to African-Americans. He was to declare, "Almighty God, Allah, who appeared in the person of Master Fard Muhammad . . . chose me to teach you.[13]

As for the immigrants, hard work, perserverance, natural growth, and the successive arrival of other Muslims enabled them to establish businesses, religious associations, and mosques. The present state of our knowledge does not permit any great degree of specificity about their activities. A few examples, however, will indicate the fruits of their early efforts toward establishing a religio-cultural presence in the United States. Albanian Muslims founded a religious society and mosque in Biddeford, Maine, in 1915, and by 1919 another had appeared in Waterbury, Connecticut. About thirty years later, if not before, they organized the Albanian-American Muslim society in Detroit.[14] An Arabic-speaking employee of Ford Motor Company built a mosque in 1921 in Highland Park, Michigan at a reported cost of about $55,000 (which unfortunately was closed a few years later).[15] At approximately the same time "Syrians" erected another in or near Ross, North Dakota (which fell into disuse round 1948).[16] This was followed by one in Brooklyn, New York in 1928, built by Polish Muslims (Tatars), and "which continues to serve as a religious and social center for their group and for other Soviet Muslims."[17] Lebanese immigrants opened a mosque in Cedar Rapids, Iowa, in 1934. Recent renovation and the addition of a Muslim graveyard attests to the determination and efficacy of that community.[18] To be sure, the immigrants founded many organizations and erected several mosques to fulfill their religious duties and preserve their cultural traditions. A large number of periodicals in their various languages and English began to appear round the turn of the century. While the majority of them were neither religious publications nor owned by their Muslim countrymen, various news items and articles served to enhance the Muslims' awareness of events in their mother countries and in their ethnic communities in America.

Since the 1950s, several important changes have occurred amongst Muslims of immigrant origin. Their numbers have increased considerably, and there is a marked improvement in their level of education and professional abilities. They have gained employment in leading American educational institutions, several government agencies (including NASA), and are represented in most of the scientific and skilled professions. Thus, they have augmented the number of American-educated offspring of earlier arrivals. Many of them came to the United States on student visas, but subsequently obtained permanent residence permits or were naturalized. A large number have become restauranteurs, grocers, a variety of other kinds of small entrepreneurs, as well as blue and white collar workers. The influx of new immigrants has heightened the awareness of those resident in America to the political issues in the old countries, and has aided cultural cohesion and the maintenance of religious practices.

With the financial support of mainly Arab governments and international Islamic organizations, several Islamic centers and associations emerged in the 1950s. They appeared in response to the mutual desire of Muslim states and Arab-American Muslims for political and cultural reinforcement. One of the first and largest is the Islamic Center of Washington, D.C., which was inaugurated by President Dwight D. Eisenhower in 1957.[19] Built by several Muslim governments which donated exquisite mosaics, carpets, and books, the Center contains a mosque, library, bookshop, and administrative offices. Initially serving the Islamic needs of the Muslim diplomatic corps in the capital, it soon became a religious resource for American universities, associations, clubs, neighboring Muslim communities and a tourist attraction. Until recently, its imams have been Egyptian graduates of Al-Azhar University (Cairo, Egypt) and various British universities. Similar, but less elaborate, centers have been opened in New York, Jersey City, Toledo, San Francisco, Chicago, Los Angeles, Detroit, Michigan City (Indiana) and other cities. Still others are in the planning or construction stage, as is the case with the center in New York City which is to be built with the help of Muslim governments.

With respect to national Islamic organizations, the most important was founded during the same period. The Federation of Islamic Associations in the United States and Canada was organized in 1954 by a second-generation Lebanese immigrant and veteran of the Second World War. A pamphlet of the Federation reads: "While in service during World War II, Abdallah Igram recognized a lack of information and misinterpretation of the tenets of Islam, the second largest monotheistic faith in the world. As a solution to the problem, he envisioned an organization that would achieve equal recognition for the American Muslim."[20] An early recipient of Arab financial support, the Federation encourages close religious ties with Islamic bodies in the Arabic-speaking countries. Several mosques and associations in the United States are affiliated with it.

If the 1950s was an important decade for the emergence of Arab-led Islamic centers and large organizations, it was also a significant period for Muslims of other foreign origins. They continued to develop means for religious and cultural preservation. For example, the Albanian communities began to publish Islamic periodicals; the Bosnians (or Serbo-Croatians) published a newspaper, and in 1955 opened a mosque, school, and social center in Chicago. The Turks, relatively more outwardly secular, and who previously had established many organizations, founded the Federation of Turkish-American Societies in 1956 to express their social and political views of which Islam is an important element.[21]

Additionally, the 1950s was a momentous decade for the general public exposure to Islam. Briefly, the impetus for this trend was (1) the greater visibility of the Nation of Islam which resulted from its growth and increasing acquisition of property, the conversion of Malcolm X and his popularity as a speaker; (2) open doctrinal disputes between the Nation on the one hand, and other African-American groups and the predominantly Arab organizations on the other; and (3) increased Pakistani, Indian, and Egyptian interest in international Islam. Because of its numerical strength, its popular appeal amongst African-Americans as an outspoken expression of many of their socioeconomic grievances, and its alleged Islamic character, the Nation of Islam was viewed as a possible ally of the Muslim world. But its doctrines were not in accord with generally accepted Islamic beliefs. Several attempts were made to ameliorate the basic divergent tenets of the movement. In view of the widespread opposition in this country, but the generally milder and sympathetic attitude of foreign Muslims, Elijah Muhammad decided in favor of numerous suggestions that he visit some Muslim countries.

In late 1959, he travelled to Turkey, Egypt, Syria, Jordan, the Sudan, Ethiopia, Saudi Arabia, and Pakistan. He was welcomed by several Muslim scholars and political figures, including the late Shaykh Mahmud Shaltut, former Rector of Al-Azhar University, and President Gamal Abdul Nasser of Egypt. Muhammad's high social and political regard for Eastern Muslims was somewhat diminished by the relatively poor social and economic conditions which he witnessed during his tour. His debates with the scholars had a dual effect upon his thinking. On the one hand, he was impressed by the efficacy of their arguments in favor of the transcendence of God, the mission of Prophet Muhammad, and the natural humanity of European-Americans. Such beliefs were in direct contrast to those he propagated as fundamental to his religious and social philosophy which made them difficult to discard. Upon his return to the United States, he spoke proudly of his statesmanlike reception, but often ridiculed the prevailing social conditions, and denigrated local and foreign Muslim scholars. While the religious hostilities between the Nation and other Muslims did not abate, there were short periods of respite. However, little hope remained of making a significant dent in the doctrinal armor of Elijah Muhammad. Foreign and American Muslims concluded that change must come from within the ranks: a planned and gradual religious redirection to be effected by the time of the aging "Messenger's" demise. A sort of Islamic unity in America was anticipated, but it could hardly be realized without the numerically dominant groups.

TWO DECADES OF TURBULENCE AND GROWTH

The sixties and seventies were decades of great change for American Muslims. Amongst the most important contributing factors were the rise of political radicalism in Africa, the Middle East and America; the defection of Malcolm X from the Nation of Islam and his subsequent assassination; the growth in the immigrant Muslim population and the founding of new organizations headed by them; the death of Elijah Muhammad and the accession of his son Warith Muhammad to the leadership of the community.

Historically, great political events in Africa have affected important segments of the African-American leadership. By the late 1950s, the Nation of Islam, or better, Elijah Muhammad, had become more observant of the changes in the Muslim world and in Africa. To him, as to many former "Black Nationalists"—clerics and laymen, Muslims and non-Muslims—Egypt had a special historical significance in the religious belief system of the Nation. Therefore, the Egyptian revolution of 1952, the nationalization of the Suez Canal and the Tripartite Aggression (Israel, Britain, and France) in 1956, and the evacuation of the Canal Zone in 1957 were all noted by Elijah Muhammad with joyous interest. The emergence of the Republic of Pakistan in 1947 and the independence of the Gold Coast (later Ghana) in 1957 were also cheerful occasions. These events had eschatalogical significance: prophetically, the "Devil" was being driven out of the "Original Man's" lands, which was an indication of the times.

Encouraged and elated by the above political occurrences, Muhammad publicly and forcefully demanded that the United States government allocate land (a state or states) to be controlled exclusively by his followers, as well as subsidize the new "Kingdom" until it would be able to fare alone. Muhammad now placed less emphasis on total divine deliverance for "God helps those who help themselves." His call for Muslim separatism reverberated in the highest political and religious circles in the Muslim world. He attracted the interest of radicals and traditionalists, irrespective of doctrinal differences. American

Muslim "militancy" became engaged to, but did not marry, foreign Muslim and African radicalism. As indicated previously, Muhammad had too much to lose nationally.

It is a truism that Malcolm X played a central role in conveying Muhammad's message in the United States and abroad, directly and indirectly. Malcolm X, however, was a keener and more responsive detector of promising political gain. He was superbly capable of implementing Muhammad's directives on the one hand, and suggesting a course of action, gaining approval (or acquiescence) and then acting on behalf of his venerable leader on the other. These traits caused him to cast a long shadow, sometimes effectively hiding Muhammad from public view. He was not oblivious to the possible opportunities for meaningful relationships with independent African and Asian countries. Nor was Malcolm X a stranger to certain diplomatic circles in New York and "Black nationalist" groups.

To be sure, Malcolm's religious beliefs were enmeshed inseparably with his activist political ideology: God aids those who *get involved* and do their utmost to change their circumstances. His public statement in 1963, relating the assassination of President John F. Kennedy to "the chickens coming home to roost," was made against the background of rising Third World nationalism. The ramifications of having said this did not threaten his sense of personal security. Further, Malcolm was probably aware that the attraction of African-Americans to Islam was due primarily to political and psychological considerations. He must have thought himself able to obtain the support of members of the Nation, foreign and African-American Sunni Muslims. His defection from the Nation, his establishment of both the Muslim Mosque Incorporated and the Organization of Afro-American Unity were reflective of his ideological position.

Malcolm X had an important effect on Muslim and African-American thought in America. His travels in Muslim and African countries in 1964—again, a period of intense nationalism—demonstrated to many Muslims and non-Muslims that Islam and political activism are not necessarily antithetical. Malcolm was welcomed officially in the mutually antagonistic countries of Saudi Arabia and Egypt. The former spearheaded an international movement for Sunni Islamic unity and disdained socialism; the latter promoted nationalism in the whole Third World, Muslim solidarity, and socialism. From Saudi Arabia he obtained "a religious license"; from Egypt he received "a religious and political charter." With such credentials he was accepted *theologically* by the majority of American Muslims—immigrants and African-

Americans—many of whom applauded, though often softly, his political pronouncements. As is well known, the 1960s was a period of great
debate in the international Muslim community: is Islam compatible
with nationalism and socialism? For Malcolm, Abdul Nasser, and
some American Muslims, they were compatible. Thus, Malcolm
exemplified to African-American radicals and Muslim-sympathizers
that political activism and Islam could be cohorts.

To African-American interest in African nationalism and the
somewhat faddish return to the roots, Malcolm X added an Islamic
ingredient. A good deal of revived interest was shown in the medieval
Muslim-ruled Sudanic states of Ghana, Mali and Songhay. Arabic,
Swahili, and Hausa names were adopted by a cross-section of African-
Americans, Muslims, and non-Muslims. Many African-Americans
adopted dress styles (excluding the dashiki) suggestive of Islam. Support for Egypt (more than for any other protagonist in the Israeli-Arab
conflict) became manifest. Travel to Muslim and African countries
increased considerably. Many exhibited a keen interest in learning
Arabic. No doubt Elijah Muhammad indirectly influenced this trend;
this point seems to have been overlooked by several students of Malcolm's post-Nation career. Elijah Muhammad, the latest in the Drew
Ali and Sheikh Daoud line, had been preaching for more than thirty
years that Islam is the religion of the "Black Man." But Malcolm said
and did things at a propitious moment in the cultural history of his
people. Malcolm X, or more appropriately, al-Hajj Malik Shabazz, was
to become a religious model and a hero to thousands of Muslims.

The real effect of his defection from the Nation and his assassination is yet to be studied. The cohesion of the Nation, however, was
demonstrated by the fact that it continued intact for ten years after his
assassination; that is, until the death of Elijah Muhammad in 1975.
Despite Shabazz's comments about Elijah Muhammad's personal life,
his reinforcement of the national and international opposition to his
former leader, the publication of his *Autobiography* and the desertion
of Muhammad's son, Wallace D. Muhammad, the Nation maintained
its strength and its public predominance over all other Islamic organizations.

Elijah Muhammad's doctrines and policies underwent basic
modifications and outright reversals with the accession in 1975 of his
son, now known as Warith Deen Muhammad. Referring to himself as
the Mujaddid (Renewer), he discarded the belief in the divinity of Fard
Muhammad, the messengerhood of his father, the evil nature of European-Americans and the superiority of one people over another. Afri-

can-Americans are called Bilalians, in reference to Bilal ibn Rabah, a one-time slave of Ethiopian parentage in Mecca, and the first appointed muezzin in Islam; he is revered throughout the Muslim world.

Imam Muhammad has received the acclaim of the national and international Muslim community and enjoys cordial relations with the U.S. government and Christian groups. He has been hosted by a number of foreign Muslim governments and organizations, including at least one in the People's Republic of China. The former hostile position of the Nation toward the United States government, and Christian and Jewish groups has given way to a concilliatory attitude toward all. In 1978, Imam Muhammad was perhaps the first major African-American to support publicly the re-election of President James Carter. This notwithstanding, a delegation from President Ronald Reagan assured the Imam that his government welcomed good relations with him. Imam Muhammad has participated in several dialogues of religious understanding with Christian ministers and rabbis. He recently initiated a drive to get ten million signatures on a "Petition for a dialogue between Imam Warith Deen Muhammad and Pope John Paul II regarding Racial Divinities in Religion."[22] In accord with Islamic doctrine, he is opposed to any representation of God. Additionally, he is contemptuous of the Christian "Caucasian image of God that makes Bilalians think inferior and act inferior, and that makes Caucasians equally artificial." The organization, formerly called the World Community of Islam in the West, has been renamed the American Muslim Mission. With branches throughout the United States, the West Indies and Guyana, and tens of thousands of members and sympathizers, the American Muslim Mission is the largest Muslim movement devoted to Islamic proselytization in the United States.

It should be noted, however, that the Nation of Islam was revived in 1977 by a formerly prominent leader in the old organization. Although "Minister Louis Farrakhan, National Representative of the Honorable Elijah Muhammad, Messenger to us all," publicly supported the doctrinal changes of the World Community, he later stated that "the effects of the changes . . . in addition to the information I gained about our people abroad, caused me to reassess the Honorable Elijah Muhammad, his teaching and program for Black people. My articulation of this caused Eman [sic.] W. D. Muhammad to announce to the entire Muslim body that I was no longer a person with whom the Muslims (WCIW) should associate, listen to, or even be given the Muslim greeting. I naturally took this to mean that I was excommunicated from the World Community of Islam."[23] As one would expect, the new Nation of Islam has attracted some of the "nationalist" and "radical" elements of the parent organization. Although it is not considered orthodox, its broad emphasis on the plight of African-Americans, and its apparent readiness to co-operate with politically similar but non-Muslim groups, makes it—at least in the short run—an important competitor of the Sunni Muslim organizations.

One should note in passing another African-American organization that attracted national and international attention in the 1970s. The Hanafi movement (named for Abu Hanifa, a prominent jurist and theologian who died in 767) seems to have emerged in Washington, D.C., in 1970, under the leadership of Hamaas Abdul Khaalis ("the enthusiastic servant of The Pure").[24] A former national secretary of the Nation of Islam in the 1950s, Abdul Khaalis was severely reprimanded because of his personal behaviour, and later left the organization. His public display of ill-feelings toward the Honorable Elijah Muhammad, whom he criticized and belittled to his former leader's aides, led to the hideous attack of 1973 on his Washington headquarters; four of his children and three other Hanafis were killed. Although the murderers were imprisoned for life, after a trial lasting almost four years, Abdul Khaalis decided to extract personal revenge.

In 1977, he and some of his followers seized, for various reasons, the Washington headquarters of B'nai B'rith, the Islamic Center, and the District Building. During the three-day occupation, he made some interesting demands: (1) cessation of the New York showing of the film "Muhammad, Messenger of God," which though partly produced with Libyan and other Arab Muslim money, was considered sacriligious by many in the international Muslim community; (2) deliverance to him of those who killed the Hanafis and Malik Shabazz, as well as two sons of Elijah Muhammad, Warith Deen and Herbert (Jabir), and Muhammad Ali, the former heavy weight boxing champion. The incident, in which 139 hostages were taken and a reporter killed, ended after the ambassadors of Egypt, Pakistan, and Iran met with Abdul Khaalis. He is presently serving a prison term.

The way in which the seige was terminated may illustrate, *inter alia,* the beginning of foreign Muslim mediation in conflicts between American Muslims and government authorities and vice versa. It is noteworthy that Abdul Khaalis offered, from his prison cell, to travel to Iran in an attempt to gain the release of the American hostages. This author is not aware that he sought a *quid pro quo* from the United States government.

The organizational growth in this period was not limited to African-American Muslims. In 1963, the Muslim Students' Association of the United States and Canada (MSA) was inaugurated with the aim, *inter alia,* of "Helping in the development of [an] Islamic personality and attitudes; disseminating Islamic knowledge and understanding; carrying on religious, cultural, social, charitable, and educational activities in the best traditions of Islam; promoting unity and solidarity among Muslims in North America and nourishing their friendly relations with non-Muslims; presenting Islam to non-Muslims as a complete way of life and a viable alternative to all other doctrines."[25] Although the MSA is directed by a group of graduates of American universities of mainly Arabic-speaking origins, actually it is much more than a student organization. With perhaps more than one hundred campus branches, the MSA is a sort of parent organization for a number of professional societies, such as the Islamic Medical Association, the Association of Muslim Social Scientists, and the Association of Muslim Scientists and Engineers. It operates an Islamic Teaching Center, a press, and a book service. It organizes regional and national conferences and seminars, coordinates the activities of centers and mosques, and collects and disseminates the obligatory tax.[26]

Muslims in America receive direct support from a truly international organization. Founded in 1962, in Mecca, the Muslim World League immediately began assisting Islamic causes throughout the world. In 1974, it was admitted as a member of the non-governmental organizations of the United Nations and opened its offices in 1976. The League is composed of three departments: United Nations Affairs, Administration, and Islamic Affairs. According to one of its publications, the Islamic Affairs Department

is rendering valuable service in disseminating the message of Islam in North America by providing imams and teachers to several Islamic centers and mosques, and through free distribution of copies of the Holy Quran and other books, brochures and other material on Islam. It has established contact with a large number of Muslim community centers and organizations, colleges and other academic institutions. It is also trying to do whatever it can, within its limitations, for the betterment of those Muslims who are, due to unfortunate circumstances, in prison. It also organizes functions on Islamic events . . . and makes use of the media to present Islamic viewpoints. In addition, the Department of Islamic Affairs also answers many inquiries on matters related to Islam, thus creating for many a better understanding of Islam.[27]

The League-sponsored First Islamic Conference of North America, held in Newark in 1977, was attended by more than one hundred and forty American Muslim organizations. In late 1981, it announced a grant of more than half a million dollars to sixteen mosques in the United States.[28]

Until the 1960s, American Muslims of foreign origins had not been active politically; some European and Asian (mainly Turkish groups), were exceptions. With the growth in the immigrant and student population, however, came a period of political activism, not in favor of Islam directly, but in cadence with the political events in the Arabic-speaking world. The most significant was the war of 1967, which affected negatively all Muslims, but especially those of Arabic-speaking descent. Political and religious sentiments were heightened considerably by the large influx of Syrians, Palestinians, and Egyptians who could relate the consequences of the war with some authenticity. A number of Arab-American associations emerged which appealed to the Islamic sentiments of American Muslims. One found it difficult to ignore the Israeli occupation of Jerusalem, in which stands the Aqsa Mosque, the third most sacred shrine of Muslims. The Israeli-Egyptian war of 1973, reinforced somewhat the recently manifested political inclination.

Events in Iran, beginning in 1979, likewise have had far-reaching but yet unstudied effects on American Muslims. The fall of Shah Reza Pahlavi in February and the accession of Ayatullah Rohallah Khumeini, despite his being a Shiah, was applauded heartily by a large number of Muslims—irrespective of ethnic origin, political inclination, or economic status. That such a traditionalist could, with considerable internal acclaim, become the ruler of one of the most Western-oriented and militarily advanced countries in the Muslim world was an almost unbelieveable occurrence. However, the persistence of the hostage crisis, which began in November, diminished greatly the Ayatullah's esteem. The incident caused widespread discussion about the Islamic legality of making hostages of foreign diplomats. In spite of the politically negative effects, the Iranian Revolution has been most favorable to the dissemination of Shiah religious literature in the United States. While a few conflicts have occurred recently between Sunnis and Shiahs (especially in Washington, D.C. over control of the Islamic Center), it is most likely that the latter will grow in number and coalesce with their Sunni brethren. Indications of this seemingly emergent trend are to be seen in several Muslim communities (for example, in Detroit, Chicago, and New York), as well as in national organizations.

PROBLEMS AND IMPLICIT SOLUTIONS

The above survey of Muslim organizations indicates that Arabic-speaking Muslim countries—particularly the Arab or Persian Gulf States—are the leading supporters of national Islamic activity in America. This is not meant to suggest, however, that American Muslims are essentially dependent on external aid or that they are controlled by their foreign donors. While petro-dollars facilitate various schemes, generally American Muslims and their donors are cognizant of the host of possible negative consequences of a patron-client relationship. There have been complaints about favoritism toward Arab-led organizations. But such protestations do not threaten seriously the overall concord amongst American Muslims.

Muslims in America are confronted daily with challenges to the Islamic way of life. Forbidden by Islam to consume alcoholic drinks, pork in its various forms and, when possible, to eat meat which has been slaughtered in an Islamically-approved manner, one must be cautious about dietary restrictions. The use of drugs and popular Western dancing, too, are generally considered forbidden or, at the very least, reprehensible. Fornication and adultery being proscribed, as well as physical intimacy with members of the opposite gender, a Muslim may suffer temptation continually. The Islamic stress upon public modesty in dress imposes certain restrictions on what may be worn by males and females. The rules of Islamic law and ethics governing relations between spouses and their offspring often conflict with acceptable and "proper" American behavior.

Cooperation among the above mentioned organizations has helped but has not made easy the adaptation of Muslims to American society. Unlike some ethnic and religious minorities, Muslims have not created adequate institutions to fortify and reinforce Islamic traditions. There is an apparent tendency toward building mosques and establishing business enterprises—restaurants, groceries, newspaper publishing houses, automobile dealerships, clothing shops, book stores, etc. Muslim professionals have opened clinics, law offices, and consulting

firms. To be sure, mosques or centers are considered central institutions to the Islamic community. They have been most beneficial for the
performance of Friday and the special Ramadan and Id (Bairam) prayers, dinners and lectures. But business enterprises—some of which sell
items not approved by Islam—generally seem to be personal ventures
which do not depend on Muslim patronage. Except in the cases of
ethnic food vendors, Muslim-owned businesses are in sharp competition with non-Muslim-owned enterprises. Therefore, they hardly serve
as a viable economic infrastructure for the community.

Significantly, there is a serious lack of Muslim educational institutions which might countervail imperfections in American society. The
existence of "Islamic Sunday schools" is noted, but they are modelled
too closely after Christian Sunday schools and are thus largely ineffec-
tive as a means of combatting the negative influences of public schools
and the media (television, radio, and magazines). A few Muslim organizations operate regular schools covering some or all of the elementary
and secondary grades; they offer many of the ordinarily required
courses in the public school system. Noteworthy, however, is their
tendency to be non-accredited because of the lack of state-required
facilities or trained teachers. This inadequacy has caused difficulties in
the passage to higher levels of education in non-Muslim institutions. It
also has discouraged many parents from registering their children in
Muslim schools. Therefore, the formative and teen years of a Muslim
are spent overwhelmingly in public schools. Though a few are in the
planning stage, and one or two others are now in existence, American
Muslims have no educationally viable colleges and universities.

Other socially supportive institutions are either non-existent or
are insufficient. These include recreational facilities for adolescents
and adults, youth camps, periodicals and books for all ages, and radio
and television programs. The establishment of counselling services
(marital, psychological, and social) have been almost totally neglected.

American Muslims have yet to produce a group of scholars who
hold postgraduate degrees in Islamic studies, that is, an American
Ulema. Numerically, there are many such persons who have studied in
Muslim and Western universities. But they are a multi-ethnic group
who are primarily employed by American universities and/or the government; thus, little of their expertise devolve on rank and file Muslims. Others are to be found in leadership positions in Islamic centers.
On the whole, they are Arabic-speaking, Indian and Pakistani immigrants whose cultural backgrounds often make difficult meaningful in-
tercourse with persons and groups of different origins. Non-immigrant

Muslims have very few university-trained Ulemas though some are presently studying abroad and in America.

In conclusion, American Muslims have succeeded in establishing a community in the United States. The task has not been easy because of external conflict with the larger American society and internal differences over doctrine. On the one hand, the American stance vis-a-vis Islam has been influenced historically by the series of Western hostile encounters—political and religious—with Muslim peoples which have distorted its perception of Islam and its adherents. Technological advancement, military superiority, and secularism have reinforced the American position. Recent interfaith discussions notwithstanding, the United States' media, textbooks and novels—powerful determinants of public opinion—have yet to approach an objective view of Islam and Muslims. Racism, in its various cloaks, has yet to be sufficiently overcome.[29] On the other hand, Muslims have been almost overwhelmed by the Western system—intellectually and materially—irrespective of their national origins. Regardless of the negative effects, this phenomenon has aided in reducing internal conflicts within the American Muslim community. The future viability of the community, however, will depend upon its ability to reduce further internal differences and to build institutions which will protest its most sacred precincts.

NOTES

1. I owe a debt of gratitude to J. W. K., O. A., S. S. N. and other modest persons who provided information useful in writing this paper. For other comprehensive surveys of Muslims in America, see Yvonne Y. Haddad, "The Muslim Experience in the United States," *The Link* 12, no. 4 (September/October 1979): 1–12; Sulayman S. Nyang, "Islam in the United States of America," *The Search: Journal for Arab and Islamic Studies* 1, no. 2 (Spring 1980): 164–82.

2. See, for example, Emily K. Lovell, "A Survey of the Arab-Muslims in the United States and Canada," *The Muslim World* (Hartford) 63, no. 2 (April 1973): 140; M. Arif Ghayur, "Muslims in the United States: Settlers and Visitors," *The Annals* (of The American Academy of Political and Social Science) 454 (March 1981) 150–163; M. Raquibuz Zaman, "Occupational Distribution of Muslim Minorities in North America," unpublished paper prepared for the Seminar on the Economic Status of Muslim Minorities, King Abdulaziz University, Jeddah, November 1981; Alixa Naff, "Arabs," *Harvard Encyclopedia of American Ethnic Groups,* ed. Stephan Thernstrom (Cambridge, Mass.: Harvard University Press, 1980), pp. 128–36.

3. Much of the current interest in this subject is due to the three-volume work of

Leo Wiener, *Africa and the Discovery of America* (Philadelphia: Innes & Sons, 1922), especially vol. 3. See also, Ivan Van Sertima, *They Came Before Columbus: The African Presence in Ancient America* (New York: Random House, 1976), especially chapters 3 and 6.

4. See Nadim Makdisi, "The Moslems of America," *The Christian Century*, August 26, 1959, 969–71; Beverlee T. Mehdi, *The Arabs in America 1492–1977: A Chronology and Fact Book* (Dobbs Ferry, N.Y.: Oceana, 1978), p. 1; Yvonne Y. Haddad, "The Muslim Experience in the United States," *The Link* 12, no. 4 (September/October 1979): 1.

5. See Carl Campbell, "Jonas Mohamed Bath and the Free Mandingos in Trinidad: The Question of Their Reparation to Africa 1831–1838," *Pan-African Journal* 7, no. 2 (Summer 1974): 129–52; *idem., Journal of African Studies* 2, no. 4 (Winter 1975/76): 467–95; Clyde-Ahmed Winters, "Muslims in Pluralistic Societies—The Case of West Indies," *Al-Ittihad* 15 (July 1978/Shaban 1398): 39–55; Douglas Grant, *The Fortunate Slave: An Illustration of African Slavery in the Early Eighteenth Century* (London and New York: Oxford University Press, 1968); Terry Alford, *Prince Among Slaves* (New York: Harcourt Brace Jovanich, 1977); Joel Chandler Harris, *The Story of Aaron (So Named) The Son of Ben-Ali* (Boston and New York: Houghton, Mifflin & Co., 1896). Apart from Alex Haley, author of *Roots,* another African-American, Khalid Al Mansour, claims Muslim origins; see Faissal Fahd Al Talal and Khalid Abdullah Tariq Al Mansour, *The Challenges of Spreading Islam in America and Other Essays* (N. P.: First African Arabian Press, 1980), p. 21.

6. Thomas W. Arnold, *The Preaching of Islam: A History of the Propagation of the Muslim Faith* (Lahore: Sh. Muhammad Ashraf, 1961), p. 465, n. 1.

7. The author is currently writing a biography of Muhammad Alexander Russell Webb and a critical edition of his works which will illuminate the early social and intellectual history of Islam in the United States.

8. Muhammad A. R. Webb, *Islam: A Lecture Delivered at the Framji Cowasji Institute, Bombay, India, Thursady Evening 10th November 1892* (Bombay: The Bombay Gazette Steam Printing Works, 1892), pp. 1, 2, 7.

9. See Arna Bontemps and Jack Conroy, *Anyplace But Here* (New York: Hill and Wang, 1966), pp. 205–208; Arthur H. Faucet, *Black Gods of the Metroplis: Negro Religious Cults of the Urban North* (Philadelphia: University of Pennsylvania Press, 1971), pp. 41–51, 72.

10. One of the best works on the Ahmadiyya and its attitude toward other religions is that of H. A. Walker, *The Ahmadiya Movement* (London: Oxford University Press, 1918). The movement was recently proscribed officially in Pakistan and has always been considered heterodox by most Muslim religious scholars.

11. *The Minaret* (New York), April 16, 1980.

12. Roi Ottley, *"New World A-Coming": Inside Black America* (New York: Arno Press/The New York Times, 1969, reprint of 1943 edition), pp. 56–57.

13. Elijah Muhammad, *Message to the Blackman in America* (Chicago: Muhammad Mosque of Islam No. 2, 1965), p. 242. The most popular studies on the Nation of Islam are C. Eric Lincoln's *The Black Muslims in America* (Boston: Beacon Press, 1961; rev. ed., 1973), and E. U. Essien-Udom's *Black Nationalism: A Search for an Identity in America* (Chicago: University of Chicago Press, 1962).

14. *The Muslim World* 11, no. 2 (April 1921): 195–96; *Harvard Encyclopedia,* p. 25.

15. *The Muslim World* 13, no. 1 (January 1923): 82–83.

16. Haddad, "The Muslim Experience in the United States," *The Link* 12, No. 4 (September/October 1979): 3.

17. *Harvard Encyclopedia,* p. 990; cf. *Twentieth Century Encyclopedia of Religious Knowledge* 2: 768.

18. *Harvard Encyclopedia,* p. 733.

19. See Muhammad Abdul-Rauf, *History of the Islamic Center: From Dream to Reality* (Washington, D. C.: The Islamic Center, 1978), pp. 74–75.

20. Quoted in Abdo A. Elkholy, *The Arab Moslems in the United States: Religion and Assimilation* (New Haven: College and University Press, 1966), p. 46.

21. *Harvard Encyclopedia,* p. 994.

22. See recent issues of *World Muslim News,* the official organ of the American Muslim Mission.

23. *Black Books Bulletin* 6, no. 1 (Spring 1978): 45. See also *Voice* (Flushing, N.Y.), May 24, 1980.

24. See John Sansing, "Hanafi Massacre, Hanafi Siege," *The Washingtonian* (February 1980): 87–96, and "No Man is Told by God What Is the Right Way," March 1981: pp. 69–77.

25. "Know the MSA," a pamphlet, n.d.

26. *Zakah* may be defined as an Islamic social tax, payable at the rate of 2.5 percent, on a Muslim's taxable possessions after the expiration of one year's ownership.

27. *Proceedings of the First Islamic Conference of North America* (New York: The Muslim World League, 1977), pp. 144–45.

28. *The Minaret,* September 1, and 16, 1981.

29. See Edward W. Said, *Covering Islam: How the Media and the Experts Determine How We See the Rest of the World* (New York: Pantheon Books, 1981).

〰〰〰〰〰〰〰〰〰〰〰〰〰〰〰〰〰〰〰〰〰〰〰〰〰〰〰〰〰

10

On Being Muslim

THE FAITH DIMENSION OF MUSLIM IDENTITY

Willem A. Bijlefeld

*P*EOPLE SHOULD NOT live by *bread* alone—and neither persons nor nations should be described and interpreted in terms of *faith* alone.[1] Probably the most serious injustice done to Islam by the Western press in recent years has been the tendency to use the word *Islam* as the magic key to unlocking the doors behind which all so-called mysteries of the Muslim world are hidden, to see Islam as the single or at least the foremost category for explaining all that is happening in Muslim nations.[2] There is no need to dwell on the irony of the fact that a religious and cultural tradition so little known in the West as Islam is, provided in 1978–79 one of the key words for the headlines of countless articles dealing with events susceptible to entirely different interpretations than the 'religious' one: "Passions and Perils: An Anxious Washington Studies the Fever in Islam," "Islam in Ferment," "The Islam Explosion," "Islamic Fanaticism Threatens World Security," "Islam Militant."[3] More recently V. S. Naipaul attracted the attention of many by the record of his visit to Iran, Pakistan, Malaysia, and Indonesia. While *Among the Believers* claims that it seeks to describe the human and political condition of these countries where Islam is significantly present,[4] the book is radically at odds with what Edward Said formulated as the necessity to take seriously "the human dimension of Islam," with honest "respect for the concrete detail of human experience," avoiding "limiting labels like 'the Islamic mind' or 'the Islamic personality.'"[5] Said's concern is that as a rule Western coverage of events in the Muslim world has almost consistently failed to discriminate between "religious passion, a struggle for a just cause, ordinary

219

human weakness, political competition, and the history of men, women, and societies seen *as* the history of men, women, and societies."[6] Where Said is questioning "how really useful . . . 'Islam' [is] as a concept for understanding Morocco *and* Saudi Arabia *and* Syria *and* Indonesia,"[7] Naipaul presents his visit to four Muslim nations as "An *Islamic* Journey"—the subtitle of the book that concludes with a section entitled "*Islamic* Winter," containing reflections on his second visit to Tehran in February 1981.[8]

Two interrelated issues are at stake. It is *at best* a modest step forward when one moves from a discussion of Islam as if it were a monolithic entity and a closed religious or philosophical system to a consideration of 900 million people[9] in this world simply in terms of their being "believers," Muslims. Islam is undoubtedly an extremely important dimension of the life of individual Muslims and Muslim societies, and the common Muslim insistence on the character of Islam as an all-encompassing way of life should not be taken lightly. But this does not mean that the complex reality of individual lives, national situations, and international relations anywhere in the Muslim world can be interpreted solely by a reference to Islam, only "Islamically." As a correlate to this, it is obviously inadequate to seek to define what Islam is and what being a Muslim implies primarily or even exclusively on the basis of observations of the actual behavior of a group—even a relatively large group—of Muslims and a study of the current condition in various Muslim societies. The observer's perspective is clearly recognizable in, for example, a description of Pakistan as "the land of faith turning into a land of plunder," and in the reminiscense of Indonesia as the land where "people floated. Whether they moved forward, into a new civilization, or backward . . . towards the purer Arab faith, they were now always entering somebody else's world, and getting further from themselves."[10] But even the most accurate description of a Muslim community does not necessarily reflect what Islam can and does mean to many Muslims. In all religious traditions and communities there are persons and events that obscure rather than reflect what many of those who live in it see as the true character of their faith. Muhammad Abduh certainly does not stand alone in his observation that "Islam is concealed from western people by a heavy curtain of Muslims," and he shares with many the awareness of the need to distinguish between the true character of the religion of Islam and "those Muslims who by their conduct have been an argument against it."[11]

That obviously creates a predicament. "A heavy curtain of Muslims" may block our vision of what Islam really is—but on the other hand we do not want to deal with Islam as an abstraction, ignoring the concreteness of Muslims' ways of life and conduct, their hopes and fears, aspirations and frustrations. We are aware of the immense variety and the ever-changing scenes in the Muslim world—regionally, culturally, politically, economically, and above all humanly. Almost blinded by the splendor of this diversity, we need to discover the common elements, that which is permanent, abiding, and distinctively "Islamic." We know that "being Muslim" implies much more than the acceptance of a particular set of beliefs, and the question of identity is for most Muslims infinitely more than a matter of private introspection.[12] Rafiuddin Ahmed provides us in his study *The Bengal Muslims 1871–1906* with an excellent example of the social, cultural, linguistic, and political ramifications of the issue of an identity crisis at a communal level.[13] Certainly in the case of the Muslim world we cannot draw sharp dividing lines between individual and communal experience, between the "spiritual" and the "material," between religion and politics, economics and arts. For any religious tradition, most definitely the Muslim, the word "faith" is misused unless it refers to a lived reality and real persons.[14] It is impossible in this introductory essay to do justice to this fully human character of faith, in this case faith as experienced and lived by those among us who are Muslims. But in restricting ourselves to the modest task of delineating some of the major themes of the Quran, we are not allowed to forget that we deal with commitments that continue to shape the lives of hundreds of millions of people.

We need to raise explicitly the question which unavoidably arises whenever an "outsider" speaks on—and to some extent, for—Islam: does a person who is not a Muslim have the mental ability and the moral right to seek to answer the question what it means to be a Muslim? The response that all that we do is simply to pass on what Muslims think and say about the subject is, understandably, far from convincing for those who raise the question, and, to say the least, irresponsibly naive. Any anthology of Muslim sayings and writings, growing out of the conviction that "the basic tenets of Islam come alive most simply in what Muslims themselves say,"[15] represents necessarily a personal choice and is a far from simple exercise.[16] Moreover, as anthologies grow larger and selections more varied, a coherent picture of what those basic tenets are becomes increasingly difficult to obtain. It does not seem appropriate to seek to protect ourselves against the accusation of a biased selectivity by simply taking shelter in the safety of a mere repetition of time-honored Muslim creedal statements or a survey of the traditional six points of the Muslim faith, and even the choice of Quranic themes and the interpretation suggested is, admittedly, a personal, subjective decision.

The legitimacy of people speaking for a religious tradition other than their own, first raised mainly as a more or less rhetorical question by some Western historians of religions, has now become, in many circles, a rather tense issue in inter-religious relationships. Many persons who year after year feel free to interpret and represent the basic tenets of a tradition other than their own turn out to be extremely sensitive, impatient, and defensive as soon as someone from the other community begins to participate in the process of trying to articulate what faith means and implies in *their* tradition. Mutuality is a painful process for many persons claiming to be interested in interreligious conversations.

While we need to remain constantly aware of the risk—especially the *moral* risk—involved in any attempt at cross-religious interpretation, we also need to realize that to shun that risk means to give in to the dangerous claims of a religious absolutism and a theological exclusivism that ultimately denies the possibility of cross-cultural and inter-religious understanding, and, most importantly, forgets that in the final analysis there can be no outsiders to "faith" if faith is a matter of being truly human.[17] Therefore we proceed and, confronted with an endless variety of data interpreted and ordered by Muslims throughout the centuries in a great variety of ways, we accept the risks of selectivity and of subjective emphases and interpretations. Embarking upon such an adventure is a pretentious imposition unless one is prepared to submit "again and again to correction by the facts"[18]—first among those facts being the reactions of those who participate in the tradition we seek to understand—a principle far more clearly articulated than implemented by many historians and phenomenologists of religion. What follows can, therefore, lay no claim to objectivity, and lacks, one might say, the authenticity of the participant's perspective. Its justification lies elsewhere. Hans Küng stated that his book *On Being A Christian* "was written, not because the author thinks he is a good Christian, but because he thinks that being a Christian is a particularly good thing."[19] In a somewhat similar manner, the following account of the faith dimension of Muslim identity is offered not because the author can claim to be a good Muslim but because he is convinced that it is a particularly good thing for all of us to begin to understand and appreciate something of what "being a Muslim" implies. Moreover, there remains the question of whether the distinction between "theirs" and "ours" is valid when we talk about faith. For if faith is the ultimate dimension of human existence, the recognition of the singular should not be jeopardized by whatever can be said about the specifics of how it is articulated in various religious traditions.

Four closely related themes will be dealt with: (1) the twofold insistence on the universal and the particular; (2) progress without innovation; (3) the balanced middle: the power of the double affirmation; and (4) the unity of God and the wholeness of *Islam*.

THE TWOFOLD EMPHASIS ON
THE UNIVERSAL AND THE PARTICULAR

One of the most common themes in recent Muslim literature all over the world is that of the universality of Islam, grounded in its recognition of the One God, infinite in majesty and mercy, Lord of the Worlds. While the frequency of the expression of this notion in our time is remarkable, all the elements of this confession can be traced back to the Quran itself, and all of them have been part and parcel of Muslim faith and thought throughout the centuries: the unity of God—the unity of the universe and the original unity of humankind (S. 2:213 and 10:19; cf. 11:118)—the unity of revelation and the oneness of religion. For our present purposes, two points seem of special importance:

1. The notion of universality is frequently elaborated in terms of a theological inclusivism as far as (particularly) the Jews and the Christians are concerned. President Sadat's speech to the Israeli Knesset in November 1977[20] and a large number of public exchanges of expressions of goodwill between Muslims and Christians have drawn the attention of many to Quranic verses stressing the bond between Jews, Christians, and Muslims, especially the unambiguous affirmation "We believe in God and in what has been revealed to us and what was revealed to Abraham, Ishmael, Isaac, Jacob, and the tribes, and that which Moses and Jesus received, and that what the Prophets received from their Lord" (S. 2:136 and 3:84) and the solemn declaration "We believe in that which has been revealed unto us and revealed unto you: our God and your God is One, and unto Him we unreservedly commit ourselves" (S. 29:46).[21] More than thirty texts in the Quran deal directly with this issue of a recognition of earlier revelations—it is the Same

God, the Only One, who is the source of all of them, not infrequently in the context of an appeal to Christians to recognize the Quran on the basis of what they themselves have received.[22] While these data are often interpreted in an exclusivistic sense,[23] sometimes the emphasis is on the positive value of different religions and communities and the necessity to recognize the Muslim community "as *a* community among communities."[24]

2. In the two-fold Muslim emphasis on the universal and the particular, an important point to note is the theological order of the two and, related to it, the issue that *particularity* in Islam is definitely not ethnic or religious *particularism*. The celebration of the revelation of the Quran, "noble," "glorious" and "wonderful," (S. 56:77; 50:1; 85:21; 72:1) a Scripture "in clear Arabic language" (S. 26:195; 16:10)[25] is placed in the context of the recognition of earlier revelation. With a slightly different emphasis than Kenneth Cragg places in his statement that "there was continuity in the Scriptural idea and discontinuity in its final incidence,"[26] I would suggest "inseparable continuity and definitive culmination" as a way to summarize the Quranic view of the interrelatedness of all revealed Scriptures.

While the New Testament order is from Jerusalem to the ends of the earth, Islam—or perhaps, rather, the Quran—starts with "the worlds" and then moves to the events around Mecca and Medina. The Quran never even hints at "a God of the Arabs" who is later on confessed to be the Lord of the Worlds: it starts with the Lord of the Worlds who *now* has also spoken to the Arabs.[27] Islam does not begin with a celebration of the revelatory event of the Quran and then proceeds to reflect on the possibility of revelation also outside the Quranic realm; it *starts* with the recognition of previous revelation and then celebrates that at last those who were without Scripture have also been included among "the People of the Book," that at last they too have become partakers of the blessings of Abraham's family—Prophethood, Scripture, and Wisdom.[28]

The wording chosen obviously intends to highlight important structural differences with at least major trends in the Hebrew Scriptures and the New Testament and the historical development of Jewish and Christian thought. There is no opportunity to go more carefully and precisely into this comparison. But the very idioms of our Scriptures show remarkable variances on this point. The Quran, e.g., does not use one single time the expression "the God of Abraham" or "the God of our Fathers" (let alone, as stated before, "the God of the Arabs"). The significant notion of the religion of Abraham denotes Abraham as the archetype of the true believer, rather than in any way

limiting God to a covenant relation with a segment of the human population. Words for "covenant" and "election" occur in the Quran, but
they have a content and emphasis significantly different from that in
the Hebrew Scriptures,[29] and so one could continue with a series of
interrelated issues. Thinking of Moubarac's provocative statement that
we find in the Quran "a history of religion rather than a religion of
history,"[30] one wonders whether—without exaggerating the distinction
between the two notions as if they were radically exclusive of each
other—one would be justified in suggesting that the Quran is concerned
with the revelatory dimension of the histories of nations[31] rather than
with revelation as history. "Islam did not arise out of the history of a
covenant with God, as in the case with Judaism. An intimate connex-
ion between God and man based on interaction in history is unknown
to Islam," Smail Balic wrote.[32]

PROGRESS WITHOUT INNOVATION

Many daily and weekly papers in the U.S.A. have in the past few years
published articles on the issue of "Islam and Modernization." With
some regularity reference is made to widespread Muslim distrust of
any "innovation." Innovations, whether they are heretical teachings or
new patterns of behavior, are often seen, we are told, as dangerously
undermining the unity, solidarity, and homogeneity of the community
of the faithful. While generalizations are as meaningless here as in the
description of any other aspect of current conditions in the Muslim
world, one cannot deny that the word *innovation* has negative connotations for a large number of Muslims.

In this connection, and not unrelated to the issue discussed in the
preceding section, one Quranic verse seems of special relevance S.
46:9, where the Prophet is instructed by God: "Say: I am not an innovation among the Messengers," "not an innovator," "no bringer of
new-fangled doctrines," "no new thing."[33] This emphasis on the continuity of revelation has led people to raise the question whether the
Quran contains the notion of a progressive revelation. The question
has been answered positively and negatively, by Muslims as well as
others, and the answer given determines or reflects the author's view
of the relation between Islam and other religions. Whenever the discussion focuses on the unity of revelation and the recognition of previous
Scriptures, the tendency is to stress that all God's messengers came

with basically the same message.[34] Whenever an appeal is made by
Muslims to other "people of the Book" to move from partial knowledge
to an acceptance of and belief in all of the Book,[35] including the Quran,
the uncorrupted embodiment of the Revelation, the emphasis is almost
bound to be on the notion of a progressive revelation, frequently
spelled out in terms of various "stages" in the history of revelation
corresponding to different levels of receptivity and comprehension.[36]

A Quranic expression often used to substantiate the thesis that all
of God's messengers stand, as it were, on the same level, undifferen-
tiated, is the declaration—in a rather common translation—that "we
make no distinction between any of them." In the light of S. 4:150 and
152 the expression referred to should be interpreted not as a denial of
different ranks but as an urgent warning that we should not discriminate against any of God's apostles, that is, we should not recognize
some while refusing to acknowledge others.[37] That seems a point of
major significance for any attempt to understand the Islamic view of
other religions. In Muslim perspective a refusal by Christians to acknowledge Muhammad and the Quran is inconsistent with their acceptance of Jesus and the Gospel, in the same manner that a Jewish refusal
to recognize Jesus is seen as inconsistent with their acknowledgement
of Moses and the Taurat. It is, therefore, this particular notion of
inclusivism that has given rise to some of the most bitter polemics
between Jews, Christians, and Muslims. The Muslims' deep-rooted
conviction of the unity of God's revelation fills many of them with
honest amazement and even bewilderment as to why a Christian whose
sincerity they do not challenge can possibly be so blinded as not to be
willing to include the event of the Quran in his or her own faith perspective. "Discontinuity" is thus seen not as brought about by, and in,
the sending down of the Quran, but by human arrogance that leads
people to an ungrateful denial of some of God's messengers and their
message; *they* are seen as being guilty of "exclusivism."

If we want to use the term progress in connection with Quranic
perspectives on the history of revelations, it is definitely not *primarily* a
matter of ever new insights and truths being added[38]—there is no innovation—but rather one of a definitive safeguarding of the revelation
against corruption and distortion, an assurance most strongly expressed in the Quranic statement that God Himself stands guard over
the Quran (S. 15:9).

There is unmistakably the tendency among many Muslims to emphasize the "permanence" of the truth of the Quran, a permanence not
challenged, in their view, by the necessity to relate their understanding
of the Quranic message to ever-changing conditions.[39] "Islam does not

need to be modernized. Islam has always been modern," wrote a leader of the World Muslim Congress some years ago.[40] Such a statement reflects, no doubt, the conviction of the "contemporaneity" of the Quran for every new generation. But it may also be related to the wider notion of the unity and continuity of all revelation: no revelation can become outdated because revelation is ultimately ahistorical. A statement by a contemporary Muslim provides a helpful illustration of this point of view that has far-reaching consequences for many of the issues in our time: "[divine guidance] . . . remains or should remain forever unaltered by time or history. . . . There is no reason to conceive of revelation as something temporal or historical."[41]

THE BALANCED MIDDLE
THE POWER OF THE DOUBLE AFFIRMATION

Although it occurs only once in the Quran, S. 2:143, the designation of the Muslim community as "a middle nation" (Pickthall) plays a significant role in many Muslim descriptions and interpretations of their tradition—"An *Ummat* justly balanced," Abdullah Yusuf Ali renders it, while Fazlur Rahman opts for "Median community."[42] Although made in a different context, Fazlur Rahman's remark on the Quranic notion of the "middle road" seems to articulate what several Muslims sense to be the characteristically Islamic vision: "the mean of the Quran" is not "a negative mean . . . from which both sides are absent," but rather "a positive, creative mean, an integrative moral organism," "the unique balance of integrative moral action."[43] Many of those who hear in this expression primarily a warning to shun excesses often work out the ethical implications as a rejection of the Christian ideal of self-denial on the one side and a denial of cruel self-assertion on the other, while on the popular-political level it is not uncommon to find this designation used in the discussion of the place of the Arab or the Muslim world as a third way in between the blocks of communism and capitalism.[44]

In whatever context it occurs, there is undoubtedly for many a powerful appeal in this refusal to accept a number of alternatives as mutually exclusive options, and rather to affirm both and to find the characteristic Muslim position in the balanced synthesis. A few illustrations of such double affirmations must suffice.[45]

Returning once more to the issue of the relation between the

Quran and earlier revelations, a widely accepted Muslim interpretation—attracting already the attention of a seventeenth-century Western Christian student of the Quran[46]—is that the "newness" of the
Quran does not lie in any new truths but in the affirmation and integration of what were one-sided emphases in the (interpretation of) the
Book of Moses and the Gospel of Jesus. The message of justice in the
Taurat (Divine justice as well as justice and retaliation in society) became integrated with Jesus' proclamation of love and forgiveness, the
latter as one-sided in the Christian context as justice was in the Old
Testament. The Old Testament understanding of the function of religion and its vision of the necessity to bring all of life under the guidance
of the Law was joined with the Christian emphasis on the need for a
personal response to God's acts of grace and its constant reminder of
the reality of the world to come.

S. 5:48, e.g., seems indeed to suggest such a process of integration and "balancing": "And therein We prescribed for them 'A life for a
life, and eye for an eye, a nose for a nose, an ear for an ear, a tooth for a
tooth, and for wounds retaliation.' But whosoever foregoes it as a
freewill offering, that shall be for him an expiation" (Arberry's translation). Whatever the difficulties in translation and interpretation are, the
basic meaning is clear: retaliation is not ruled out—an eye for any eye
has still its validity—but the option for a voluntary charity, a remission
of the retaliation, is always there.

Far more pronounced in the Quranic proclamation is the other
double affirmation mentioned already: that of this life *and* the next.
The Islamic concern with this-worldly affairs has received a one-sided
emphasis lately in many superficial or seriously distorted descriptions
of the phenomenon of Islamic resurgence. The relevance and
significance of one of the major issues at stake, namely the role of
religion in and for society, can perhaps most easily be illustrated by a
reference to Fazlur Rahman's article "Islam: Challenges and Opportunities."[47] Noting "the multiple phenomena of lawlessness and chaos" in
Western society and observing that "Western civilization is a giant now
fully corroded from within," Fazlur Rahman suggests a crucial distinction between Islam and Christianity, the latter now weakened "even as
a spiritual force," but in a sense traditionally inadequate in as far as it
"almost never oriented either the polity or the other social institutions
of the Christian peoples, except for marriage. Islam, on the other hand,
has had, as its central task—and this is its very genesis—to construct a
social order on a very ethical basis. In the execution of this task, its
very spirituality, that is, a genuine morality, is at work: it is asceticism

in this world."[48] While "at the moment . . . the Muslim community is not prepared to play this role . . . and does not know how to recover and reconstruct Islam," Islam has a tremendously important role in and for the world at large: "For the world, at this critical juncture of its history, appears to offer a unique opportunity for Islam to play its due role in the construction of a viable future for humanity."[49]

A description of Islam as critically concerned with the order of *this* world needs to be complemented, as indicated above, by a reference to the Quranic reminder of the transitory nature of "the enjoyment of the life of the world" (S. 42:36; cf. S. 40:39; 10:24; 18:45–46; 87:16–17), its admonition that "the life of the world is only play, and idle talk, and pageantry, and boasting among you, and rivalry in respect of wealth and children" (S. 57:20). "This life of the world is but a pastime and a game. Lo—the Home of the Hereafter: *that* is Life" (S. 29:64; cf. S. 6:32; 47:36). "The life of this world is but comfort of illusion" (S. 3:185; cf. S. 46:20).

The notion of "asceticism *in* this world" is not unrelated to this awareness of the world to come and our human accountability to God: when "hell will be set afire, and paradise brought nigh, a soul will know what it has earned" (S. 81:12–14)—a theme recurring most frequently in the earlier suras of the Quran but definitely present in late Medinan suras as well.[50]

"Revelation *and* Reason" is another double affirmation often emphasized,[51] not entirely unrelated to the view of both history *and* nature as equally important realms of revelation and the understanding of Islam as both the final and the primal religion.[52] That in a Muslim catechism with a question and answer format[53] each question receives a double answer, the first one based on reason, the second one on Quranic texts, would normally not be seen as a "compromise" in the negative sense, since many Muslims would challenge the thesis that there exists "always and in all religions a relationship of distrust between revelation and reason."[54]

THE UNITY OF GOD AND THE "WHOLENESS" OF ISLAM

Especially in past centuries several "outsiders" have suggested that there is a major inconsistency in what these observers interpreted as the most characteristic "double affirmation" of Islam: its fundamental

testimony to "God *and* Muhammad." We need to begin to grasp the
crucial significance of "that eloquent 'and' that links the Unity of God
with the Apostleship of Muhammad,"[55] while doing justice to the persistent Muslim insistence that Islam is absolutely uncompromising in
its affirmation of the Unity of God—the One to Whom "none is equal"
(S. 112:4),[56] who does not share His power and majesty with anyone (S.
17:111; 18:26; 25:2, 27:60–61) who has no "associates" and no "offspring."[57] Only in passing can we refer to the tragic distortion of the
reality of the faith of Muslims by those who in the past insinuated that
the radical monotheism of Islam reduces the confession of the Oneness
of God to the level of arithmetics. At stake and implied in the witness
that "there is no God but He"[58] are, among many other notions, the
richly diverse elements of the recognition of His majesty and power,
the affirmation of His sovereign freedom,[59] the celebration of His being
"our sufficiency" (S. 65:3, 3:173; 8:64; cf. S. 39:36), the assurance of
His self-commitment to mercy (S. 6:12, 54),[60] and the awareness of our
total dependency on Him.

The confession that there is "none besides Him" is, in Muslim
perspective, in no way compromised by the "and" of "God and His
messenger," but receives its ultimate foundation in the second part of
the Muslim affirmation of faith; for it is exactly in and through the
revelation of the Quran and the prophethood of Muhammad that the
testimony to the Oneness and Unity of God is brought to its utmost
clarity and defended against all kinds of distortions.

One can hardly overstate the powerful impact which the Prophet
has on the daily lives of Muslims,[61] the significance of his exemplary
role, the earnestness of the devotion which remembers him, in short, of
the continuing desire to "celebrate" him.[62] Ignoring or downplaying this
aspect of Islam is as much of a distortion of the Muslim tradition as
interpreting it as being inconsistent with the first part of the Islamic
witness.

Exactly because God is One, the response to Him needs to be
"undivided." The Arabic word "islam" expresses in a most succinct
manner the interrelatedness of the recognition of the Oneness of God
and the totality of the commitment it requires. The archetype of this
proper response to God is Abraham. He approached his Lord "with an
undivided heart," and he and his son "submitted" when God tested
them—using two interrelated expressions of the Abraham narrative in
S. 37:84 and 103 (cf. S. 2:131).

In this unquestioning commitment to God the elements of obedience and humility clearly play an important role. But there are other

aspects as well, among them especially a sense of security, peace, tranquility, confidence and assurance,[63] and very importantly the element of gratitude.[64] As the signs of God's power and majesty in this world are as clear as "the imprints of His mercy" (S. 30:50), so awe and gratitude are interrelated in the human response.

This total commitment is possible only because there is none besides God worthy to be worshipped and obeyed. As there is "none besides Him," so there is no realm of life unrelated to Islam as a response to Him. Whatever in any given situation the need may be for differentiating between roles and functions of people within the community of believers and in the society at large, Islam cannot be reduced to the kind of creedal affirmation that would forget to ponder and give thanks for the most diverse signs of God's active involvement in all of life. S. 30 lists the rest found in the relationship between spouses, the plurality of languages and colors, the quickening rain after a dry spell, and "herald winds that give you a taste of His mercy" as "signs" alongside that of the sending of His messengers (verses 20, 21, 22, 23, 24, 25, 46).[65]

Abu Hurayra's report on something the Prophet used to say seems to summarize much of what has been said and to hint at much more that has been left unspoken:

O Lord of Everything
O Sender down of the Law, the Gospels and the Quran . . .
Thou art the First and there was nothing before Thee
Thou art the Last and there is nothing after Thee
and Thou dost hide Thyself and there is nothing
    beyond Thee.[66]

NOTES

1. "Faith is a quality of the whole person. It has, therefore, as many dimensions as has personhood," W. Cantwell Smith wrote, *Faith and Belief* (Princeton, N.J.: Princeton University Press, 1979), p. 158. In the following article the word *faith* is not used in as sharp a distinction from the *belief* as Smith wants to maintain, but in full awareness of the

fact that "faith is a response to what one indisputably knows to be of divine origin," Wilfred Cantwell Smith, "Faith as *Taṣdīq*," in *Islamic Philosophical Theology*, ed. Parviz Morewedge (Albany: State University of New York Press, 1979), p. 113. For a recent discussion of Smith's position see Donald Wiebe, "The Role of 'Belief' in the Study of Religion. A Response to W. C. Smith," *Numen* 26 (1979): 234–49 and Wilfred Cantwell Smith, "Belief: A Reply to a Response," *Numen* 27 (1980): 247–55.

2. This point is emphasized strongly by Edward W. Said, *Covering Islam: How the Media and the Experts Determine How We See the Rest of the World* (New York: Pantheon Books, 1981). See below notes 5, 6, and esp. 7.

3. These titles have been selected arbitrarily from a long list of headlines of articles dealing primarily with political, social, and economic events and developments in Muslim parts of the world, but all of them using the word "Islam" in the title. The articles here mentioned appeared in *New York Times*, Dec. 9, 1979; *U.S. News and World Report*, Dec. 10, 1979; *New Republic*, Dec. 8, 1979; *Journal Inquirer*, Nov. 30, 1979; *Christian Science Monitor*, Dec. 14, 1978, respectively.

4. V. S. Naipaul, *Among the Believers: An Islamic Journey* (New York: Alfred A. Knopf, 1981).

5. Said, *Covering Islam*, pp. xxxi, 152.

6. Ibid., p. 7.

7. Ibid., p. xv; see also p. xix (". . . I do not believe as strongly and as firmly in the notion of 'Islam' as many experts, policymakers, and general intellectuals do; on the contrary, I often think it has been more of a hindrance than a help in understanding what moves people and societies") and pp. 38, 53, 56–60, 77ff.

8. Naipaul, *Among the Believers*, pp. 401–30.

9. Estimates of the world total of Muslims continue to vary widely, from the consistently low figures in the *Encyclopaedia Britannica* (the *1982 Book of the Year* estimate is 592,157,900) to the high of more than one billion given in many Muslim sources. Of interest are the data in the *World Christian Encyclopedia*, ed. David B. Barrett (Nairobi: Oxford University Press, 1982), p. 6. While his figures for the present are much lower than commonly estimated, he anticipates an increase of almost 95,000,000 between 1980 and 1985 and of more than 477 million between 1980 and the year 2000.

10. Naipaul, *Among the Believers*, pp. 86 and 305 respectively.

11. The first quotation is found in Charis Wady, *The Muslim Mind* (London: Longmans, 1976), p. xvii (from a letter from Dr. Hassan Hathout), the second quote is from Muhammad Abduh, *The Theology of Unity (Risālat al-Tawḥīd)*, trans. Ishaq Musaad and Kenneth Cragg (London: George Allen and Unwin, 1965), p. 154.

12. Nadav Safran rightly observed in his review of Anwar el-Sadat's *In Search of Identity* (New York: Harper and Row, 1978) that Mr. Sadat meant by it "the search for a practical philosophy of life and guiding ideals and goals, rather than a narrow psychological sense of one's self"; *New York Times Book Review*, May 7, 1978.

13. Rafiuddin Ahmed, *The Bengal Muslims, 1871–1906. A Quest for Identity*. (Delhi: Oxford University Press, 1981), esp. Ch. IV: "A Crisis of Identity: Muslims or Bengalis?"

14. See Wilfred Cantwell Smith, *Faith and Belief*, pp. 48–49: "Faith, in Islamic theology, was set forth as first a personal relationship to truth *(tasdiq)*: a recognizing of it, appropriating it to one's self, and resolving to live in accord with it."

15. Wady, *The Muslim Mind*, p. xvi.

16. The critical issue is not, using Khurram Murad's words, that "an anthology selects, necessarily, only what the selector's eye discerns as suitable, and only in such

measure and such arrangement as he judges to be appropriate"—Khurram Murad, in a review of Kenneth Cragg and R. Marston Speight, *Islam from Within: Anthology of a Religion* (Belmont, Calif.: Wadsworth, 1980), in *The Muslim World Book Review* 2, no. 1 (Spring 1982): 5. Nor is it that "the anthologist's own understanding, preferences, priorities, even inner dispositions" are reflected in his choice of material. The crucial question is whether anyone attempting a "descriptive" introduction to a religious tradition—either in the form of an anthology or in some brief observations as offered here—is critically aware of those preferences and priorities, and at least indirectly deals with the criteria for what is considered "suitable" and "appropriate" by stating openly the objective of his presentation.

17. "The locus of faith is persons" Wilfred Cantwell Smith insists; *Faith and Belief*, p. 158. But in seeing faith as "the prodigious hallmark of being human" (p. 142), Smith in no way denies its transcending dimension: "Faith is that quality of or available to humankind by which we are characterized as transcending, or are enabled to transcend, the natural order—an order both in and beyond which, simultaneously, it has been normal, we may observe, for men and women to live."

18. G. van der Leeuw, *Religion in Essence and Manifestation* (Gloucester, Mass: Peter Smith, 1967), p. 685.

19. Hans Küng, *On Being A Christian* (Garden City, N.J.: Doubleday, 1976), pp. 20–21.

20. The English translation is included in el-Sadat, *In Search of Identity: An Autobiography*, pp. 330–43; the reference to S. 2:136 is in the concluding paragraph, p. 343.

21. Already in the twelfth century a Bishop of Sidon, Paul of Antioch, brought together the Quranic texts he considered as speaking in favor of Christ and the Christians, including the verse here mentioned as well as, among others, S. 5:82; 42:15; 10:94; 3:55; 22:40 and texts dealing with the Quran "authenticating" previous Scriptures, those speaking highly of the Injil and of Christ and his Virgin Mother. See Paul Khoury, *Paul d'Antioche, Évêque melkite de Sidon (XIIᵉ S.)* (Beirut: Impr. Catholique, n.d.), Arabic text pp. 59–83 (Arabic section), French trsl. pp. 169–87.

22. Most of these texts are enumerated in my "Some Recent Contributions to Qur'anic Studies, I" *MW* 64 (1974): 96.

23. Si Boubakeur Hamza, e.g., denies that there is a single Quranic text validating any non-Islamic beliefs *after* the revelation of the Quran: "Outside Islam there is no salvation." *Le Coran* (Paris: Fayard-Denoël, 1972), I, 32, 137, 237, 242, 247–48.

24. See especially Fazlur Rahman's comments on S. 5:48 in *Major Themes of the Qur'ān* (Minneapolis-Chicago: Bibliotheca Islamica, 1980), pp. 166–67. It occurs in an Appendix ("The People of the Book and Diversity of 'Religions'") which appeared originally under the title "Christian Particularity and the Faith of Islam" in *Christian Faith in a Religiously Plural World,* ed. Donald G. Dawe and John B. Carman (Maryknoll, N.Y.: Orbis Books, 1978), pp. 69–79.

25. These and all other texts referring to the fact that this revelation was given in the Arabic language (S. 12:2; 20:113; 39:28; 41:3; 42:7; 43:3) occur in suras of the Meccan period and cannot be used as an argument on which to base the thesis that there was a development from a religious "Islamism" in Mecca to a nationalist, political "Arabism" in Medina, as Julian Obermann suggested in 1955; see for further references my "A Prophet and More Than A Prophet?" *MW* 59 (1969): 21, note 88.

26. Kenneth Cragg, *The Event of the Qur'ān* (London: George Allen and Unwin, 1971), p. 61.

27. Not in a "communal electionist" sense, as if God, after an earlier choice of

other communities which then became disobedient, now has finally chosen the Arabs (see note 29 below), but rather with the emphasis on the tremendous responsibility now that God has spoken also to them through a messenger from among them, speaking their own language.

28. S. 29:27 speaks about "Prophethood and Scripture" having been established by God among the descendants of Abraham; S. 4:54 uses the language of "Scripture and Wisdom" having been bestowed upon Abraham's descendants; and S. 45:16 the three words, "Scripture, Wisdom and Prophethood" are combined, having been given to the children of Israel. Cf. also S. 3:79 (81) and 6:89. This is obviously not to deny that the Quran also affirms the universality of God's revelation; "Every community has its messenger"; S. 10:47; 16:36; 17:15; 23:44; 30:47; cf. also S. 13:7 and 35:24.

29. Cf., e.g., Fazlur Rahman's remark that "the whole tenor of the Qur'ānic argument is against election" (with a reference to S. 2:124) and his observations on the Quran's "strong rejection of exclusivism and election"; *Major Themes of the Qur'ān*, pp. 165–66. The language of God "choosing" or "electing" is indeed very rare in the Quran, and never in the sense the word has in the Hebrew Scriptures. The verb *khara*, VIII, is used for Moses in S. 20:13, for the Children of Israel in 44:32, and in a general sense (whomever He wills) in 28:68. The verb *safa*, VIII, is used in connection with Noah, Adam, the family of Abraham, and the family of Imran in S. 3:33; Abraham, Isaac, and Jacob in 38:47; Abraham in 2:130; Moses in 7:144; Tabut (Saul) in 2:247; Mary in 3:42, and in a more general sense (His servants whom he has chosen) in 27:59 and 35:32.

30. Y. Moubarac, *Abraham dans le Coran* (Paris: J. Vrin, 1958), p. 139, note 2, with a reference to S. 3:17. On the same page the remark occurs that Islam "est une religion de la tradition plutôt que de l'histoire."

31. Used in the more general sense of groups of people, communities. A great number of Muslim writings speak about the immutable laws of God governing the rise and fall of civilizations and communities, their destruction due to their turning away from God's commandments, becoming oppressive, etc. A wide variety of such views and statements is discussed in Yvonne Yazbeck Haddad, *Contemporary Islam and the Challenge of History* (Albany: State University of New York Press, 1982); see, e.g., pp. 101, 105, 112–113 and 118 as well as the Appendices, esp. no. E ("Islam Looks at History" by Muhammad Kamal Ibrahim Jafar, pp. 174–80) and no. G ("The Qur'anic Interpretation of History" by Imad al-Din Khalil, pp. 188–204). One of the Quranic expressions relevant in this context is the challenge to travel over the earth and to see what the end was of those who gave the lie to the truth (S. 3:137; 6:11; 16:36) and to become wise by seeing what happened to those (sinners) who lived before (S. 12:109; 27:69; 30:9, 42; 35:44; 40:21, 82; 47:10).

32. "The Image of Jesus in Contemporary Islamic Theology," in *We Believe in One God*, ed. Annemarie Schimmel and Abdoljavad Falaturi (New York: The Seabury Press, 1979), p. 2.

33. In or according to the translations of A. J. Arberry [*The Koran Interpreted* (London: Oxford Univ. Press, 1964; first publ. 1955)], J. H. Kramers [*De Koran* (Amsterdam: Elsevier, 1956 and reprints); "Niet ben ik een nieuwlichter onder de boodschappers"], A. Yusuf Ali [*The Meaning of the Glorious Qur'ān* (Cairo-Beirut, n.d.; first publ. as *The Holy Qur'an*, 1934)], and Muhammad Marmaduke Pickthall [*The Meaning of The Glorious Qur'ān* (Mecca-New York: Muslim World League, 1977; first publ. 1930)] respectively. Muhammad Asad, allowing in a footnote for the translation here given as an alternative rendering, gives as his first choice: "I am not the first of [God's] apostles," basing this on the interpretation given by Tabari, Baghawi, Razi, and Ibn Kathir; *The Message of the Qur'ān* (Gibraltar: Dar al-Andalus, 1980).

34. See Fazlur Rahman's remark: "These messages are universal and identical": *Major Themes of the Qur'ān,* p. 163. An interesting qualification is given by Muhammad Asad in his footnotes to S. 46:9: "the Qur'anic doctrine of the identity of the *ethical* teachings propounded by all of God's prophets" (italics added).

35. The believers (Muslims) are addressed in S. 3:119 as "you who believe in all of the Book," in a passage dealing with the relation between them and "the People of the Book," Jews and Christians. Asad translates the beginning of vs. 119 as follows: "Lo! It is you who [are prepared to] love them, but they will not love you, although you believe in all of the revelation," and adds to these last words the footnote "i.e., including the revelation of the Bible." Whether one opts for that interpretation or—as seems preferable to me—reads with Arberry and others "you believe in the Book, all of it," the distinction remains between the true believers who accept all of God's revelation, including, particularly, its final embodiment, and those who refuse to acknowledge part of it.

36. The idea of a progressive revelation is, e.g., expressed by Mohammad Abd Allah Draz in his remark: "In the revelations of the Qur'an, as in every previous revelation, a new and original contribution is added to the earlier ones." "The Origin of Islam," in *Islam—The Straight Path,* ed. Kenneth W. Morgan (New York: Ronald Press, 1958), p. 34.

37. The expression referred to is found in S. 2:136, 285; 3:84. The idea of different "ranks" is found in S. 2:253. "We make no distinction between any of them," is the translation given in, among others, Pickthall, Muhammad Zafrulla Khan, *The Qur'an* (London, Dublin: Curzon Press, 1971; 3rd rev. ed. 1981), and Muhammad Asad. The last mentioned clarifies the meaning in his footnote to S. 2:136: "i.e., we regard them all as true prophets of God." Preferable, since it is less open to misunderstanding, is Arberry's: "We make no division between any of them." On the issue itself cf. Fazlur Rahman: "If Muḥammad and his followers believe in all prophets, all people must also and equally believe in him. Disbelief in him would be equivalent to disbelief in all, for this would arbitrarily upset the line of prophetic succession." *Major Themes of the Qur'ān,* p. 164.

38. The examples of a somewhat different emphasis given above do not render this observation invalid. Many Muslims emphasize as one of the distinctions that whereas all other prophets and messengers were sent to a particular "tribe," the Prophet Muhammad's role and function are for all of humankind.

39. The only issue raised with some frequency among Muslims is whether the notion of "immutability" also applies to some very specific legal commandments and prohibitions in the Quran. A few references can illustrate the variety of positions held. Ismail R. al-Faruqi, emphasizing that the Quran is "imperishable because God declared Himself its protector and guardian," speaks about the limited number of verses dealing with legislation (hardly 500 out of 6,342) as "of lesser importance than the rest," and sees this as a reason for the ongoing validity and applicability of the Quran: "They [Muslims] hold that God will not need to send another revelation, partly because He has placed in human hands an imperishable and definitive statement of His will, that is the Qur'ān, and partly because He wishes people themselves to discover and to elaborate the means by which the will of God is henceforth to be realized. It is not by accident therefore that the Quranic revelation is not prescriptive in the main; it is because the divine plan relegated lawmaking to humankind, as long as the principles and values that the prescriptive laws embody are those which God has revealed" *Islam* (Niles, Ill.: Argus Comm., 1979), pp. 36–37. The need to distinguish clearly between "legal enactments" and "moral injunctions" is emphasized in many of Fazlur Rahman's writings. Rejecting the principle that "although a law is occasioned by a specific situation, its application nevertheless be-

comes universal," Fazlur Rahman maintains that it is exactly in order to do justice to the *ratio legis*—the "intention" of the law, the reason for its being enunciated—that specific laws have to be changed in changing circumstances: "When the situation so changes that the law fails to reflect the *ratio,* the law must change," *Major Themes of the Qur'ān,* pp. 47–49. A similar position is represented by Smail Balic, for example, in his article "Das Schari'a—Verständnis in pluralistischer Gesellschaft," *Islam und der Westen* 1, no. 1 (Jan. 1981): 2–3, where he stresses the need for a historical-critical study of the Quran ("Ein historisch-kritisches Qur'an—Verständnis stellt sich als unumgängliches Erfordernis ein") in order to be able to discover the meaning (purpose, intention) behind specific legal injunctions. In order to stress the fact that such an attempt is totally inacceptable to many (most) other Muslims, we conclude with the final sentence of Falaturi's article mentioned before. With reference to the discussions that took place at the conference in Freiburg, Germany in November 1974 he writes: "Muslims vigorously opposed any reference to an *historical* understanding of the Koran which might in any way put into question the existence of Islam and its laws as proclaimed by Muḥammad," *We Believe in One God,* p. 73.

40. Inamullah Khan, "Islam in the Contemporary World," in *God and Man in Contemporary Islamic Thought,* ed. Charles Malik (Beirut: American University of Beirut, 1972), p. 12.

41. Falaturi, "Experience of Time and History in Islam," in *We Believe in One God,* p. 65.

42. F. Rahman, *Major Themes of the Qur'ān,* p. 145.

43. Ibid., p. 28.

44. "The essence of Islam is to avoid all extravagances on either side. It is a sober, practical religion," reads the beginning of the footnote Yusuf Ali has at S. 2:143. And in discussing Sayyid Qutb's view of the West and of the struggle between capitalism and communism, Yvonne Haddad writes, introducing a quotation from Sayyid Qutb: "There is no doubt that victory for Islam is assured because of its self-evident superiority and because Islam occupies what he calls the all-important middle position. Islam offers the world a balance that is 'not to be found in idealistic Christianity nor in dogmatic communism, but in a middle position about life. [Islam] as an ideology balances pure spirituality and moderate practical materialism and forms from them a system for the conscience and a way of life, an everlasting vision for humanity.' " Y. Haddad, *Contemporary Islam,* p. 91. The quotation, in Haddad's translation, is from Qutb's *Nahwa Mujtama Islami* (Cairo, n.d.), p. 32.

45. See also, e.g., a passage in Anwar al-Jundi, *al-Islam wa Harakat al-Tarikh* (Cairo, 1968), p. 496, summarized as follows in Haddad, *Contemporary Islam,* p. 86: "Islam is the only system that provides for the coming together of body and spirit in man, of worship and works in life, of the world and the hereafter in religion, and of heaven and earth in the universe."

46. Dominicus Germanus (1588–1670) composed an "Interpretatio Alcoranus Literalis cum scholia," still unpublished, to which Sr. J. Marita Paul Colla is devoting a doctoral dissertation (forthcoming, Hartford). In the context of his discussion of the meaning of *al-Rahman* and *al-Rahim*—for which he accepts as the common Muslim interpretation that the words refer to God's grace in this world and the next—Dominicus quotes in Arabic and translates passages from Al-Kashani and others, and finally one from Ibn Kamal, describing the Jews as devoted to the worship of "external bodily pleasures and sensual appetite," the Christians as tending towards "the internal and the light of the World of holiness," while Muslims, truly worshipping the one God alone, are

called to "rejoice in all things in this world and the next." Scholion on the Proemialis (Surat al-Fatiha).

47. *In Islam: Past Influence and Present Challenge* (in Honour of W. Montgomery Watt), ed. Alford T. Welch and Pierre Cachia (Edinburgh: Edinburgh University Press; Albany: State University of New York Press, 1979), pp. 315–30.

48. The references quoted are from *Islam: Past Influence,* pp. 328, 329, 330 respectively.

49. Ibid., p. 327.

50. One can hardly overemphasize the frequency and intensity of the Quranic admonition that in all actions all persons stand constantly under God's judgment, and its emphasis on ethical conduct. In elaborating this point, many Muslims stress the fact that the notion of "salvation," in the Christian sense, has no place in the Quran and in Islamic thought "For Islam, there is no particular 'salvation': there is only 'success *(falāh)*' or 'failure *(khusrān)*' in the task of building the type of [ethico-social] world order we are describing"; Fazlur Rahman, *Major Themes of the Qur'ān,* p. 63. For a few other examples of Muslim discussions of the notion of "salvation" see my "Other Faith Images of Jesus: Some Muslim Contributions to the Christological Discussion," in *Christological Perspectives,* ed. Robert F. Berkey and Sarah A. Edwards (New York: Pilgrim Press, 1982), p. 206 and p. 298, note 51.

51. For a general discussion of the relationship between revelation and reason in Islam see A. J. Arberry's *Revelation and Reason in Islam* (London: George Allen and Unwin, 1957). In several Muslim publications, also at the popular level, emphasis is laid upon the "rational" character of Islam, not infrequently with references to Muhammad Abduh-Rashid Rida's statement about the complete harmony of the revelation God has granted in His uncreated Book, the Quran, and that found in His Created Word, Nature. In other Muslim expositions the emphasis is not so much on "reason" in a strictly intellectual sense, but rather on man's reasonableness, his conscience, his original orientation towards God, his inner disposition. Cf. S. 30:30 and the data in Jane I. Smith, *An Historical and Semantic Study of the Term Islam* (Missoula, Mont.: Scholars Press, 1975), pp. 123, 124, 193, 201. A very significant recent contribution to the discussion of the issue of intellect and revelation is Seyyed Hossein Nasr's *Knowledge and the Sacred* (New York: Crossroad, 1981). In the chapter "Scientia Sacra" (pp. 130–59) he writes (p. 148): "Although the Intellect shines within the being of man, man is too far removed from his primordial nature to be able to make full use of this divine gift by himself. He needs revelation which alone can actualize the intellect in man and allow it to function properly."

52. This double characterization of Islam as "final and primal religion," used in my "Islam's forstaelse af sig selv, I–II," *Nordisk Missions Tidsskrift* 74, no. 2 (1963): 37–46; no. 3 (1963): 25–37, became a widely accepted way of introducing Islam following Seyyed Hossein Nasr's elaboration of it in his *Ideals and Realities of Islam* (Boston: Beacon Press, 1972; originally published in 1966): "Islam, the last religion and the primordial religion—the universal and particular traits" (pp. 15–40).

53. An interesting contribution to the discussion on the background of the question-and-answer format as used in religious instruction (with references to Pijper, Huizinga, etc.) is made by A. van Selms, *'N Tweetalige (Arabiese en Afrikaanse) Kategismus* (Amsterdam: Noord-Hollandsche Uitg. Mij., 1951), pp. 25–28.

54. Van Selms, in the publication just mentioned, sees this double answer as a "compromise," since he assumes that there is a constant tension between reason and revelation in all religions; ibid., p. 30.

55. Kenneth Cragg, *The Call of the Minaret* (New York: Oxford University Press, 1956), p. 67; cf. also p. 69, "Small conjunctions often carry profound significance. There is none more tremendous than that which links the One God with the human instrument of His revelation and His will, in the creed and devotion of Islam."

56. This sura is often described as containing the essence of the whole Quranic message. See also S. 42:11 and numerous verses that emphasize the incomparability of Him "other than Whom there is none"—in many instances in the language of praise and thanksgiving; S. 2:255; 3:2; 24:35; 28:70; 59:22–24; 68:13 and passim.

57. A terminology used in several passages dealing with the polytheists (for example, S. 6:100–101; 16:57, 62; 17:40; 37:149, 152, 153; 43:16–18; 52:39; 53:21–22; 72:3), as well as in the context of a criticism of a notion current among Christians (4:171, 172; 2:116, 19:35).

58. A clause occurring in this form twenty-four times, with the variants "no God but I" in S. 16:2; 20:14; 21:25; "no God but Thee" in S. 21:87; and "besides Whom there is no God" and "no God besides Allah" in S. 9:31; 20:98; 37:35; 38:65; 47:19; 59:22,23.

59. A notion not unknown from their own tradition to many Western polemicists who interpreted this *in the case of Islam and the Quran* as "arbitrariness" and "capriciousness." The "whom He wills" language plays no doubt an important role in the Quran, but it is an expression of the freedom of the God in Whom people are called to put their trust and in Whom they are invited to take refuge. The difficulty, clearly, remains to do justice to both the latter aspect and the notion of the sovereign freedom of God. If they are seen in the tension of their interrelatedness, it becomes obvious that there is no justification for a typology of Islam as that given by, for example, Gustav Mensching: "Die Religion des demonischen Willensmacht und der vollkommener Ergebung"; *Vergleichende Religionswissenschaft*, 2nd ed. (Heidelberg: Quelle & Meyer, 1949), pp. 57–59. Although only the second part of this characterization is used in the title of the section on Islam in his later study, *Die Religion* (Stuttgart: C. E. Schwab, 1959), the author's assessment of the Quranic witness of God has not changed, as is evident from the following statement (p. 59): "Dämonische Willensallmacht ist der Gott Mohammeds, eine Willkürwille, von dem alles Lebendige abhängt."

60. In no way is this expression to be treated as a single "prooftext"—the Quran abounds with verses stressing the mercy of God. "The immediate impression from a cursory reading of the Quran is that of the infinite majesty of God and His equally infinite mercy," Fazlur Rahman, *Major Themes of the Qur'ān*, p. 1.

61. "No one can estimate the power of Islam as a religion who does not take into account the love at the heart of it for this figure [the Prophet] . . . the love of this figure is perhaps the strongest binding force in a religion which has so marked a binding power," Constance E. Padwick, *Muslim Devotions. A Study of Prayer Manuals in Common Use* (London: S.P.C.K., 1961), p. 145.

62. Cragg and Speight, *Islam from Within*, pp. 67–70: "Celebrating Muhammad."

63. Also the confidence and assurance that the ultimate triumph and victory are with God, His Messenger and those who obey them, no matter how much other persons and powers may try to extinguish God's Light. See, for example, S. 9:32; 61:8; 58:20–21; 5:56, etc. The pattern of the Noah and all other "punishment" stories will continue to be repeated until the final judgment day.

64. Many have drawn attention to the Quranic language that the decisive choice for all persons, in their response to God, is that between gratitude and ingratitude, S. 14:7; cf. 76:3 and 2:152. Rudi Paret lists at S. 10:12 and 10:22 more than twenty verses dealing with the theme of people's (un)gratefulness in their answer to expressions of God's goodness. See also S. 14:34; 17:67; 22:66; 42:48; 43:15; 80:17 and 100:6, verses

listed by Paret at 11:9–10; *Der Koran Kommentar und Konkordanz* (Stuttgart: W. Kohlhammer, 1971), pp. 218, 220, and 232 respectively.

65. In a variety of ways the Quran describes God's sending of messengers and prophets as an, or perhaps rather as *the,* expression of His mercy; for some references see *Christological Perspectives,* pp. 212–13 and p. 301, notes 97–99.

66. Muḥammad b. Abdallah al-Khatib, *Mishkat al-Masabih* (Lucknow, AH 1319) X, ii, 2, as translated in Margaret Smith, *The Way of the Mystics* (London: Sheldon Press, 1976; first pub. 1931), p. 143.

Index

Abbas, Shah, 160, 162
Abbasi, Riza-yi, 141
Abbasid Caliphate, 13, 72, 149
Abd al-Wahhab, 194n.
Abduh, Muhammad, 21, 102, 220
Abdul Latif, Shah, 119, 227
Abdus Sabur, Salah, 119
Abjul-Nassar, 208
Abu Bakr, 71, 75
Abu Najib, 122
Adawiyya, Rabia al-, 114
Afghani, Jamaluddin, 21
Africa: political effects on United
  States, 206–207; slave trade in, 196
Ahimsa, 12
Ahmad, Ghulam, 200
Ahmad, Jalal Ali, 21
Ahmad, Muiz al-Dawla, 13
Ahmadiyya movement: appeal of, 200;
  Ghulam Ahmad, 200; precepts of, 200
Ahmed, Rafinddin, 221
Akbar, 15
Alchemy, 62, 115
Algeria: life style of, 24; revolution in,
  10, 24
Ali, 71, 75–76
Ali, Abdullah Yusuf, 227
Ali, Noble Drew, 199–200
Ali, Syed Ameer, 11, 21
Ali, Yusuf, 236n.
Allah. *See* God
Allegory: of Banyan tree, 113; of
  elephant, 113

Almagest, 59
Almoravid dynasty, 15
American Islamic Propaganda Move-
  ments, 198–199
American Muslim Mission, 209
Amin, Salih, 193
Among the Believers (Naipaul), 219
Ansari, Abdullah-i, 126
Antinomianism, 7, 118
Apologist school, 11, 48
Arab-Israeli conflict, 9–10, 98, 212
Arab socialism, 37, 39
Arabesque style, 144
Arabian Nights, 15, 35
Arabic, 55
Arabism, 233n.
Arafat, Yasir, 22
Arberry, A. J., 237n.
Architecture, 50, 53, 153–156
Aristotle, 56, 66n.
Armenians, 28
Arnaldez, Rodger, 9
Art, 53, 66: "Arabesque" style, 144; ar-
  chaeological perspectives, 163, 169;
  and the artist, 138–141, 163, 169; cal-
  ligraphy, 141–143, 160, 163–164;
  ceramics, 149, 163–165; of the cities
  and middle class, 163–165; city-coun-
  try tension in, 151–153; collecting,
  162; and commerce, 163–165; conflicts with religion, 141–149; embroidery, 165; figural, 137, 145, 149, 156,
  169, 178; of Nomads, 165–169; oral

THE ISLAMIC IMPACT

was composed in 10-point Times Roman and leaded 2 points by Coghill Book Typesetting Co.,
with display type in Legend by Dix Type;
printed sheet-fed offset on 55-pound, acid-free Glatfelter Antique Cream,
Smythe-sewn, and bound over binder's boards in Joanna Arrestox,
also adhesive-bound, with paper covers printed on Corvon 220-13 by
Niles & Phipps Lithographers, Inc.,
by Maple-Vail Book Manufacturing Group, Inc.;
and published by

SYRACUSE UNIVERSITY PRESS

SYRACUSE, NEW YORK 13210